READING THE MIDDLE AGES

READING THE MIDDLE AGES

An Introduction to Medieval Literature

Theodore L. Steinberg

McFarland & Company, Inc., Publishers

Jefferson, North Carolina, and London

LIBRARY OF CONGRESS CATALOGUING-IN-PUBLICATION DATA

Steinberg, Theodore L. (Theodore Louis), 1947–
    Reading the Middle Ages : an introduction to medieval literature
/ Theodore L. Steinberg.
        p.   cm.
    Includes bibliographical references and index.

    ISBN 0-7864-1648-3 (softcover : 50# alkaline paper) ∞

    1. Literature, Medieval — History and criticism.   I. Title.
PN671.S74   2003
809'.02 — dc21   2003010126

British Library cataloguing data are available

Cover art ©2003 Art Today

Manufactured in the United States of America

McFarland & Company, Inc., Publishers
  Box 611, Jefferson, North Carolina 28640
  www.mcfarlandpub.com

For my father and mother —
Sherman and Regina Steinberg

Contents

Preface

Probably none of us would choose to go back to living in medieval Europe. Just the unpleasant aspects of day-to-day life, such as the pungent odors of an unwashed society with no sanitation systems, would quickly overwhelm us — let alone the more serious problems like disease and the scarcity of food. But of course our reactions would depend on our knowledge of the present. For medieval folk, the Middle Ages *were* the present. They did not sit around waiting for the Renaissance or wishing that someone would invent television. They had to confront the world as it existed, as they knew it, with bad odors, food shortages, short life expectancies, inadequate medical knowledge, and all the other disadvantages that we can think of from our modern perspectives. We might marvel that people survived under such conditions, but in fact they did more than simply survive. They created a culture that was in many ways magnificent. The remnants of that culture, its art, literature, music, and philosophy, demonstrate its magnificence and illustrate for us the ways in which people who lived in quite different material circumstances responded to the universal challenges of human existence. Their responses to those challenges may be very different from ours, in which case the contrasts are instructive; but in many cases we will see that their responses were surprisingly similar to our own, a phenomenon that is equally instructive.

This book is intended for several audiences, but it is primarily for students. That is to say, it is primarily for anyone who wants to find a way into the study of medieval literature. Such a person may or may not be enrolled in a college. Matriculation status is irrelevant. All that is important is the desire to learn and the willingness to try to suspend twenty-first-century sensibilities and enter the world of the Middle Ages. That world may be confusing and self-contradictory — much as our present world is — but it also has a beauty and a logic of its own, qualities

1

that are worth knowing. Just as we can never know exactly what it would be like to be another person, so can we never know what it would be like to have lived in another time. But just as literature can help us in our quest to understand other people, so can it help us to understand other times.

This book will attempt to cover a lot of ground. The Middle Ages lasted about a thousand years, which is a long time for anyone but a geologist or an astrophysicist to cover. Furthermore, the Middle Ages was an international phenomenon, and the works that will be discussed come from England, France, Iceland, and Italy. And finally, in the spirit of multiculturalism, this book will attempt to overcome the picture of the Middle Ages as a monolithic culture, European and Roman Catholic. Consequently, there will be chapters on the literature of medieval Jews, who formed the largest minority group in medieval Europe, and on *The Tale of Genji*, the supreme literary work of medieval Japan. Of course, the picture that will emerge will still be incomplete, but this book promises only an introduction. Its intent is to lure the reader into the fascinating world of medieval literature. Its author believes, with the Roman poet Horace and his Renaissance follower Sir Philip Sidney, that literature should both teach and delight. If this book helps readers to learn about medieval literature and leads them to enjoy that literature, it will have accomplished its goal.

There are few references in the pages that follow to secondary materials on medieval literature. Readers who are particularly drawn to individual works should certainly consult the vast secondary literature that exists for most of them. There are, however, several references to contemporary novels. Purists might prefer to overlook those references.

I would like to thank Minda Rae Amiran, Brian Gastle, Scott Lightsey, and Gillian Steinberg for reading the manuscript closely and making helpful suggestions. Of course, I take responsibility for any flaws in what follows, but those readers should certainly share in the blame. As always, my greatest debt is to my wife, Phyllis.

Introduction

One of the most popular Roman literary works during the Middle Ages was Ovid's *Metamorphoses*, a collection of mythological stories that are often delightful but that also contain motifs that can be troubling, such as rape, incest, murder, and mutilation. One of the first stories in the book tells of Phoebus Apollo's love for a young woman named Daphne, who has no interest in loving the god and tries to run away from his advances. As he catches up to her, she prays for help and is transformed into a tree, the laurel tree, which then becomes sacred to Apollo. In the fourteenth century, Petrus Berchorius wrote a commentary on the *Metamorphoses* that he called the *Ovidius Moralizatus*, that is, *Ovid Moralized*. His was only one of many attempts to demonstrate the morality, the ethical and religious lessons, of Ovid's often risqué stories, and his commentary reveals important aspects of medieval thought. On the story of Daphne and Apollo, for example, he gives several interpretations, as he often does. He first says "that Phoebus signifies those who desire worldly glory.... The beautiful girl Daphne is worldly glory which is so loved by such people that they follow her as much as they are able" (137). Soon, however, Berchorius says, "Phoebus can signify the devil and Daphne the Christian soul because the devil never ceases enticing that virgin — that is the soul — with temptations so that he subjugates her through her evil consent and destroys her by sin" (139). These two interpretations are obviously quite different from the way modern readers would approach Ovid's stories — and they also differ from each other — but Berchorius presents them both as equally valid. A contemporary reader might regard Berchorius' approach as postmodern because it accepts shifting perspectives and apparent contradictions with equanimity. For a medieval reader, or a modern-day medievalist, there is nothing "postmodern" about this approach. Those shifting perspectives and apparent contradictions are all perfectly ordinary, as long as they lead to morally acceptable positions.

The literary text, like the world, is there to be interpreted, to reveal its Christian content. The medieval commentator (and the commentators were all men) knows where he wants to end up — with a moral or religious truth — and he is willing to take any road that will get him there. As we will see, Berchorius' approach to Ovid in many ways typifies the Middle Ages.

Before we go any further, we should ask what we mean by the term "Middle Ages" and what they came in the middle of. The easiest definition of the Middle Ages is that it was the period from roughly A.D. 500 to A.D. 1500. Of course, historical epochs neither begin nor end at precise moments. They are the result of processes. We may say that the Atomic Age began on August 6, 1945, when Hiroshima was destroyed, but we could also say that it began somewhat earlier, when the bomb was tested, or even earlier, when a critical mass was achieved at the University of Chicago, or even earlier, when scientists like Madame Curie began investigating the atom, or even earlier, when the ancient Greek philosopher Democritus posited the existence of what he called atoms. So it is with the Middle Ages. It is convenient to think of them as beginning in about the year 500, with the collapse of the Roman Empire, and ending in 1500, with the beginning of the Renaissance. They came in the middle, between Classical Antiquity and the Renaissance. But the Roman Empire did not collapse all at one time, and the Renaissance began at different times in different places throughout Europe. It began, for instance, in the early fourteenth century in Italy but not until the early sixteenth century in England. The first great Renaissance writer was the Italian poet Petrarch, who lived before Chaucer and whose work Chaucer adapted; but Chaucer is still a medieval writer. In short, historical boundaries are inexact. At the same time, however, they are undeniable. Many scholars today think of the Renaissance as the Early Modern period, but no one thinks of the Middle Ages that way. However great the distance is between our time and the Renaissance, the distance between us and the Middle Ages is in many ways far greater, though, as we will see, we still have much in common with the people and the concerns of the Middle Ages.

Of course, if a historical period lasts a thousand years, that thousand years can be subdivided into other periods. For a long while, people who lived after the Middle Ages looked back on those thousand years as a time of superstition and ignorance, of barbarism and inhumanity; and just as we, in our time, might refer to an idea as "Victorian" in order to disparage it, they referred to the era that preceded theirs in disparaging terms. Such disparagement of earlier periods is extremely common.

It allows us to assert our superiority without actually having to do anything superior. Even now, when we hear about some particularly barbaric act, we are likely to say that it sounds medieval, that it reminds us of the Middle Ages. We conveniently ignore the fact that the twentieth century was probably the most barbaric century in human history. If we think of the Middle Ages as barbaric, however, then we can view our own failings as a throwback, as acts that characterize an earlier time rather than our own. And if we think of the Middle Ages as the Dark Ages, we seem to make the distance between them and us even greater.

But the Middle Ages are not the same as the Dark Ages. The Middle Ages consist of the thousand-year period that came between the fall of Rome and the Renaissance, and the European Dark Ages are the first couple of centuries of those thousand years. It is hard for us to imagine what the fall of Rome meant to people who were then living. That collapse is analogous, perhaps, to the collapse of the Soviet Union in our time, though with profound differences. One difference is that Rome had existed for centuries rather than just decades, and another is that the mere idea of the Roman Empire pervaded people's lives. When the empire ceased to exist, Europe became a site of chaos. As we saw earlier, Rome did not collapse in a single cataclysm. Chaos had been descending for a long time. But when it became clear that the idea of Rome had ceased to exist, chaos took over. There were no nations in the modern sense of the word; there were no longer provinces. There was no central authority to build or maintain roads, to offer security, to provide justice. There were relatively small groups of people, which we might call tribes, who lived in a fairly constant state of hostility. Given the need for self-defense and for self-preservation, these tribes had little time and few resources to lavish upon such luxuries as learning. Learning, whether of classical or of scriptural texts, was confined to the monasteries and was always in danger of eradication.[1] It seems almost miraculous that the political and cultural heritage of Rome did not entirely disappear at this time, though it did become thoroughly combined with Christianity. Those few centuries after the fall of Rome were in many ways a dark age, though even in those centuries there were some bright lights.

Even greater light appeared in the eighth century with the rise of Charlemagne. Charlemagne was not only a warrior and a conqueror, he was also a patron of learning. He sponsored scholars and established schools where those scholars could study and rescue ancient texts. So much important work was done in his time that we refer to the era as the Carolingian Renaissance, the rebirth in the time of Charlemagne. Charlemagne was crowned emperor of the West by the Pope on Christmas in the year 800, and although the empire fell again into some chaos in the years after his death, we can see the combination of classical and Christian motifs that characterized the Middle Ages in the name that was given to the western empire in 962, the Holy Roman Empire. While we recognize that this empire was neither holy nor Roman, that combination represented an ideal for many medieval thinkers.

The combination of the classical and the scriptural was not only an ideal, however; it was also the source of a problem. In the early centuries of Christianity, when many people became Christians, either voluntarily or involuntarily, without fully understanding the meaning of Christianity, they remained attached to the classical, mythological stories that they enjoyed, including the works of Virgil and Ovid. Many early Christian writers railed against these works as lies about false gods who were actually servants of the Devil or demons themselves. Other Christian writers, however, found another way to approach these works, a way that enabled them to continue to read such works under Christian auspices, as Berchorius did with Ovid. They argued that the pagan writers had somehow been smart enough to see glimpses of Christian truths even without the benefit of divine revelation. Consequently, their writings, while not precisely religious, did contain those Christian truths in a disguised, allegorical form. Virgil's *Aeneid*, the story of Aeneas' flight from Troy and his struggle to find and found Rome, was interpreted as the story of the human soul making its way from this fallen world to the eternal world of God, and every episode in the poem was interpreted according to this scheme. And Ovid's *Metamorphoses*, a series of often sexually explicit stories, was also understood as an allegory of Christian truths, as Berchorius demonstrates.

This combination of the classical and the scriptural became even more important in the next "renaissance" during the Middle Ages, the renaissance of the twelfth century. The twelfth century marked a real turning point for Europe in a number of ways. It was in this century, for instance, that nationalism as we know it became obvious. Through a very gradual process, nations, in the modern sense, began to appear. In architecture, the twelfth century marks the end of the heavier, bulkier Romanesque style and the beginning of the Gothic style[2]; and in art it marks the beginning of a more naturalistic, though still clearly medieval, approach to representation. The twelfth century was a time when people began to pay more attention to the world around them, to nature, and to themselves as individuals.

The twelfth century also marked a vital change in Western thought, largely because of the influence of Aristotle. During the Middle Ages, almost no one in western Europe could read Greek, and the works of Aristotle had not been translated into Latin, which was the scholarly language of the time. (Even the works of Plato were not known in Europe except for half of one dialogue and the reports of Christian neo–Platonists like St. Augustine, to whom we will return shortly.) Through a complicated series of events, Aristotle's works, especially his works on logic, were introduced into western Europe in the twelfth century, and some people, like Peter Abelard, began to apply Aristotle's logical criteria to the Bible and to earlier religious writers. According to Aristotle's criteria, both the Bible and the writings of the Church Fathers contained logical contradictions, and much of the philosophical work of the next several centuries was devoted to analyzing and often explaining away those contradictions. This combination of Aristotelian and biblical thought was called scholasticism; and though it may have eventually degenerated into empty logical argumentation, in the twelfth century it represented an important new way of thinking. In later chapters we will examine works from the twelfth, thirteenth, and fourteenth centuries that illustrate the developing thought of those centuries.

THE RELIGIOUS CONTEXT

As this discussion indicates, religion played a central role in medieval life, more central, perhaps, than we can easily imagine. During the Middle Ages, religion dominated virtually every aspect of life, and when we talk about religion in the European Middle Ages, we mean (aside from Judaism and a few heretical sects) Roman Catholicism. Our views of the religious situation may be somewhat skewed, since all of our records were written by people who had been trained by the Church. Even so, it is clear that, to an extent that nearly exceeds our imaginative abilities, religion permeated people's lives. Even if few people could read the biblical texts, everyone heard the stories of the Bible in sermons or saw them depicted on the walls of churches. And everyone attended church.

Aside from the Bible, the most important source of Christian teaching in the Middle Ages was the fourth- and fifth-century bishop of Hippo in North Africa, St. Augustine. Augustine wrote volumes and volumes of works in which he refuted heresies and proclaimed a vision of Christianity that relatively quickly became the dominant view of the Western Church. Among his most important works are the *Confessions*, his spiritual autobiography, and a very long work called *The City of God*. The latter work took him many years to write, but its composition was stimulated by a specific question. Augustine's contemporaries and coreligionists wanted to know how they could respond to the charge that Christianity had weakened Rome and led to its collapse. After all, Christianity had become the official religion of Rome in the early fourth century, and by the beginning of the fifth century the Germanic tribes were well on their way to overrunning the empire. Augustine began *The City of God* to respond to this question, but as the years passed, the book developed into a theoretical work on the history of the world.

Augustine's answer — and please keep in mind that Augustine's long and complex book cannot be summarized in a single short paragraph — was based on a Neoplatonic understanding of Christianity which, because of Augustine's influence, became the basis for medieval Christianity. Augustine argued that there are actually two cities that we must consider, the City of Man and the City of God. The City of Man was founded by the biblical Cain and shares the frailties of the world: It is temporary and changeable, subject to time and decay. Those qualities define this world, which, though made by God, who proclaimed it to be good, is subject to, and apt to lead us into, sin. The other city, the City of God, is eternal and unchangeable. On earth, these two cities seem intermingled, but they are really quite distinct. Too often, according to Augustine, we are ensnared by the transitory pleasures of the City of Man, the pleasures of this world, and we forget that our goal should be eternal residence in the City of God. We are only visitors, sojourners, pilgrims in the City of Man, and the goal of our pilgrimage should be the City of God. For Augustine, the Church represents the City of God in the world, but, with a medieval love of allegory, he found many other symbols for these cities. The Old Jerusalem, the actual historical city, was the City of Man, while the New Jerusalem, the heavenly city described in Revelation, is the City of God; or Babylonia was the City of Man and Jerusalem was the City of God. (A point to note here is that in such allegorical presentations, the symbols can easily be transformed: In the pairing of Jerusalem and Babylon, Jerusalem, the historical city, represents the City of God, whereas in the pairing of the historical and the visionary Jerusalem, the historical city is the City of Man. So it is with medieval allegory: The allegories are not constant and must therefore be examined in their contexts.) Augustine's answer to the question his friends asked, then, is that Rome is the City of Man and as such is subject to change. Rome may well fall, but in the great scheme of things, measured against the eternity of the City of God, Rome is at best inconsequential and at worst an inducement to sin. Our focus should be on the City of God; the tribulations of this world, except for their purifying effect on human beings who understand them correctly, are temporary and insignificant. (It is worth recalling that the allegorical reading of the *Aeneid*, a poem that Augustine loved, makes Troy the City of Man and Rome the City of God, which, as the seat of the papacy and of the Church, it ideally was.)

Augustine, of course, was neither the first nor the only person to put forth such doctrines, but he expressed them the most clearly and forcefully, and his influence can be felt though the Middle Ages, the Renaissance, the Reformation, and well into the eighteenth century. The problem is that, as with so many religious ideals, it is easier to profess than to carry out what Augustine says. We need only look at the great medieval churches, whether Romanesque or Gothic, to see buildings that were built to honor God, to represent the City of God on earth, but that do so by glorifying the City of Man. Those buildings were not built free of charge, nor were they built by volunteer laborers. They cost a fortune, and people were coerced into building them. In fact, the cathedrals were often built in competition with each other. The development of the Gothic style in the twelfth century meant that cathedrals could be built higher and higher, and there was virtually a contest to see who could build the highest and most magnificent cathedral until the one that was being built at Beauvais collapsed. Such behavior is hardly what Augustine had in mind.

In fact, this example of the cathedrals expresses a theme that will run through this book, a theme that characterizes much of the thought and the literature of the Middle Ages. The kind of Christianity that dominated medieval Europe was both highly idealistic and quite demanding. It held up ideals of perfection and demanded that Christians try to live by those ideals. Because human beings are imperfect, or, in Christian terms, fallen, that demand could not be met. Consequently, medieval Christians were constantly confronted with evidence of their failure to live up to what was expected of them.

An example will illustrate this point. In Exodus 21: 23-24, we read that if a woman is injured and dies, the responsible party will "render life for life, Eye for eye, tooth for tooth, hand for hand, foot for foot...."[3] Around the time of Jesus, Jewish rabbis understood this passage to mean not that a person who injures someone should be injured in return, for such a system would benefit no one. Rather, they understood it to mean that an injured person was entitled to suitable compensation, that the value of the injury should be assessed and an equivalent amount should be given to the injured person. This system was highly civilized, since it prevented the injured party from either receiving no compensation or from acting out of vengeance and seeking excessive compensation, possibly through the use of violence.

This system recognizes and regulates the human desire for vengeance. In Matthew 5: 39, however, Jesus takes regulation even further: "if one strikes thee on thy right cheek, turn to him also the other." In other words, the injured party should avoid not only vengeance but any kind of compensation. Clearly a world in which people could behave as Jesus instructs would be better, but equally clearly, Jesus is describing an ideal that few can reach. While the Old Testament expresses many ideals, it makes allowances for human failures. The New Testament makes few such allowances.

Of course, Christianity is based on the premise of human sinfulness. While both Judaism and Christianity believe that Adam and Eve ate the forbidden fruit in the Garden of Eden, that episode played almost no role in the development of Judaism, whereas it became part of the central story of Christianity, which taught that the whole human race was besmirched by Adam and Eve's sin and that the only possible route to salvation, to eternal life in Heaven, was through Jesus' death on the cross, which atoned for that original sin. The medieval Christian, then, had to deal with what seem to us to be superhuman standards and the knowledge that because of human sinfulness, he or she could never meet those standards.

There were, naturally, several possible responses to this dilemma, all of which we will see represented in the literature. People could simply persevere, attempting to reach the ideal even though they knew they would not be successful. Even if they failed to reach the ideal, they would still be better than if they did not try. Or they could develop an exaggerated sense of their sinfulness, a focus on the inability to live up to the ideals. Or they could simply give up in the face of their inevitable failure to attain those ideals. As we will see, this conflict between idealistic demands and human realities became central to much of the literature and can be found not only in the realm of religious thought but in other areas such as chivalry and in matters of love. It can be found in the works of St. Augustine and in the works of another of the founders of medieval thought, Boethius.

Boethius, who lived in the late fifth and early sixth centuries, wrote a number of works, but he is best known for *The Consolation of Philosophy*, a work that is written in a mixture of verse and prose. Boethius, who had held a high governmental position in Ostrogothic Rome, wrote the book while he was in prison awaiting execution on a trumped-up charge. As the book opens, he describes himself lamenting his fate in terms that we might consider quite normal. After all, he has fallen from a high position and is facing death. Suddenly, however, a woman appears before him, a woman whose magical abilities would have immediately indicated to a medieval reader that she was an allegorical figure. In fact, she is Philosophy, and, as the book's title indicates, she has come to offer Boethius consolation. Her consolation really is consoling, which helps to explain why this short book has remained so popular for so long and why it was so important during the Middle Ages. Philosophy leads Boethius, through logical arguments, to see that much of what he has valued, the materialistic aspects of his life, is transient and ultimately worthless, the result of Fortune (another personified abstraction). By the end of their conversation, Boethius has come to an understanding of what is truly important in human existence. He has, in modern terms, gotten his priorities straight and therefore can understand what constitutes true happiness as opposed to the superficial happiness that is provided by material objects or earthly glory.

Boethius' teachings are in many ways similar to those of Augustine, though Boethius arrives at his conclusions primarily through reason while Augustine arrives at his primarily through faith. Together, however, they provided a foundation for medieval thought, for medieval attitudes towards the world, towards what is important in the world, and towards how human beings should exist in this world. It should be noted that neither of them says that the world is inherently evil — after all, on every day of the biblical creation story, we read that "God saw that it was good" and on the sixth day "God saw all the things that he had made, and they were very good." The problem is not so much with the world as it is with human beings who misuse the things of the world. Nevertheless, there were both individuals and groups during the Middle Ages who renounced the things of this world in a variety of ways. Hermits, particularly in the early centuries of the Middle Ages, withdrew from the world and lived alone in the wilderness. Monks lived in monasteries, where they were supposed to work and pray. Although the monastic ideal often became corrupted and required reform, the ideal itself expressed central beliefs about medieval Christianity's attitude toward the world. And individual ascetics often denied themselves food or drink for long periods or wore hair shirts, rough garments that would irritate the skin and serve as a constant reminder that the temptations of worldly comfort should be rejected, that true bliss and true happiness were spiritual and would only be fully attained after death. But of course, even if many people felt that such ways of life expressed the ideals of Christianity, most people chose not to follow them.

LITERACY AND READING

Once again, then, we see a huge gap between the publicly proclaimed and accepted ideal and the reality that did not and could not live up to that ideal. It is difficult for us to know how people in the Middle Ages dealt with that gap. It certainly plays a role in the literature that we will be examining, but there are differences between that literature and the literature of later eras that we must keep in mind. One difference between then and now is that through much of the Middle Ages, literacy was confined to a relatively restricted population that consisted mostly of members of the clergy. And, while we know that there were a number of literate women, most of the writing that we have from the Middle Ages was done by men. Thus, medieval writing represents a relatively small segment of the population, a segment that often had its own peculiar concerns. For example, medieval literature (and theology) is full of misogyny, hostility toward women. We might assume from reading such literature that misogyny was characteristic of the Middle Ages until we realize that most of these misogynistic works were written by members of the clergy, men who had taken vows of chastity but who, having normal sexual feelings, were tempted by the mere existence of women to break those vows. Consequently, they might well have regarded women as the tool that the Devil used to undermine their commitment to chastity. It is hardly surprising that men in such circumstances would have produced misogynistic texts.

Even when writers produced more secular texts, their writings were intended for a relatively small audience among the upper class. Surely the lower classes also enjoyed hearing stories and poems, but because those stories and poems existed orally and were not written down, they have disappeared. What remains is what was written down, a factor that brings us to the complicated issue of studying literature from what we call a manuscript culture.

When we read medieval literature, we must always remember that this literature was written before the invention of the printing press in the fifteenth century. Some social critics say that the invention of personal computers in the late twentieth century is comparable to the invention of the printing press, but the truth of that statement remains to be seen. We do know, however, that printing created tremendous changes. Before the invention of printing, writing or copying a book was both time-consuming and expensive. The time factor is easy to understand. Imagine how long it would take to copy the Bible or *The Canterbury Tales* by hand. We have become so accustomed to photocopiers, computers, and scanners that we can barely think about the time and effort it took to transcribe a single copy of a text. Furthermore, even when we write by hand, we use ballpoint pens, not the quills that medieval scribes utilized; and we use paper that comes with lines already marked on it. Medieval scribes occasionally used paper, but the preferred medium was parchment, made from the skin of an animal. Parchment was durable, but it was also expensive, as was the ink, which was made from plant matter. Lines had to be incised on the parchment and then the whole text had to be copied legibly by hand, either by copying an already existing text or by taking down a text as it was being read aloud. In either case, errors and new readings were bound to enter the texts. In addition, punctuation barely existed in the Middle Ages and spelling had not yet been standardized. Finally, scribes were not shy about changing the words they were copying, either through misunderstandings or because they preferred to say things in other ways.

The result of all these complications is that a medieval text exists in a very different state from a modern one. A modern text, which may exist in thousands of copies, will have been proofread by its editor and its author. Punctuation and spelling are expected to conform to certain standards, and every one of those thousands of copies will contain the identical text. If the text is reprinted with changes, it will be listed as a new edition. Medieval texts, on the other hand, may exist in single copies, as is the case with the manuscript of *Beowulf* and the *Pearl* manuscript. One might think that having a single text would be easy, since there would be no chance of alternate readings. Such is not the case. In *Sir Gawain and the Green Knight* (part of the *Pearl* manuscript, which is technically known as MS Cotton Nero A.x.) a major character's name appears only once, and it is impossible to tell whether that name is Bertilak or Bercilak. When we look at a work that exists in many manuscripts, the problems multiply. Scribes may have changed words through simple error, or they may have misunderstood the text they were copying, or they may have tried to improve the text. And usually we do not know which manuscript (if any) belonged to the original author, so that we cannot arrive at anything like an authorized text. In the case of Chaucer's *Canterbury Tales*, we cannot even know the order in which Chaucer would have wanted to tales to appear. And the lack of punctuation makes the situation even more complicated. It often happens that punctuation affects meaning; if we cannot be sure where a sentence ends and another begins or where quotation marks belong, we are bound to run into interpretive difficulties. Thus, we must keep in mind that whenever we read a modern edition of a medieval work, we are relying on the skills of a modern editor, someone whose skills must be respected but whose editorial judgments — which manuscript version should be used? where should commas, periods, and quotation marks appear? — are open to dispute.

Furthermore, reading habits were also different in the Middle Ages. We know, from descriptions and artistic representations, that people did read alone, but even when they did, they did so differently from us. In his *Confessions*, St. Augustine mentions one oddity about his teacher, St. Ambrose: when Ambrose read, he did so silently and without moving his lips. Apparently, even reading to oneself was a kind of oral exercise. But we also know that many of the works we are about to examine were not intended to be read to oneself. They were intended for oral recitation. One implication of this fact is that medieval literature should not be read silently. Actually, like poetry from every age, it should be read aloud, slowly.

People in the Middle Ages may not have had radio or television or many of the other forms of entertainment that we enjoy, but they still liked stories and adventures. After meals people might well have gathered together to hear a poet read or to hear someone else, perhaps a professional reciter, tell the latest stories or recite old favorites, the way friends today might get together to go to a movie or to watch a television show. Once again we can see that while people in the Middle Ages differed from us, they were also like us in many ways.

THE MEDIEVAL POET

Perhaps a major difference between them and us is that our most popular forms of entertainment are not poetry recitations. We might argue that we have more choices in how we spend our time, but the medievals did other things as well. There is, however, another factor at work here, a change in the way both poetry and the poet are perceived. As a result of developments since the time of Descartes, and particularly under the influence of the Romantic poets, we tend to think of poets as people who have a gift, as people who are not only good at using words but who are good at looking inside themselves and describing their deepest feelings. When Percy Shelley writes in his "Ode to the West Wind,"

> Oh! Lift me as a wave, a leaf, a cloud!
> I fall upon the thorns of life! I bleed!

we think we know what he means. Though English teachers might warn us that Shelley is using a persona, we tend to think that the poet is indeed describing himself in these lines, that he is calling out from the depth of his soul. Those insistent exclamation points and that plaintive "Oh!" give the impression that the speaker is truly in distress, and our interest in the "self," in our innermost beings, reinforces this impression. Medieval poetry is quite different.

The difference can be seen in the names we use for the poet. The original meaning of the word "poet," which comes from the Greek word *poiein*, is "to make." In medieval England, appropriately, the poet was often referred to as a "maker." On the one hand, this title was a simple statement of craftsmanship. The poet could indeed make poems, as the carpenter could make shelves or as the goldsmith could make jewelry or implements. On the other hand, at least by implication, the maker was analogous to the Maker, that is, to God, who created the world out of language, just as the poet creates worlds out of language. (This idea finds a full expression in Sir Philip Sidney's *Apology for Poetry*, a work of the Renaissance.) The medieval poet not only does not explore his self, his innermost being, but the medieval poet would not have understood what those words meant. For the Romantic and post–Romantic poet, the world is filtered through individual consciousnesses, each of which is capable of creating its own truth. For the medieval poet, the world is out there to see; if one sees it clearly, one recognizes Truth (or if one knows Truth, one will discern it in the world).

Since the Romantics, lyric poetry has predominated, because it is so suitable for expressing the concerns of Romantic and post–Romantic poets. In the Middle Ages, lyric was subordinate to narrative poetry; and while there are beautiful and moving medieval lyric poems, they are quite different from their modern counterparts. Many, naturally, are religious in nature:

Now goth sonne under wod	Now the sun goes beneath the woods;
Me reweth Marye thy faire rode	I pity, Mary, thy fair face.
Now goth sonne under tree	Now goes the sun under the tree;
Me reweth Marye thy sone and thee.	I pity, Mary, thy son and thee.

Undoubtedly the poet truly felt pity for Mary and for her crucified son, so the poem is an expression of his real feelings, but all medieval Christians felt such pity, so the poet is not merely expressing a personal feeling. He is expressing an appropriate feeling, what everyone should feel while contemplating the horror of the crucifixion. The poet underscores the crucifixion motif by using the words "wod," "rode," and "tree," all of which refer to the cross. He is not, however, searching his soul. He is, rather, allowing this momentous event in salvation history to touch his soul. The event exists "out there," in the world, and the poet acknowledges it.

There are many other medieval lyrics that may seem more personal. Many of these poems deal with love, especially with the problem of loving someone who does not return the feeling. We might be tempted to see personal expression in these poems, but they are no more personal than is a country-western song about unrequited love. Medieval poets do not examine themselves. They examine the world, which they believe exists independently of their perceptions, and they examine that world in the light of the ideals that their religious beliefs established. Characters in medieval literature may occasionally demonstrate psychological depth, though even then we must be careful not to take the concept too far, but medieval authors are not interested in self-analysis.

Nor are medieval authors interested in anything like what we call realism. Characters and settings seldom receive physical description. We never learn whether Beowulf is tall or short, fair or dark. We do not know what he ate for breakfast, what he wore, what his home looked like, or what he did to relax. We are told only what we need to know, that he was a hero, a powerful fighter, a man of integrity, a good king. The same is true of other characters and places. The writers make no attempt to help us picture them. At the same time, the reader must be aware that when a writer includes a detail, there must be some reason for that inclusion. We can make an analogy between this literary technique and the techniques of medieval art. Anyone who looks at a medieval painting or manuscript illumination is bound to be struck by its unreality. Such paintings tend to be two-dimensional, with human figures in postures that would be impossible for real human bodies to assume. Trees or plants, if they are included at all, are schematically drawn, and backgrounds consist of flat color or textured patterns. There is little or no sense of perspective in these paintings: the main characters are large and the minor characters are small.

The casual viewer of such paintings might attribute these odd qualities to a lack of skill: Medieval artists were simply primitive, unable to render reality realistically. Of course, nothing could be further from the truth. Certainly the Middle Ages had its share of incompetent artists, just as every age does, but thinking of medieval artists as primitive reveals more about us than it does about them. It reveals our assumption that we know what constitutes reality, that our conventions offer the only way to represent reality, that our perceptions are correct and other cultures' perceptions are not. Art historians have spoken about the rediscovery of linear perspective in the Renaissance, as though linear perspective somehow provides a more legitimate mode of visual expression than did the medieval techniques. Such views are ethnocentric and ignore the legitimacy of other perspectives.

In fact, we can argue, those medieval techniques, whether in art or literature, are perfect expressions of medieval perspectives. If medieval artists had needed linear perspective, they would have used it. That they did not use it indicates that they did not need it in order to present their vision of the world, a vision that differs significantly from ours. We locate reality in the phenomenal world, which we study empirically. We observe things closely so that we can determine how they work, whether on the grand scale of the cosmos or the subatomic world of quantum mechanics. From all of these observations we try to draw conclusions, to find patterns. Renaissance artists attended autopsies so that they could better understand how the human body works, so that they could portray it accurately. These kinds of observation were largely irrelevant to the medievals, who did not locate reality in the phenomenal world. That phenomenal world was important, because God created it and saw that it was good, but that world existed largely as a system of symbols that gave evidence of a higher reality.

We can say that for the medievals, God had written two books, the Bible and the book of Nature. The Bible revealed the Truth to human beings, though even the Bible was seen as an elaborate system of signs that had to be read correctly. For example, the Old Testament was read as history, but it was also seen as a foreshadowing (as it still is for many people) of the New Testament. Thus, every episode and every character in the Old Testament potentially has a New Testament counterpart. For example, in Genesis 22, Abraham is commanded to sacrifice his son Isaac. As they approach the place of sacrifice, Isaac carries the wood that will be used for the sacrifice. This story was seen as the foreshadowing of the Crucifixion, when God sacrificed his son on the wooden cross, which Jesus carried to the place of sacrifice. The Old Testament story is called the type, while the New Testament story is the antitype; the whole system is known as typology. Medieval biblical commentaries and art works are full of such typology, which makes everything in the Bible somehow symbolic.

The other book that God wrote is the book of Nature, the created world, which, like the Bible, is a symbolic system. The symbolic value of natural objects may come from their biblical associations (snakes, and their cousins the dragons, are obviously evil because of the serpent in the Garden of Eden), from their natural characteristics (the sunflower follows the sun just as the Christian soul should follow God), or from what has been called "unnatural natural history" (the pelican was thought to nourish her offspring by pricking her breast with her long beak and allowing them to ingest her blood, just as the body of Jesus was pierced and his blood provided the means to everlasting life). What should be clear in all of these cases is that worldly phenomena bespeak a greater reality, a reality located in the world of religious truth. That is the reality that concerned the medievals. Thus, when they painted or when they wrote, they were not overly concerned with what we consider realistic depictions of the phenomenal world; and even when they dealt with what might be considered secular subjects, they used the style that they knew. Thus, there are no receding backgrounds in medieval art because the artists were depicting actions against what we might call a background of eternity.

Occasionally, we must admit, this attitude toward realism has its amusing side. In Chrétien de Troyes' *Lancelot*, Lancelot is in the middle of a sword fight when he realizes that his beloved Guinevere is watching him from a tower at his back. Because he is so much in love, he turns to gaze at her, while he continues to duel with his opponent, who is now at his back. Even if it were possible for him to conduct a duel with a formidable opponent behind his back, Lancelot was likely to be killed. No matter. Lancelot perseveres. Undoubtedly Chrétien intended his audience to smile at this somewhat absurd scene, but the scene also makes a serious point about Lancelot's love and about the power of love in general.

In reading medieval literature, then, we must be prepared for such incongruities; and when we encounter them, we cannot dismiss them as evidence of medieval naiveté or primitiveness. We have to try to see and understand them on their own terms. We have to think medievally.

THINKING MEDIEVALLY

So what does thinking medievally mean? First, it means that we have to think in terms of the Bible. As the great medieval scholar Morton Bloomfield said of William Langland, people in the Middle Ages "spoke Bible" (37), so we always have to look for biblical parallels and references. Second, we need to be aware of their symbolic systems and their passion for order and symmetry. This passion shows itself in small ways, for instance in the legend that the wood of the cross came either directly or indirectly from the Tree of the Knowledge of Good and Evil. The same tree whose fruit brought sin and death to the world brought the possibility of everlasting life. This passion can also be seen in larger structures, like cathedrals. (A cathedral, incidentally, is not simply a large church. It is the church which, regardless of its size or magnificence, contains the throne, or kathedra, of the bishop.) The great Romanesque, and even more the great Gothic cathedrals, are not simply astounding feats of architecture. They symbolize the entire universe.

These cathedrals were always built in the shape of a cross. Of course, in order to see this shape clearly, an observer would have to be above the cathedral, which was generally impossible since the cathedral would have been the tallest building in a city. Occasionally that cross (or cruciform) shape would be obscured by a series of chapels built at one end, but it is always there. Furthermore, cathedrals are always built with the altar facing east, the direction of Jerusalem. Thus the eastern end is associated with the rising sun and the crucifixion, while the west end, in contrast, is associated with the Last Judgment. Although there is much more that is symbolic about the cathedrals, only one more point will be mentioned here. As we noted earlier, the Gothic style allowed cathedrals to be built taller than ever before. The architects designed those buildings so that when a person enters, that person's eyes immediately look up, not only to the ceiling of the cathedral but in the direction of God.

Thinking medievally also involves being prepared for sudden juxtapositions. In medieval literature and art, we often find two or more scenes placed next to each other with no explanation or transition. We, the audience, must make the necessary connections, which may depend not on the overt action in the scenes but on the thematic or symbolic subtext. We will see examples of this technique in our discussions of the literary works.

Another kind of juxtaposition involves ideas. We live now in an analytical age. We like to break ideas down to their constituent parts. The Middle Ages were a more syncretistic time. The medievals liked to bring together all kinds of ideas and show how they pointed in the same direction. They were like modern physicists, who are looking for a Grand Unified Theory that will unite all the forces of nature, except that the medievals already had the theory—their religious view of the world— and sought as many ideas from as many sources as possible to illustrate the universality of the theory. They even liked puns, because puns showed connections between disparate things that might otherwise not seem connected. The reference a couple of paragraphs ago to "the rising sun and the crucifixion" could just as well have been written in English "the rising Son and the crucifixion," and the connection between "sun" and "Son" would have added layers of meaning to the statement.

ON TO THE LITERATURE

There is, of course, much more that could be said by way of an introduction to medieval literature, but it is time now to move on to the literature itself, where many other points will be considered. Even so, the reader who turns back to the beginning of this introduction, to the brief quotations from Berchorius, will recognize a number of the points that have been discussed: the religious and moral orientation, the allegorization of both literature and experience, the attitude toward phenomenal realism, and the juxtaposition of not only unrelated but apparently contradictory ideas.

"So why," one might ask, "should we bother studying such alien material? What value does it have?" There are a number of answers to these questions. English literature has its roots in the Middle Ages, and, because writers read other writers, medieval literature has influenced everything that came later. In addition, many of our customs and ways of thinking have their sources in the Middle Ages. Of most immediate interest, perhaps, the modern university began in the Middle Ages, and when students don caps and gowns for graduation, they are putting on medieval garb. More importantly, medieval people faced the same basic human problems that we face, and it is worth our while to understand how they stated those problems and to see what their solutions were. And finally, medieval literature is worth reading simply because it is enjoyable. Reading this material about knights and ladies, heaven and hell, saints and sinners puts us in touch with minds that were alive hundreds of years ago and that continue to live through the literature. We may not have access to an actual time machine, but literature is a good substitute. We are about to take a journey through hundreds of years of the Middle Ages. We have to do so largely through translations, and even so, the journey may occasionally be difficult. Nevertheless, it is a journey worth making.

I. *Beowulf*

ON DIGRESSIONS

Students often groan when *Beowulf* is mentioned. This reaction is somewhat puzzling and very disappointing for those of us who love this remarkable poem, but those groans may simply be a response to a poem whose plot seems hard to follow. One function of this chapter is to explain why it seems that way and then to demonstrate that it really is not so difficult.

(I would just like to offer one bit of advice here: pay close attention to this paragraph. I will explain why later.) English teachers, like people in other professions, often have certain experiences in common. When people first meet me and learn what I do for a living, they tend to respond in one of two ways. One response goes, "An English teacher? I'd better watch my grammar." Several years ago, as I was about to undergo an angioplasty, the cardiologist walked into the cath lab and announced, "He's an English teacher, so watch the way you talk." I hastened to assure everyone that at that moment I did not particularly care how they talked, as long as they were good at what they were about to do — which they were.

The other thing people say when they learn I teach English is, "I've read some Shakespeare in Old English." Shakespeare's plays are emphatically not written in Old English. Shakespeare, writing in the late sixteenth and early seventeenth centuries, was using Early Modern English. Even Chaucer, writing in the fourteenth century, did not use Old English. His language was Middle English. As we will see in a later chapter, Middle English is difficult but not at all impossible for modern readers to read. *Beowulf*, however, is written in Old English, and Old English is, for those of us living in the twenty-first century, a foreign language. Old English began to disappear as a spoken language after 1066, when William of Normandy invaded England with his Norman-French army, who, as victors at the Battle of Hastings, became the ruling class. At first, the linguistic result of Hastings was that the rulers spoke the French of Normandy while the conquered peoples of England spoke Germanic Old English (which has also been called Anglo-Saxon). Thus, Richard the Lionhearted, that famous English king who ruled England from 1189 to 1199, spoke French, not Old English or Middle English or anything that could be confused with English. However, as society changed over the next couple of centuries, the Norman French and the Germanic Old English gradually coalesced to become Middle English (which existed in a variety of dialects); and eventually Middle English developed into Modern English. Modern English is undoubtedly developing into another form that linguists will discuss in centuries to come.

Here is a sample of Old English, the first three lines of *Beowulf*, to demonstrate what Old English was like:

> Hwæt we gardena   in geardagum
> þeodcyning   þrym gefrunon
> hu ða æðelingas   ellen fremedon…

First of all, there are two letters in this passage that no longer exist in English (though they should)—þ and ð, both of which represent the "th" sound. There are, however, a number of words in this passage that do exist, in different forms, in Modern English. "Hwæt" became Modern English "what" (which is why words like "what," "which," and "why" are really supposed to be pronounced with the "h" sound first—"hwat," "hwich," and "hwy"). Old English "we" became modern "we," "hu" became "how," and "ða" is a form of "the" (which is a bit more complicated, because Old English is a highly inflected language — that is, nouns, adjectives, and articles take different forms depending on how they are used). One other linguistic aspect of this passage should be noted: the tendency (still found in modern German) to create compound words by combining nouns. Thus "geardagum" is a compound word made up of "gear" (which would have been pronounced "ye-ar"), meaning "year" and "dagum," meaning "days." Literally "geardagum" means "yeardays," which we understand to mean "in days gone by." Similarly "þeodcyning," which combines "þeod" and "cyninga," means "peoplekings" or "kings of the people." *Beowulf* is full of such constructions. Another construction that Old English verse uses is kennings, picturesque ways of naming people or things. *Beowulf* contains many such phrases, like "whale's path" for the sea or "throne house" for castle.

Another point to notice about the opening of the poem is the style of the verse. Each line is divided into two parts, and what holds each line together in the original is not rhythm and rhyme, as in more modern verse, or the length of syllables shaped into strict feet, as in ancient Greek and Latin verse, but alliteration. The techniques of alliteration are complex and have furnished the battleground for numerous academic conflicts, but the main point is that in almost all lines there are two words that alliterate in the first half-line and one in the second half-line. This technique gives Old English verse a sound all its own. As we will see, this verse form again became popular in written verse in the fourteenth century.

There are many fine translations of *Beowulf.* One recent verse translation that captures the sound and feeling of the original and is wonderful for reading aloud (as the poem was intended to be read) is by Frederick Rebsamen. A good, very literal prose translation is the one by E. Talbot Donaldson.

(Reader, pay close attention to this paragraph, too.) I met E. Talbot Donaldson several years ago at a conference on the Middle Ages. Conferences can be very exciting — there are exchanges of new ideas, research projects can be developed, and scholars can test their insights on colleagues in shared disciplines. Occasionally, however, there are scholars who besmirch the ideal. Instead of simply disagreeing with other scholars, they try to belittle them. Of course, the greater humiliation falls on those who engage in such tactics, but their intended victims also suffer. Professor Donaldson, however, who was one of the great scholars in his field, never stooped to such activities.

No one knows how *Beowulf* was put together. The poem, like so many works from the Middle Ages, is anonymous, and we cannot even be sure what century saw its composition. All that we know for certain is that it exists in a single manuscript (now in the British Library) and that that manuscript was nearly destroyed in a fire. (It is frightening to think that this great poem was almost destroyed, and we might wonder how many other works actually were destroyed before they could be rescued.) *Beowulf* was probably composed as *The Iliad* and *The Odyssey* were, orally, with passages being added or changed over the course of time, until someone finally wrote it down. The manuscript itself dates from around the year 1000, but the poem is clearly older than that, and we can see from its mixture of Christian and non–Christian elements that it contains a number of different layers. While analyzing those layers is a fascinating and worthwhile enterprise, for our purposes we should simply accept the poem as it exists and try to understand it, because whoever did write it down knew what he was doing and created a masterpiece.

That last point requires explanation. The final "author" of this poem did know what he was doing, even though the poem often seems to ramble off in arbitrary digressions. The central story of *Beowulf* is quite simple: Beowulf, as a young warrior, rescues the Danish people by killing two monsters, Grendel and Grendel's mother. Fifty years later, long after he has become king of his own people, he saves them by killing a dragon, though he himself dies in the process and we are given to understand that his people's days are numbered. Told in this way, the story does not seem to amount to much. Of course, as is the case with all stories, a great deal depends on how the story is told, and Beowulf's battles with the three monsters are certainly exciting. They are, without question, the best-known parts of the poem.

The rest of the poem is taken up with stories about the Danes, the Swedes, the Frisians, the Franks, and the Geats (pronounced Ye-ats; these are Beowulf's own people), stories that often appear completely unrelated to the main story of Beowulf and the monsters. It may look like the *Beowulf* poet was just adding lines to draw his story out, but all of those minor stories, those digressions from the main story, are truly central to the poem.

At this point we must pause to consider the role of digressions in literature. In our ordinary, everyday conversation, we often begin talking about a subject only to interrupt ourselves and digress to another subject. Frequently, when we try to return to the original subject, we may find that we have forgotten what it was and worry that we are losing our minds. Authors, too, often use digressions, and good writers do so purposefully; often the digressions in a work can give us greater insight into what the work is actually saying. In medieval literature, digressions frequently rely on the technique of juxtaposition discussed in the introductory chapter: the author makes no explicit connection between the main text and the digression, leaving that job up to the reader. As readers, then, we must understand the digressions and their relationship to the main story. They may, for instance, take the story further or they may offer a contrast to it. In any case, there are thematic connections between the main story and the digressions. As we will see, the digressions provide another perspective from which to observe the story, and as always, the reader must know what the perspective is.

Now we can return to these paragraphs earlier in this chapter that asked the reader for special attention. Both of those paragraphs contain a digression, though each functions in a different way. The chapter's second paragraph contained a story about English teachers that appeared to have nothing directly to do with *Beowulf,* but that little story may have made a reader smile and may even have induced the reader to continue reading. It also made a connection with Old English that was important for understanding the language of the poem, and it illustrated the digressive nature of *Beowulf.* Five paragraphs ago there was another digression, this time about a great scholar and about purported behavior at scholarly conferences. Again, this paragraph seems unrelated to *Beowulf,* but in fact the poem is about heroes, and E. Talbot Donaldson could be seen as a hero to scholars who believe in a particular approach to the scholarly life. Furthermore, as should become clear shortly, the behavior of scholars at conferences as it was described is closely linked to one of the main points being made in *Beowulf,* so the digression actually foreshadows the rest of this discussion. In more formal scholarly writing, we would not find such digressions, but if the reader sees how they function in this chapter, he or she will also be prepared to deal with the numerous digressions that occur throughout *Beowulf.*

If we assume that authors control their material, we must also assume that there is nothing in a great literary work that does not have a function. Great writers do not digress because they have nothing else to say or because they have lost their train of thought. Digressions perform vital functions in furthering our understanding, as Jonathan Swift recognized in his *Tale of a Tub,* half of which is made up of digressions, including "A Digression on Digressions," which is also what these last few paragraphs have been.

And now that this digression is over, we can return to *Beowulf. Beowulf* is full of digressions, a whole series of stories or parts of stories that appear to be woven through the main stories about Beowulf and the monsters using a technique called interlacement. These digressions are often told without regard to chronology, and they assume that the poem's original audience would have recognized not only the names of characters but also the stories associated with those characters. (Most editions of the poem provide the background information that we need, since characters like Healfdene and Ongentheow are not part of our cultural context, though they were for the original audience.) Our task, as we read the poem, is to see what links together the main story and the digressions. We will examine some of the links, but there are many more than we can consider in a brief chapter.

OF KINGS AND MONSTERS

The poem opens, strangely enough, with a digression, this one about a king who plays no role in the main action of the poem, Scyld Scefing. Scyld's immediate importance is that he is the ancestor of Hrothgar, who is the king of the Danes and who needs Beowulf's help; but Scyld serves another purpose as well, which can be seen near the poem's beginning when the narrator says, "That was a good king!" Scyld Scefing, who was found by the Danes as a baby floating on a ship in the sea (somewhat like Moses or the Assyrian king Sargon II), grew up to be a remarkable king. What made him so good? He lived by the ideals that should govern a ruler: As a young man, he gave gifts to his retainers, thereby ensuring their loyalty later in his life and allowing him to lead his people with confidence through times of war and peace. Scyld, through a deft combination of generosity and valiant deeds, has protected his people from all the evils that threaten them, which is the job of a king. Furthermore, through what may look to us like bribery but which was interpreted as generosity, he builds a fellowship of warriors who remain loyal to him. That hint of bribery, however, requires attention. Scyld is a good king, he will protect his people, and his retainers should be loyal to him because their loyalty benefits the whole kingdom. At the same time, if their loyalty can be bought for a handful of gold, both its sincerity and its value become doubtful. Thus, this passage praising Scyld raises vital questions about the organization and the values of his society, questions that will become more pressing as the poem continues. Scyld's son Beowulf (or Beow, not to be confused with the hero of the poem), and his grandson Healfdene continue this tradition. The next king in line is Hrothgar, and Hrothgar, too, appears to be a good king, but strange things happen during his reign.

That reign seems to begin successfully, so successfully that Hrothgar decides to build a magnificent hall, called Heorot, in which to entertain his retainers. Perhaps Hrothgar is flaunting his wealth and power, but he does not, on the surface, seem to have done anything terribly wrong. Nonetheless, the building of Heorot rouses the ire of Grendel, a local monster, who twice attacks the hall's inhabitants, killing large numbers of them and frightening the rest away, so that Hrothgar's treasure hall stands empty and the usually fierce Danes are terrified.

On one level, all we have here is a good adventure story containing warriors, kings, and a monster; but if we regard it only as an adventure story, we miss the point. Let us begin to look more deeply by starting with Grendel. What kind of a monster is he? Although Grendel is never described in any detail, we do learn later on that he is roughly human in shape. He is huge and very strong — on his first attack he seizes thirty warriors and later he gobbles one down — but he is no fairy tale giant. In fact, the vagueness of his description is purposeful. It makes him seem more terrible by allowing him to be vaguely human combined with something more mysterious, for, as the narrator tells us, Grendel is descended from Cain, the first murderer, the killer of his brother. The narrator, like many other readers of Genesis 4:15, interprets the mark of Cain not as a protective device (as the Bible indicates) but as a punishment, a sign of his status as an outcast. We must remember that after Cain killed Abel, God asked where his brother was, to which Cain responded by asking one of the most important questions in the Bible: Am I my brother's keeper? Although that question is never answered directly, the context makes clear that the answer is an emphatic "Yes." Much of *Beowulf* dramatizes the question and its implicit answer. Grendel's descent from Cain indicates his sinful nature; he embodies the spirit of fratricide. But there is even more to Grendel, for St. Augustine in *The City of God* had identified Cain and his son Enoch with the city of man, the city of this transitory and sinful earth, as opposed to the eternal and pure city of God. This fact may help us understand why Grendel has not attacked the Danes before the completion of Heorot: this magnificent hall has been built to celebrate Hrothgar's great deeds and is therefore a monument to the works of men and a distraction from the city of God. The things of the city of man belong to this descendant of Cain, who founded the city of man.

But at this point the situation becomes even more complicated, as, just before Grendel's first attack, we are told that in the hall, the scop (the bard) had been reading a creation story that sounds very much like the one in Genesis (and like the earliest Old English poem we have, Caedmon's Hymn); and yet after Grendel's attack, the narrator tells us that the Danes offered heathen sacrifices because making such sacrifices was their custom. These Danes, the narrator explains, did not know God, that is, the God of Christendom. Apparently what we have here is a Christianized reinterpretation of an originally pagan story. In the original story, the Danes offered sacrifices to their gods. The Christian narrator retells the story but comments on it from his own religious point of view. As we saw in the words of Berchorius in the Introduction, Christianity tended to interpret all other cultures in its own image. So *Beowulf*, a pagan Germanic story, was given a Christian coloring, though we can often see the seams where the two perspectives were brought together. This explanation would also help us to understand the frequent references throughout the poem both to God and to "wyrd," an Old English word that means fate or destiny.

What we have, then, is a story about a monster who is descended from the fratricidal Cain and who attacks a monument that glorifies human accomplishments. Now let us consider one of the narrator's very brief digressions. Just after he describes Heorot, he tells us that the magnificent new hall awaited its destruction by fire, a destruction that would result from some kind of feud between a father-in-law and his son-in-law. For us, this is a confusing passage, because we do not ordinarily know the circumstances of Heorot's destruction; but for the poet's audience it made good sense. This digression eliminates some of the suspense of the main story because it tells us that Grendel, despite his fierceness, will not destroy Heorot but that the building will be destroyed as the result of a conflict between two members of the same family, that is, between Ingeld and Hrothgar. As we consider this digression, we should also consider another one: After Beowulf defeats Grendel, there is a celebration in Heorot, and the narrator tells us that all of the Danes drank together in good fellowship, including Hrothgar and his nephew Hrothulf. Everyone seemed bound together in unity, the narrator says, because treason had not yet shown itself. Passages like these abound in *Beowulf*, woven into and around the three larger stories of the battles with the monsters. The first digression indicates that Heorot will be destroyed in a family feud, and the second one takes the idea of a family feud even further, for the audience of *Beowulf* would have known that after Hrothgar's death, his nephew Hrothulf seized the throne from the young man he had promised to protect, Hrothgar's son Hrethric. This betrayal is not just a family feud. It is treachery, the opposite of the loyalty that Scyld Scefing inspired (or bought) with his gifts. It is the betrayal of one's word and of one's family, and it is made even more horrible when, during the feasting, Hrothgar's wife Wealhtheow walks through the crowd of celebrating warriors and sees her husband and his nephew sitting together, apparently united in friendship and loyalty. Hrethric's mother takes pleasure in seeing the family so clearly united, but she does not know, as the poem's audience does, that Hrothulf will be the instrument of her son's downfall. This dramatic irony (when the audience knows something that the characters do not) magnifies Hrothulf's treachery and makes his victims, Hrethric and Wealtheow, even more pathetic.

The question we must consider, though, is the relationship between these stories that are told as digressions and the main story of Beowulf's fight with Grendel. In effect, they are the same story: Grendel, the descendant of Cain, tries to destroy Heorot and threatens Hrothgar's reign, but Grendel does not succeed. Ingeld, however, does destroy Heorot, and Hrothulf does end the reign of Hrothgar's son; and both Ingeld and Hrothulf, like Cain, succeed by turning on members of their families. The only difference between them and Grendel is that Grendel, who is unsuccessful, is obviously evil, while Ingeld and Hrothulf, who do succeed, conceal their evil behind an appearance of fellowship. This pattern is repeated throughout the poem. Grendel, Grendel's mother, and the dragon all pose threats to human society, but they are all outside of that society and are all obviously evil. Therefore, they can be opposed and destroyed by Beowulf. The more dangerous threats to society, the ones that actually succeed, have human sources and frequently involve deception or some other human failing. Anyone looking at the monsters would recognize immediately that they are evil and must be countered, but how can we tell what evil lurks in the hearts of men? The monsters, then, provide most of the poem's excitement, but their major role is to contrast one form of evil — open, obvious, and opposable — with another form of evil — subtle, deceptive, and difficult to recognize let alone combat.

Virtually every one of the subplots that are woven into the fabric of *Beowulf* in the digressions has this relationship to the main story, even if those subplots operate in different ways. For example, when Beowulf arrives at the Danish court and announces his intention to fight Grendel, he is challenged by another foreign warrior, Unferth. The narrator tells us that Unferth is hostile to Beowulf because he is jealous of any man who might gain more worldly glory than himself. That comment, of course, is a giveaway, for in the Christian context of the poem, a concern for one's own worldly glory betrays a most unChristian attitude. Furthermore, it reflects Unferth's hypocrisy. Unferth, like the Danish warriors, has been afraid to stay in Heorot at night to challenge Grendel, but, motivated by his pride, he resents Beowulf's attempt and tries to shame the young warrior. Significantly, during Beowulf's eloquent defense of himself against Unferth's accusations, he mentions that Unferth had killed his own brothers, and once again we can see that Grendel is not the only descendant of Cain in the poem. Unferth's story is never told, but clearly he is a fugitive in Hrothgar's court as a result of some family problem. To Unferth's credit, after Beowulf defeats Grendel, Unferth praises him; and before Beowulf fights against Grendel's mother, Unferth lends him his sword. Unferth, then, is not a two-dimensional villain —

no one in the poem is. He is much more like a real man who has had to
deal with the complexities of his life and apparently has not always dealt
with them successfully.

THE TROUBLE WITH GEATS

Even when the characters in the poem are not guilty of fratricide or
treachery, however, they freely exhibit the failings of human beings. We
can see this point by looking at the behavior of the warriors who accompany Beowulf on each of his three adventures. During Beowulf's battle
with Grendel, his companions watch with drawn swords, ready to help
their leader if they have to. Later, as Beowulf plunges into the water to
fight with Grendel's mother, they wait on the shore. And finally, when
Beowulf fights with the dragon, his retainers, with the exception of the
loyal Wiglaf, actually run away. Again, the battles are exciting, but the
clear decline in the responses of Beowulf's companions is far more important, for another major theme of the poem concerns the origins and
declines of societies. The poem opens with Scyld Scefing, the founder
of Danish glory, and it tells, too, of the destruction of that glory after
the death of Hrothgar. The histories of several other peoples are also
retold, but the clearest focus is on Beowulf's people, the Geats.

Beowulf is surely a great hero, but there are indications in the poem
that something is rotten in the state of the Geats, and the rottenness
comes primarily from their king, Hygelac. Beowulf is supremely loyal to
Hygelac, who, after all, is also his uncle (a good contrast with the situation at the Danish court); and at one point Beowulf tells Hrothgar that
Hygelac would always be willing to send him aid. Nevertheless, when
Beowulf returns from Denmark to the Geatish court, Hygelac's first words
to him are a rebuke for having risked his life by going to Denmark.
Hygelac claims that he would have preferred to allow the Danes to settle their own monster problems, but probably what he really means is
that he feared losing Beowulf, his best warrior. Because Hygelac knows
how important Beowulf is to his own continued existence, he selfishly
urged the hero not to be generous and help the Danes, not to combat
the predations of Cain's descendant. Consequently, it is no surprise when
we learn in another digression that Hygelac meets his end leading a raid-
ing expedition against the Frisians, an expedition that had no legitimate
motives but that resulted from Hygelac's pride, his attempt to dominate
another people. Though Hygelac opposed Beowulf's obviously heroic

venture, he finally brought destruction to himself and ultimately to his people because of his pride and his greed. Not only has he been unwilling to encourage an active response to evil, but he himself will act wrongly out of a desire for booty.

The decline of the Geats, then, is another focus of the poem, and it is interesting that Beowulf undertakes the battle with the dragon at least in part so that he can obtain a treasure that will allow the Geats to pay tribute to the Swedes. Beowulf knows that the Geats are no longer able to defend themselves and must buy off their enemies. It is even more interesting that Wiglaf, who assumes power after Beowulf's death, will not allow the Geats to use the treasure. He knows that buying off the Swedes is a stopgap measure — it may remind us of Scyld buying the loyalty of his retainers — and that the Geats will either have to defend themselves properly or disappear. The poem concludes with the lament of an unnamed Geatish woman who remembers the past glory of the Geats and who quite rightly fears for the future of a people who have forgotten the values that a civilization needs if it is to continue in existence. As we know, the Geats did disappear.

Hygelac, however, is far from being the only deficient ruler in the poem. Even Hrothgar, who seems so concerned for his people, lacks some attributes of the ideal ruler. We have already seen that the building of Heorot was problematic, but even more troubling is his behavior when Grendel attacks. Instead of trying to protect his people or set an example for them, Hrothgar abandons the hall along with everyone else. And even when Beowulf arrives to challenge Grendel, Hrothgar does not stay in Heorot. Instead, while Beowulf puts himself and his men in the way of danger, Hrothgar goes to bed with the queen. There is no little irony in the poet's use of heroic language as he describes the king going off to the comfort of his wife's bed while a foreign hero tries to solve the kingdom's problems. We might think back to the narrator's line about Scyld Scefing, "That was a good king," and consider whether the same words could be applied to Hrothgar at this point — or to Hygelac or to any number of other rulers in the poem.

We should not think, however, that Hrothgar is a terrible king. Just before Beowulf is ready to leave the Danes, Hrothgar delivers a long speech that resembles a sermon. He emphasizes to Beowulf the vicissitudes of human existence and the transitoriness of human happiness, and he urges the young warrior to guard against evil and to make the correct choice between earthly, material rewards and spiritual, eternal rewards. Hrothgar's words here are very much like those of Boethius: Instead of focusing on the fleeting joys of this world, look to the eternal, to that which has real value. Hrothgar may not succeed in doing so himself, but he generally tries to do what is correct and he, aside from Scyld Scefing and Beowulf, is the only person about whom the poet says, "He was a good king." But if even Beowulf is unable to assure his people's safety after his death, how much less is the flawed Hrothgar able to do so.

BEOWULF AND THE QUESTION OF EVIL

The contrast between these good kings, between Beowulf and Hrothgar, is illuminating. One of the reasons for the persistence of evil in the poem is people's reluctance to oppose it actively. Naturally the Danes and the Geats could not guard themselves against the monsters because, until those monsters attacked, no one knew they existed. Nevertheless, once their existence was known, only Beowulf was willing to fight against them. The Danes mourned and worried, and they offered sacrifices, but they never actually took action against the evil. Beowulf alone showed an awareness that thinking about evil and acting against it are two different things.

But the monsters, as we have seen, clearly represent evil. While we know that they must be fought, even if we are not willing to fight them ourselves, the poem forces us to confront a more difficult problem: How are people supposed to respond to the evil that lies within them? As bad as the Grendel family is, the Danes can still exist. Their downfall comes from the evil within Hrothulf, that human evil which harms everyone. Such is the pattern of the whole poem: Monsters are obviously evil, but the more subtle evils of Hrothulf, Finn, Heremod, the Heatho-Bard warrior, and others all work to prevent peace and stability, signs of civilization, from becoming reality. If the Grendel family are descended from Cain, at least they have an excuse for their actions, for they are traditionally outcasts from civilization. What excuse can there be for the pride and treachery that seem to control the lives of human beings; and how can this pride and treachery be controlled? Over and over, the *Beowulf*-poet makes these points and asks these questions, not simply by repeating himself but by showing a multitude of variations on the themes.

Amazingly, the poet uses his female characters in much the same way that Homer did in *The Iliad*. Wealtheow, Hygd, Hildeburh, and the unnamed Geatish woman all demonstrate graphically the suffering that is caused by the treachery and failings of men, whom they trust and on whom they depend. These women all contribute to the tone of sadness that pervades the poem. Yes, of course the poem celebrates the heroism of Beowulf in his battles with the monsters, but the poem also looks deeply at the unhappiness of human life, especially the unnecessary, man-made unhappiness. The celebration of Beowulf, vanquisher of monsters, forms the main story; the digressions, however, by presenting the failures of human beings, place that main story in a context, and each set of stories illuminates the other.

Beowulf clearly offers a sophisticated look at the values that make a society great and whose absence can make a society disappear. For a long time, it was common to refer to the Middle Ages as the Dark Ages. It is true, as we saw, that for a couple of centuries after the collapse of the Roman Empire, Europe was in a chaotic state, a state that might have been called "dark." But no one could possibly think that a remarkable, exciting, and insightful poem like *Beowulf* could be the product of a "dark" age. It is a poem of high literary and philosophical sophistication. It is a poem that even now tells us something about our lives. Certainly it depicts barbarism, which often hides under a surface respectability, but in many ways that depiction is characteristic of the twentieth century, a century that saw, for example, the barbarism of the Holocaust emerge from what might have been the most civilized nation in the world. At the same time, the poem depicts a vision of civilization, of cooperation, and of individual and group responsibility to which we can still aspire. The thought that this poem exists in a single manuscript that was nearly destroyed by fire is indeed frightening. It is a poem that should command our closest attention. Because the poem focuses on the fates of nations, especially the Danes and the Geats, rather than on individuals, it should be considered an epic, one of the finest epics of the Middle Ages and probably one of the finest of all times.

Another great epic from about a century later that might appeal to readers who enjoy Beowulf is the French *Song of Roland*. That poem is quite different — it lacks monsters, although it contains some spectacular warriors — but it, too, focuses on a vital moment in the history of a people. Its technique also differs from that of *Beowulf*, but these two poems reflect styles and concerns that characterize an important phase of the Middle Ages. In the next chapter, we will look at a phase that began in the twelfth century and lasted for several hundred years.

II. Chrétien de Troyes

One of the odd things that happens when we consider history is the way time seems to become compressed. For instance, if we are asked about ancient epics, we might well mention *The Iliad* and *The Aeneid*, without fully realizing that those works were written down almost eight hundred years apart. The equivalent would be classifying a work written in about 1200 with something written this year. There are bound to be some major differences. The same is true of even shorter periods. A novel written this year would differ significantly from a novel by Jane Austen, just as there are differences between *Beowulf* and the romances of Chrétien de Troyes, written in the late twelfth century. The contrast between the earlier epic and the later romances illustrates an important point: We speak of the Middle Ages as though it was a homogeneous period of a thousand years, but the reality is that numerous changes took place during that millennium. One century was not like another.

Beowulf represents an earlier part of the Middle Ages, and for all its considerable sophistication as a literary work, the picture it presents of society is fairly limited. We see little of everyday interactions. Most of the action centers on warrior life. Beowulf has no friends and certainly no love interest. (In *The Song of Roland*, that other great medieval epic, Roland has a fiancée who appears in the poem just long enough to drop dead when she learns that Roland has died.) Chrétien's romances are quite different, and many of the differences reflect developments that occurred in the twelfth century.

The twelfth century was indeed a remarkable time. It has justifiably been called a renaissance. Thanks to a number of factors, such as the Crusaders' contacts with non–European peoples, the arrival of the works of Aristotle in Europe, certain technological innovations, and the gradual coalescing of duchies and smaller kingdoms into nations, the twelfth century was an exciting time, full of interesting people — Peter Abelard, Bernard of Clairvaux, Henry II of England and his wife Eleanor of Aquitaine, and many, many others. It was a time that produced a renewed interest in the natural world and in the lives of individual human beings. Many of these interests are obvious in the romances of Chrétien de Troyes.

While we know the name Chrétien de Troyes (as opposed to the anonymous author of *Beowulf* and so many other medieval works), we know almost nothing about him. Apparently he was from the French city of Troyes ("de Troyes" is not his last name — it means "from Troyes"), but beyond that, we know little aside from the few hints that he gives us in his works. Nevertheless, he had a profound effect on medieval literature, an effect that continues even into the present. One of Chrétien's achievements lay in popularizing the romance genre. *Beowulf*, as we saw, was an epic, a work dealing with a pivotal moment in the history of a people and focusing on the people as a whole rather than on individuals. With the developments of the twelfth century, authorial focus began to shift to individuals, who are the subjects of romances. One of the best of the early romances is the French *Roman d'Eneas*. *The Aeneid* is an epic, the story of the founding of Rome. Aeneas, naturally, is an important character in that story, but the focus is on Rome and on his part in the creation of that city. The twelfth-century retelling of Virgil's poem, however, changes that focus, as the epic becomes a romance, the story of a great hero and of his love life. (It is essential here to note that the word "romance" as used to describe a genre has to do originally with the fact that these works were written in a Romance language rather than in Latin. Romantic love developed in those romances, but they are not called romances because they contain such love.) Chrétien's romances are such excellent examples of the genre that they helped to further its popularity.

Another of Chrétien's accomplishments concerns his contribution to the popularity of stories about King Arthur. Stories about King Arthur may have been based on some vague historical recollection of a great warrior, but King Arthur as we know him from literature never really existed. Before Chrétien's time, the legendary Arthur had been mentioned in Geoffrey of Monmouth's Latin work *The History of the Kings of England* and a few other works, and there were also oral legends about Arthur, but there was no cult of Arthurian literature. Chrétien took these stories, none of which had been developed in great detail, and created a new fictional universe, a universe that many other writers, from the Middle

Ages to the present, would use in their own ways. The situation is analogous to what happened in Greek drama: Certain historical situations — the Trojan War or the battle at Thebes — were available, as were characters with clearly identifiable characteristics — the wily Odysseus, the beautiful Helen. Writers were free to use these characters and situations as they saw fit, so that Euripides could even suggest that Helen of Troy had never been in Troy. After Chrétien, as more and more Arthurian stories were composed, the whole cycle took shape, from Arthur's conception to the fall of the Round Table and Arthur's death, using characters like the valiant Gawain, the adulterous Lancelot, the nasty Kay, and others whom Chrétien had described, for Chrétien comes at the beginning of Arthur's literary career. In many cases he seems to be dealing with already established characters like Kay; but in other cases, he seems to have invented both his characters and their situations. In either case, the excellence of Chrétien's romances contributed to the popularity of Arthurian literature.

Chrétien wrote five romances (along with other works, some of which have been lost), and there are a number of controversies about some of those works. *Erec and Enide* is the first romance and is clearly Arthurian, though Erec played only a minor role in subsequent Arthurian literature. The second romance, *Cligés*, is only tangentially Arthurian in the sense that two of the major characters visit Arthur's court. The last three romances concern some of the more famous Arthurian knights: *Yvain or The Knight with the Lion*, *Lancelot or The Knight of the Cart*, and *Perceval*, a romance that also features Gawain. *Erec and Enide* and *Yvain* are in many ways companion pieces, although information in the romances themselves indicates that *Yvain* and *Lancelot* were composed simultaneously. Consequently, we must try to understand these romances both on their own and in conjunction with each other.

Another complication in *Lancelot* is that Chrétien tells us that the subject and the meaning of the story were given to him by the noblewoman Marie de Champagne, who had an abiding interest in questions concerning love and who sponsored some of the major writers of her time. And a further complication in this romance is that Chrétien turned the task of finishing it over to another poet. Some scholars have speculated that he did so because he disapproved of the subject and meaning, while other scholars have speculated that the whole romance undercuts the meaning that Marie supplied. No definitive resolution of these questions is possible, for several reasons: We do not know exactly what Marie asked of Chrétien, we do not know why he did not finish the romance himself, and Chrétien's writing ordinarily contains so many levels of irony that we have difficulty ascertaining what his attitude may have been.

Finally, *Perceval* also presents a number of problems. This romance is the longest of all, and it appears to be divided into relatively distinct sections, one dealing with the adventures of Perceval and the other with the adventures of Gawain. And the romance is clearly unfinished. Again, scholars have speculated on explanations for these unusual characteristics. Chrétien might have died before completing the romance, or he might have been working on two separate romances, neither of which he completed but which someone who followed him combined. Whatever the explanation, *Perceval*'s lack of a conclusion led several medieval writers to add continuations to the poem. These continuations, which run to thousands of lines, develop the stories of the poem, including that concerning the Holy Grail. Chrétien does little to explain this mysterious object, but in the continuations and in later Arthurian works, like the Vulgate Cycle and Thomas Malory's *Morte Darthur*, the Grail story is developed at great length.

There are excellent modern prose translations of these romances, but we must remember as we read them that Chrétien wrote in the most common French verse form of the Middle Ages, short rhyming couplets. Chrétien's Old French does not differ from Modern French as much as Old English differs from Modern English, but there are significant differences. Here is a sample passage from *Yvain*:

Cuers et oroilles m'aportez	Heart and ears give me
car parole est tote perdue	for words are totally lost
s'ele n'est de cuer entandue.	if they are not understood by the heart.
De cez i a qui la chose oent	There are some who hear the thing
qu'il n'entandent, et si la loent;	they don't understand, but they praise it;
et cil n'en ont ne mes l'oie,	they can only hear
des que li cuers n'i entant mie…	since their heart understands nothing.

(*ll.* 150–156)

Not only does this passage present Chrétien's verse, but it also illustrates important points about what he says. We might regard these words as fairly obvious — we must understand what we hear — but Chrétien is actually referring to the words that Jesus often uses. For instance, in Matthew 13, Jesus tells the Parable of the Sower (which Chrétien also cites at the beginning of *Perceval*), and he concludes with the words, "He that hath ears to hear, let him hear," after which he explains the allegorical meaning of the parable to his disciples. Jesus is telling them that they have to go beyond the literal meaning of the words in order to understand what the words really mean. Chrétien's reference to the Bible here is typical of what he does. He is not a theologian, and he is not delivering sermons, but he does rely heavily on a biblical background for his narrative, just as a contemporary author might rely on references to popular culture.

In our time, students often think that literature contains "hidden meanings," which only English teachers are capable of finding, but as Jesus indicates, that view is not correct. Meanings are generally not hidden — what kind of sense would it make for authors to write something and hide its meaning? — but we must know how to read, or, as Jesus says, listen. If we hear the Parable of the Sower and think it is only about a man who tried to plant some seeds, we miss the most important part of the story; if we understand the literal meaning of the story and its larger implications, as Jesus explains them to the disciples, then the story becomes far more meaningful. This way of reading was quite important for the medievals, who expressed it by using the analogy of a nut or a grain of wheat: In order to get to the meat, the nourishing part of the plant, we have to get past the shell. Just so, the reader must understand both the literal meaning and the meaning that lies beneath it.

This method of reading raises the question, "Why doesn't an author just say what he or she means?" The answer is that authors do say what they mean, but what they mean is complex, not reducible to a convenient aphorism. Furthermore, as Jesus knew when he used the parables, those stories offer not only a meaning but a striking way of expressing that meaning. The story makes the meaning stand out, and it also makes it easier to recall. So Chrétien, in the passage above, reminds the reader, near the beginning of *Yvain*, that while he is about to tell a good story about knights and damsels and giants, this story is not an idle entertainment, a series of empty adventures. Rather it has a deeper meaning (not a hidden meaning) to which its audience should attend. Certainly if *Yvain* has such a serious level of meaning, Chrétien's other romances do as well. Our job, then, is to go beyond the surface of the story, as important as that surface is, to see what lies beneath.

One way of regarding these romances is to see them as commentaries on elements that were current when they were written, things like marriage customs or international relations. Such matters are unquestionably vital, but they require a detailed knowledge of the twelfth century; and even with that knowledge, they often must be approached speculatively. A better approach for those who are reading these romances for the first time might be to focus on the subject that is at the center of all of them, love. Our modern notions of romantic love actually originated in the twelfth century, and love, or its personification as Love, plays a major role in these romances. (Medieval manuscripts, incidentally, do not distinguish between love and Love. That distinction is added by modern editors or translators as an aid to modern readers.)

EREC AND ENIDE AND *YVAIN*

Love is certainly central in *Erec and Enide*, which tells the story of this young couple's very brief courtship and marriage and the longer period of adjustment that followed. Chrétien begins by announcing that he is telling this tale in order to teach and that he will tell it well, as opposed to other people, who tell it badly. The story itself begins on Easter. Chrétien, in fact, often identifies the time when a story takes place by citing a religious holiday, just as we might say, "Oh, that happened around Christmas last year." We have to be aware, however, that these religious holidays had a special significance for Chrétien's audience. Easter for them was not associated with bunnies and chocolate, though undoubtedly they did enjoy the renewal of nature at least as much as we do. But Easter was also full of religious significance. It commemorated the Resurrection, which for Christians was the most important event in the history of the world. As we will see, it was also a significant holiday in terms of the action of *Erec and Enide*.

After Chrétien's brief introduction, the action of the romance begins as Arthur announces that he is reviving the custom of the white stag: Whoever kills the white stag is allowed to kiss the most beautiful lady. At first glance, this custom may seem chivalrous and even romantic, but Gawain immediately discourages Arthur from reviving it because it will lead to dissension in the court, since every knight has a lady whom he considers the most beautiful. Clearly Gawain's warning is well-founded, but Arthur ignores it. We see in this exchange an important aspect of Chrétien's romances. We tend to think of Arthur's court as a glorious place, and we tend to think of Arthur as a glorious king. In some versions of the Arthurian stories, the court and the king are indeed glorious, but not in all versions. Chrétien's picture of the court and the king is seldom glorious. Instead, the court often seems nearly decadent, and the king, as is the case in this episode, behaves frivolously. Gawain is quite correct in his assessment that the hunt for the white stag may prove divisive, and Arthur has no good reason for reinstating it. Furthermore, it is highly inappropriate for Easter, but Arthur will not be dissuaded until later on, when his knights are already disturbed. From the very beginning of Chrétien's first romance, then, we can see the lack of perfection in Arthur's court.

Erec, however, seems to rise above this corruption. He does not take part in the hunt, and when one of Guinevere's ladies-in-waiting is struck by a dwarf whom she encounters in the woods, Erec goes after the miscreant despite being unarmed. This adventure, of course, gives him the opportunity to meet Enide, who is the most beautiful lady in the world. (Chrétien's readers must get used to having the heroine of each romance described as the most beautiful lady in the world.) Erec and Enide quite naturally fall in love at first sight, another convention in these romances, though Chrétien gives us reasons to wonder about their love. Enide must indeed be beautiful, and Erec regards her as something of a trophy, while Enide, who lives in poverty, realizes that if she marries Erec and he becomes a king, she will become a queen, which is not a bad career choice for a poor young girl. She acquiesces to him in everything, even when he insists that she come to Arthur's court wearing her usual rags so that Guinevere can give her fine clothing. These two beautiful young people appear to be using each other very nicely. And when Arthur declares her the most beautiful lady, deserving of his kiss, none of the other knights objects. What we see, then, if we look beneath the surface of the Arthurian court, is a kingdom whose king is frivolous and likes to kiss pretty girls and whose people are attracted to superficial glories.

Strangely enough, we never learn Enide's name until the day of her wedding, which takes place on Pentecost. Although Pentecost is little noticed now, it was an important holiday in the Middle Ages, for it marks the descent of the Holy Spirit as related in the Book of Acts. There is an implication here that this marriage is potentially special, though we must pause for a moment to consider some aspects of medieval marriage. We are accustomed to courtship and marriage as free choices that people make, but in the Middle Ages, particularly for the upper classes, marriages were arranged. They were not based on love but on political or economic expediency. Not only would the couple not have been in love, but they may never have met before the wedding. Love, if it developed, came later, which explains in part why so many medieval love stories involve adultery. People certainly felt love, but that love had no necessary relationship with marriage. We might recall that the ancient Greeks had separate deities for love and marriage, Aphrodite and Hera. The same distinction held true in the Middle Ages. Consequently, if Erec and Enide married each other for ulterior motives, there was nothing odd in that action. What is unusual is the possibility that they might really love each other! In this connection, Chrétien makes an allusion to a story that seems to have been frequently on his mind, the story of Tristan and Isolde. He only mentions, before describing the delights of the wedding night, that no Brangain was substituted for Enide, but that casual reference recalls the whole story of Tristan and Isolde, of their adulterous love (caused, in most versions, by a love potion) and the machinations they use to be together and to deceive King Mark, who is Isolde's husband and Tristan's uncle. While Erec and Enide are not like Tristan and Isolde, still their love is purely physical. They gaze at each other and what they see goes to their hearts, leading them to kisses and to other activities too delicate for Chrétien to mention.

After the wedding and the subsequent tournament, Chrétien's narrator tells us that Erec seems to have been a total success, for he is as attractive as Absalom and as well-spoken as Solomon. Again, superficially these comparisons seem like compliments, but for those who have ears, who can hear the deeper meaning, these comparisons are damning. Absalom, after all, was the son of King David who took great pride in his appearance, particularly in his luxuriant hair, who rebelled against his father's rule, and who died when his hair got caught in a tree and made him a target for David's soldiers. Comparing Erec to Absalom, then, is no compliment. Solomon, too, had his problems. In Sunday school stories, we may have learned that Solomon was the wisest man who ever lived, but the rest of the Bible story is not so positive, for Solomon, in addition to building the temple to God, had seven hundred wives and three hundred concubines, many of them foreign, and he built temples to their gods as well. There were serious discussions in the Middle Ages about the state of Solomon's soul, about whether he would have been taken to Heaven when Jesus harrowed Hell or whether he would have faced eternal damnation. Again, then, comparing Erec to Solomon is no compliment. Nor is it a coincidence that when Erec and Enide return to Erec's homeland, they go to church and the narrator takes the opportunity to provide a brief summary of the Christian story of sin and redemption, for Erec is about to lapse even further into sin.

Erec's feelings for Enide, we are told, are so excessive that he begins to neglect his knightly duties. We have already seen how frivolous Arthur is, so we have an idea of the seriousness of Erec's failure. Furthermore,

Erec's feelings for Enide are described more in terms of lust and physical attraction than in terms of real love. Erec, that is, neglects his duties in favor of the physical pleasure Enide provides. His actions lack reason; and when he overhears Enide lamenting his declining reputation, his reaction is totally irrational. He takes her out on the road with him and forbids her to speak to him. Enide tries to obey, but several times, when she thinks he is in danger, she speaks up to warn him. Her love puts him first, which is how love should operate. He begins to understand that she truly loves him, but he does not know how to respond.

The turning point comes when, after a grueling battle, Erec loses consciousness. He and Enide are found by the Count of Limors, who immediately develops his own lust for her and tries to force himself upon her. At this point, Erec revives, kills the count, and scares away everyone else. Once again we have a good story that has a deeper significance, for Erec's revival from a deathlike state recalls the Resurrection, a reference that gains force when we realize that Limors means "the death." In other words, Erec comes back to life and kills the Count of Death. The Christian overtones of the story are unavoidable, though they must be treated carefully. While they remind us that the poem opened on Easter, the commemoration of the Resurrection, they do not mean that Erec *is* Jesus. Rather, he relives in his own life the experience of Jesus; he incorporates that experience, becoming Christ-like, as all Christians were expected to do. That accomplished, he can be fully reconciled with his wife, whom he now loves properly rather than selfishly. Chrétien's narrator even calls the pain the lovers have suffered their penance, adding to the religious significance of their adventure.

It would seem at this point that with the lovers reconciled in a holier kind of love, the story might end, but there is more, for Erec now must face the Joy of the Court. In this challenge, Erec must fight against a knight whose prowess is attested to by a long row of severed heads from previous battles. Again, the Joy of the Court is an exciting adventure that has deeper connections with the rest of the romance. After Erec defeats the knight (as we expected he would), the knight explains that he has been in the garden where the battle takes place ever since he promised his beloved lady anything she asked for and she demanded that he stay in the garden until another knight can defeat him in battle. This story presents some interesting problems. First, the knight is obviously unhappy with his lady's demand, which is unreasonable and has resulted in the unnecessary deaths of numerous knights. That demand, however, is an assertion of her power over him. Surely he could have refused her, though that course would require him to break his oath, which raises the question of whether he is bound by an oath to do something so unreasonable or even unethical. The fact that he has acceded shows how much he was like the earlier Erec, who was also so taken with his beloved that he distorted his obligations as a knight; and paradoxically, he is glad to have been defeated, for his loss sets him free.

The situation is made even more complex by being set in a garden. This garden has no walls, though it is inaccessible except at a designated entrance. Regardless of the season, its trees bear fruit, which cannot be removed from the garden, and its flowers bloom. It also contains every kind of bird and plant. As Chrétien so often does, he relies here on the reader to make an association, this time between the garden and Eden. This fallen Eden, with sinful love at its center, is redeemed by Erec, who thereby establishes himself as the victorious knight that he should be. And having achieved this status, Erec also deserves to succeed his royal father on the throne. At his coronation, he wears a robe that displays the attributes of Geometry, Arithmetic, Music, and Astronomy, the quadrivium (four of the seven liberal arts). Erec, the warrior, now knows about love and the other subjects that will make him a good ruler, better even than the frivolous King Arthur.

This romance, then, typifies Chrétien's work. It tells a good story, full of romantic love and adventures, but it does so with an abundance of biblical and religious references that help to focus our attention on the serious issues that the story raises, issues involving questions of moral and religious behavior, which, for Chrétien, are the same. We can see this same combination of elements in the other romances, particularly *Yvain*, which is a companion piece to *Erec and Enide*. Erec's problem was neglecting his knightly duties for love, while Yvain's is the opposite, neglecting his obligations to his beloved in favor of knightly deeds. But *Yvain* is a much darker poem.

Chrétien begins this poem by telling us that after dinner on Pentecost, a group of knights were discussing love, a subject, Chrétien says, that is not held in as high regard as it used to be. In King Arthur's day, love was respected and had a good effect on its adherents; but now (in the twelfth century) love is just an empty word. Chrétien implies that his story will illustrate something about true love, but Chrétien likes to play tricks with his audience.

The romance does not get off to a good start, as Arthur abandons this knightly conversation and goes to bed with the queen, who detains him for so long (doing what? one wonders) that he falls asleep. This beginning bodes ill for both Arthur and the subject of love. During Arthur's absence, Calogrenant tells a story that may be honest but that shows him defeated in battle. Some years earlier, at a magic spring, he poured water onto a stone, which caused a huge storm, after which a knight appeared and unhorsed Calogrenant. The knight's story is an odd one, filled with marvels like a hideously ugly bullherd and a magic spring, but the whole romance is filled with unnatural elements like dragons, giants, a magic ring, and magic ointment, so everyone accepts Calogrenant's story as true.

Yvain, however, is intrigued by the story, and without a road map he sets out to find the spring. Like Erec at the start of his story, Yvain sets out alone and ultimately meets his lady. Yvain does so, however, after killing her husband, which is not necessarily a good way to win a lady's favor. Naturally he falls in love with Laudine at first sight, and he is helped by her lady Lunete, whom he had helped previously.

Erec's romance with Enide, we may recall, was rather odd. Yvain's courtship of Laudine is even stranger. He has just killed her husband and fallen in love with her, so that when the narrator tells us that this behavior shows us how noble love is, we may suspect that he is being ironic. Nevertheless, with Lunete's prompting, Laudine agrees to meet and then to marry him, even though she knows that Lunete is trapping her in an affair that she does not want. At the same time, with her husband dead and her knights weak, she needs someone to defend her country. Thus, Yvain marries her out of love, though it is a rather sudden love, while she marries him because she needs a valiant warrior — any valiant warrior. Clearly this relationship is off to a rocky start.

And it becomes even rockier when Yvain's good friend Gawain persuades the newly married knight to set off on a jousting tour. Gawain shames Yvain by claiming that love has made him soft, that he needs to be a "man" and not be tied down by his wife. In fact, what Gawain says is that Yvain should not be like Erec. Laudine gives Yvain permission to leave for a year — though no one considers who will protect the country for that year — but Yvain, who claimed to be so deeply in love with her, stays away longer. Their actions thus undercut both of their alleged reasons for having entered into the marriage. Yvain's behavior is the opposite of Erec's. Erec doted too much on his beloved, while Yvain forgets his commitments to his lady. When he realizes his mistake, he is too late, for Laudine renounces him and he goes mad. Much of the rest of the romance, as we might expect, concerns his winning her back; but even though he appears to be successful, *Yvain* has a much less happy conclusion than does *Erec and Enide*.

Yvain's adventures before the reconciliation, however, are quite exciting. Early in those adventures, Yvain rescues a lion who is fighting with a serpent, after which the lion accompanies him. This action is difficult to interpret. On the one hand, the battle between those two creatures is clearly allegorical: The serpent represents the devil, while the lion, for a number of reasons, is associated with Jesus; Yvain chooses the right side. On the other hand, it is difficult to understand why Jesus would need Yvain's help and why Chrétien makes the point that Yvain had to cut off part of the lion's tail in order to help him. And it is equally difficult to understand why the lion, when it thinks Yvain has died, tries to kill itself. Chrétien's romances contain many passages that present such difficulties, and while we may not be able to explain them, they are fun to contemplate.

Other episodes are less difficult to explain, though they are equally challenging in other ways. For example, Yvain discovers that Lunete is facing execution for having arranged his marriage to Laudine, and he offers, after some highly competitive lamenting, to serve as her champion. (Two minor comments need to be inserted here. One is that Lunete says she tried to find a champion at Arthur's court, but no one would defend her, a rather bad reflection on that court. And the other is that she explains that Gawain is away from the court searching for the queen, a reference to the plot of *Lancelot*, which was being written at the same time.) Yvain leaves Lunete to find lodging, but when he does, he learns that his host's sons are likely to be killed and his daughter seized on the next day by an evil giant. Yvain, of course, could save them by fighting with the giant, but, as he explains, he is already committed to rescuing Lunete. If the giant arrives early enough, Yvain will fight him, as long as he will be free to rescue Lunete at noon. Certainly this episode has a comic side — poor Yvain has to hope the giant shows up or he will have to leave the host's children to their fate while he saves Lunete. At the same time, the episode raises serious moral questions about his duties as a knight. What are those duties? Whom should he rescue? Should he rescue Lunete, for whose predicament he is largely responsible, or should he rescue the five children of his host, to whom he also owes an obligation? And should Lunete be held responsible for her role in persuading Laudine to make a bad match? Fortunately for everyone involved, none of these questions have to be confronted, since the giant arrives early and Yvain defeats him in time to rescue Lunete. But Chrétien does not let either his characters or his audience get off quite so easily, for Yvain's next adventure raises similar questions, and this time the questions must be addressed.

Two sisters are disputing after their father's death. The elder sister claims the entire inheritance, while the younger wants the inheritance shared. Gawain agrees to fight for the elder, though he demands that she keep his participation a secret. We are not told why he does so. One possibility is that, like so many knights, he simply wishes to remain anonymous, but another possibility is that, like Arthur himself, Gawain does not believe in the elder sister's argument, which raises the question of why he agrees to defend her. Eventually Yvain, who is known only as the Knight with the Lion, agrees to defend the younger. Thus Yvain and Gawain, such great friends, face each other in battle without knowing each other's identity; and the narrator goes into great detail explaining how Gawain and Yvain can simultaneously love and hate each other. This passage (*ll.* 5992–6081) is both interesting and amusing. In almost a hundred lines, Chrétien uses the methods of scholastic disputation to prove absolutely nothing.

Scholasticism is the system of argumentation that arose in the twelfth century under the influence of Aristotle's works on logic. It involves the use of strict logical reasoning, which Chrétien parodies in trying to explain how two close friends can try so hard to kill each other. Of course, logic cannot explain what is going on, which at this point may be amusing but soon will not be. As night begins to fall, the combatants pause, and soon their identities are revealed, at which point they each defer to the other, claiming to have been bested in battle. Again, these actions seem like the height of courteous behavior, except that their behavior ignores the cause in which they are fighting, that is, the justice of the sisters' claims. In fact, all thoughts of justice, which should be their primary concern, are dismissed as both knights courteously claim defeat. To make matters worse, Arthur, who has been enjoying the battle so much that he has refused to intervene, finally does so, telling the elder sister he has known the whole time that her claim was unjust and that she should renounce it or he will declare Yvain the winner and give everything to the younger sister.

What is going on here? Near the beginning of *Erec and Enide*, Arthur explained that one of the duties of a king is to uphold justice, but justice seems to have played no role in this episode. If Arthur knew what was just from the beginning, he should have said so — that is the duty of the king. Instead, he has arranged for a really entertaining battle, with no consideration for the justice of the case or the possibility that someone could be injured, a state of mind that the two champions share. Chrétien can play with scholastic argumentation, proving that they love and hate each other simultaneously, but no such argumentation is necessary to illustrate the point that Arthur's court shows no concern for justice or for righting wrongs. Arthur and the rest of the court are quite willing to forget about justice as long as they can have a good time. If Chrétien parodies scholasticism, he also parodies the protestations of royal courts that their concerns are the right ones.

The poem's conclusion reinforces the sense of superficiality and moral ineptitude that this episode has highlighted, for Laudine is once again tricked by Lunete into accepting Yvain. Husband and wife appear to be reconciled, and the narrator gives us a happily-ever-after conclusion, but we have to wonder whether the narrator expects to be taken seriously. That reconciliation, like the original match, has been brought about through trickery and deception. Yvain's behavior in the sisters' quarrels makes us question his integrity, and Laudine's acquiescence to being tricked again raises other questions about her. If the feeling they share can be described as love, then we might want to contemplate what Chrétien means by that term. We should certainly recall the narrator's words at the beginning of the romance, when he said that people no longer know how to love the way they used to. If what we have seen in the romance — lust, trickery, abandonment — amounts to love, perhaps Chrétien is saying that the changes have been for the better. What appears to be a love story is something else indeed. It is a story that illustrates the corruption and hollowness of Arthur's court and of the cult of love. It is, in many senses, a negative version of *Erec and Enide*.

LANCELOT AND PERCEVAL

Even more negative, if that is conceivable, is *Lancelot*. As was mentioned earlier, Chrétien says that this story and its significance were given to him by Marie de Champagne; at the end, Godefroi de Leigni tells us that he finished the romance, with Chrétien's permission. Scholars have speculated that perhaps Chrétien found the tale distasteful, which we could surely understand, and abandoned it, allowing Godefroi to complete it. That scenario is plausible, but it is not necessary. *Lancelot* is certainly distasteful, but a major difference between it and *Yvain* is that the corruption in *Lancelot* lies on the surface, whereas the corruption in *Yvain* lies in the subtext, where those who have "ears" can "hear" it.

The story of *Lancelot* involves the well-known motif of Lancelot's love for Guinevere, the wife of King Arthur. This love, which later writers developed in even greater detail, presents numerous problems. If Arthur's court has appeared frivolous or disengaged from morality in the previous romances, in *Lancelot* it appears to be totally rotten. Lancelot owes loyalty to his king, but instead he commits adultery, a violation of one of the Ten Commandments, with his king's wife. Other knights know of the adultery but say nothing, and Arthur himself possibly knows of it without commenting on it (as is certainly the case in later romances on the subject). In short, the rottenness of Arthur's court starts at its very center. Thus, at the romance's beginning, a knight appears at court and announces that he holds many of Arthur's subjects as prisoners and that Arthur cannot save them. Arthur, who apparently has not noticed that any of these people had gone missing, replies that if he cannot rescue them, he will just have to cope with their loss. This is hardly the response that we would expect from King Arthur, or from any competent ruler, and it indicates the degeneracy of the court. When the stranger knight announces further that he will free the prisoners himself if a knight from the court will lead Guinevere into the forest and then defeat him in battle, Arthur allows Kay to undertake the task. Kay appears in four of Chrétien's romances, always as a nasty braggart who invariably suffers defeat at the hands of those he torments, so Arthur's choice of Kay as Guinevere's guardian betrays either a lack of judgment or a deficiency in his love for his wife — in fact, given Arthur's behavior in these opening pages (as well as in the other romances), no one should be surprised that Guinevere prefers someone else. Naturally Kay is defeated and Guinevere is taken captive.

Gawain and an unnamed knight, Lancelot in disguise, attempt to find Guinevere, but when Lancelot's horse dies, Lancelot confronts what he and everyone else in the poem regard as a major moral decision: Should he ride in a cart, which the narrator tells us is a symbol of punishment and shame, in order to learn her whereabouts or should he maintain his dignity and avoid the cart? For the space of two steps he hesitates while Reason and Love argue within him. Then he jumps into the cart. Throughout the rest of the poem, Lancelot is known as the knight of the cart, although Guinevere later rejects him because he hesitated briefly before going to find her. Lancelot loses both ways. Despite his dedication, he loses both his reputation and his beloved over this trivial incident, the former because of what he did and the latter because of what he did not. Furthermore, in terms of verisimilitude, the whole episode has an amusing side: People in the most distant parts of the kingdom, including Guinevere, who has been held hostage, know about his behavior. Today, with email and twenty-four hour news stations, perhaps news of some-one's misdeeds would spread that quickly, but not in the twelfth century. Chrétien seems to be making a point about foolishness and misplaced priorities. Everyone cares about whether he entered the cart or whether he hesitated. No one, however, seems terribly concerned about the abduction of numerous people, including the queen, or about the adulterous relationship at the center of the romance.

This focus on absurdity runs throughout the romance. For instance, as he tries to find Guinevere, Lancelot encounters a beautiful young woman who invites him to spend the night at her home, but with the condition that he agree to lie with her for the night. Lancelot, the adul-terer, expresses his reservations, but needing shelter for the night, he fin-ally accedes even though he hates the idea. After the lady stages an assault against herself, from which Lancelot rescues her, she goes to bed with him, but he is careful not to touch her. For someone having an adulter-ous affair with his queen, he is indeed scrupulous. Perhaps he really does love Guinevere.

Further absurdity enters the story when Lancelot recognizes Guin-evere's comb by the blond hairs that adhere to it; when Lancelot is so immersed in contemplating his love for Guinevere that he fails to hear another knight challenge him; when, having found Guinevere, he breaks through the bars of her prison and cuts off part of his finger without noticing the injury, and when, consequently, he leaves a trail of blood, also without noticing it. There is also the absurdity of Guinevere's anger over his hesitation to mount the cart when he finally arrives to rescue her. In short, virtually all of the major characters in the poem are so smitten by what they take to be love that they behave in ways that are irrational and morally obtuse and that certainly violate obvious religious strictures. Chrétien does not write in ignorance of normal behavior. Rather, he goes to great lengths to point out how ridiculous and wrong his characters' behavior is. They certainly suffer great shame, he says, but they are ashamed of the wrong things. Getting into a cart and hesitating to get into it are irrelevancies. Lancelot and Guinevere should be ashamed of their adulterous behavior, but they never are. And Arthur should be embarrassed by his performance as king, but he never is. When Kay is accused of committing adultery with Guinevere, thanks to the trail of blood that Lancelot left in the room where they both slept, Lancelot defends the purity of both Kay and Guinevere, as though he himself were not sinning by deflecting his guilt. For such behavior he should feel shame.

In *Lancelot* and in his other romances, Chrétien relies on well-known and publicly accepted standards of behavior — for kings and queens, for knights, for Christians in general — and shows how far from the ideals his characters are. In part, he simply demonstrates a general failure to live up to the ideals that his society proclaims, but he goes beyond that simple social criticism, for he knows that Christianity sets an impossibly high standard that necessarily exceeds human capabilities. Human beings therefore must fail, no matter how assiduous they may be in trying to fulfill their responsibilities. This motif can be seen in much medieval literature, and it is particularly clear in medieval Arthurian literature. Some three centuries after Chrétien, Thomas Malory develops the idea in his *Morte Darthur*, in which Arthur and his knights try to establish an almost utopian kingdom founded on the Christian knight's duty to defend the weak and the downtrodden, to right wrongs, and to establish justice. But almost immediately after the establishment of the Round Table, things start to go wrong, sometimes through honest errors and sometimes through normal human — but unchristian — behavior, until finally the kingdom collapses. In the world as medieval Christianity conceived of it, such a utopia could not exist. Rather, it lived up to its etymological meaning of "no place." (Actually, the word "utopia" did not enter English until the early sixteenth century, but the ideal of a perfect state existed earlier.)

Chrétien deals more overtly with the religious implications of his romances in *Perceval*. It is difficult to read *Perceval* without thinking about the later development of the Grail legend, and it is nearly impossible to devise a full interpretation of a poem that is unfinished. Without knowing how Chrétien intended to end the poem, interpretations of the part we have are even more tenuous than usual. We can, however, with some assurance contrast the two major sections of the poem, one dealing with Perceval and the other with Gawain. Perceval is a "holy fool," the kind of character that Dostoyevsky refers to in the title of his novel *The Idiot*. His innocence and his naiveté are both appealing and dangerous, creating difficulties for himself and for others. His failure to ask the question that will cure the Fisher King and bring fruitfulness to the wasteland is lamentable; but we can guess that Chrétien would have allowed him to learn enough to return and correct that error, as opposed to Gawain, who can never achieve such a feat. But that guess must remain a guess. Oddly enough, it is strangely fitting that *Perceval* remains unfinished. First, as we saw earlier, its lack of a conclusion led to the composition of several continuations and of other works like Wolfram von Eschenbach's *Parzival*, based on the same legend. But also, there is so much about *Perceval* that is unworldly and mysterious that its incomplete state seems totally appropriate.

Finally, we should briefly consider *Cligés*, Chrétien's least Arthurian romance. Set largely in Greece, Constantinople, and Germany, *Cligés* is often viewed as an anti–Tristan and Isolde story. That story, which later became incorporated into the Arthurian cycle, tells of the love between Tristan and Isolde, despite Isolde's marriage to Tristan's uncle. It also tells of the various subterfuges used by the lovers to meet and carry on their affair and of the affair's tragic conclusion. The story was very popular in the Middle Ages, existing in a number of versions. Chrétien even tells us in the introduction to *Cligés* that he wrote a version. Several times in the romance, the lovers, Cligés and Fenice, distance themselves from Tristan and Isolde, saying that they do not want to be thought of in the same terms as those two lovers. Those disavowals, of course, have the effect of making us think of Tristan and Isolde, for Fenice, like Isolde, is married to her lover's uncle. This uncle, though, had promised Cligés' father that he would never marry, so Cligés may be justified in maintaining his love for the woman who is now his aunt. Furthermore, thanks to a magic potion, the uncle has never consummated their marriage except in his dreams. By making the uncle wicked and by leaving the marriage unconsummated, Chrétien makes the Tristan and Isolde story even more complex. Is Cligés justified in cuckolding his uncle? Does he, in fact, cuckold him? If the marriage is unconsummated, are Cligés and Fenice committing adultery? Are their attempts to distance themselves from Tristan and Isolde merely a form of self-justification, as if to say, "Those two were clearly adulterers, but we are far superior to them?" Once again, Chrétien uses his romance to raise difficult questions and to make us, his audience, consider those questions in relation to such clearly stated ideals as "Thou shalt not commit adultery." Chrétien does not provide easy answers to these questions (and neither, as we will see in the next chapter, does his contemporary, Marie de France), nor does he allow us to ignore them.

Here we come to one last point concerning Chrétien. His romances are full of elements that had not appeared earlier in medieval literature: an awareness of his characters' psychology and of their interior lives. In a work like *Beowulf*, we only know what Beowulf is thinking from what he actually says. Chrétien, however, enters his characters' minds. What they think might not strike us as terribly accurate reflections of the way people really think — his characters often seem to think in terms of scholastic disputation, lining up logical arguments on both sides of an issue, or their inner thoughts may take the form of a debate between allegorical personifications like Reason and Love. Nevertheless, Chrétien's forays into his characters' interior worlds reflect the twelfth century's increased interest in the individual. In this area, Chrétien is something of a pioneer. We may regard those psychologizing passages as somewhat naïve from our perspective, but if we can play a mental game and put ourselves somehow back in the early twelfth century, looking forward to what Chrétien was doing, we might get a sense of how revolutionary he was.

The works of Chrétien de Troyes are fun to read. His stories flow well, they entertain, they teach us about the time when they were written, and they help us to understand what it means to be a human being in this world, however different our world may be from the one in which they were composed. Chrétien may have been a pioneer in several ways, but he was not the only pioneer in the twelfth century. His contemporary, Marie de France, was equally so, though she went, as we will see, in different directions.

III. The *Lais* of Marie de France

MEDIEVAL WOMEN WRITERS

It is almost a commonplace to say that women were regarded as lesser beings throughout the Middle Ages. They were regarded as the property of their fathers and then of their husbands, they had few legal rights, and, because of the lack of contraception and the state of medical knowledge, they spent much of their lives pregnant and many of them died in childbirth. Life in the Middle Ages was difficult for everyone, but it was especially difficult for women. At the same time, women's lives were far from hopeless. The case has been made, for instance, that women's lives in the Middle Ages were in some ways less constrained than they became later. We regard the Renaissance as a time of rebirth, as a great leap forward for mankind. It may indeed have been such a leap for men, but not for women. In England, Elizabeth I was the greatest ruler of the Renaissance, but she did little to ease the path to prominence for other women, and in many ways she made the path more difficult. Once again we have to be wary of the tendency to equate "medieval" and "primitive." As recent research has illustrated, medieval women lived vital and productive lives and were often prominent in public affairs. We have already encountered Marie de Champagne, who sponsored Chrétien's *Lancelot*, and her mother, Eleanor of Aquitaine, was one of the most fascinating women of the Middle Ages; but there were numerous other women, with both secular and religious backgrounds, whose lives and accomplishments deserve more attention.

Another stereotype about the Middle Ages concerns literacy. Certainly literacy was not nearly as widespread as it is now, but neither was illiteracy universal, and we have evidence that there were many literate women. One sort of evidence can be found in paintings of the Annunciation, that moment when the angel Gabriel announces to Mary the role she will play in the Incarnation. In many paintings of this scene, Mary can be seen reading a book. Medieval artists, of course, did not try to depict historical scenes with any kind of historical accuracy. Biblical and mythological figures wear medieval garb and engage in medieval activities, which means that medieval artists, in depicting Mary with a book, would have seen nothing odd about a literate woman. In addition, we have other illuminations that depict female scribes. And of course we have works by a number of female writers.

The manuscript culture of the Middle Ages had a special effect on the works of female writers, because medieval culture was still highly patriarchal. Thus, many medieval works are anonymous and might have been written by women. More important, medieval scribes were undoubtedly reluctant to copy works by women, which were taken less seriously than works by men (a situation that remained true through the nineteenth and even into the twentieth centuries). There were, however, exceptions to this rule. The works of female mystics, for example, were accorded a certain respect. Women were mostly excluded from formal religious study, but a number of women had mystical experiences that they wrote about (or dictated to men, who wrote them down). The works of Hildegard of Bingen and Margery Kempe belong in this category.

But there were also female authors of less overtly religious works whose writings have survived. Christine de Pizan, for example, wrote a number of important works, including a response to the offensive sexism of *The Romance of the Rose*. One of the finest female writers of the entire Middle Ages was the twelfth-century author of a number of fables and lays, Marie de France. Although we can assign her name to these works, "Marie de France" (Marie of France) is rather like "John of New York": it tells us fairly little. Based on hints within her works, scholars have tried to determine exactly who Marie might have been, but as is so often the case, such determinations are speculative. What we do know is that Marie was a woman, that she was French, and that she apparently lived for a time in England, where, we have to remember, French was the language of the upper classes. As far as the *Lais* are concerned, we cannot even be sure that Marie wrote them all. All twelve appear together in only a single manuscript, and Marie mentions herself in only one, but there can be little doubt that the same person wrote them all and that that person gave serious attention to a number of issues that specifically affected women.

This collection of lais (lays, in English) is Marie's best-known work. What is a lai? It is a short narrative poem related to the ballad. We might think of lais as the medieval equivalent of short stories, as opposed to the longer narratives that were the romances. The shortest of Marie's lais, "Chevrefoil," is 118 lines long, while the longest, "Eliduc," is 1184 lines long. Compared to the 6808 lines of *Yvain*, these poems are short indeed, but the stories they tell have far simpler plots as well. Marie indicates with some regularity that she has heard these stories elsewhere before she wrote them down, that she has not invented them but only that she tells them well; and it is certainly possible that they originated as oral tales. Or Marie may simply be relying on the medieval commonplace of denying originality. In either case, she correctly says that she tells the stories well. Whether she invented them or not, these stories are enjoyable and relevant both for medieval and modern tastes.

THE LAIS

For instance, the lai called "Les deus amanz" ("The Two Lovers") seems as applicable to our society as it did to Marie's twelfth-century society. This lai, Marie says, is based on a true story and was originally made into a song by the Bretons. The problem with these assertions is that the first is highly unlikely, as anyone who reads the lai can see; and if we cannot believe the first assertion, we may choose not to believe the second either. The lai tells of a king who has an only daughter whom he loves so much that he tries to prevent her marriage, a most unnatural attitude for the Middle Ages. Anyone who wants to marry her must carry her up a mountain. We are not told how much she weighs, or how high the mountain is, but we do learn that no one can accomplish the task and eventually potential suitors stop trying. Then a young man falls in love with her and she with him, so she sends him to her aunt in Salerno, which was a center for medical studies, to obtain a potion that will give him the strength to take her up the mountain. At what must have been great expense and effort, he does so, then returns to face the challenge. As they start up the mountain, he does well, but twice when she feels him tiring and offers him the potion, he refuses to take it. When he reaches the summit, he falls down dead; the poor princess is so upset that she dies, too.

What a strange story! We might well feel sorry for all the characters. The king, who adored his daughter, has lost her; and the two lovers are both dead. But there is another way to look at the story. The king, through his selfishness, has prevented his daughter from knowing love or marriage (or the combination thereof) and has caused her death. And her lover, through his pride, has done the same. He has traveled all the way to Salerno, and the potion is right there for him to take, but apparently he is too macho to use it. Isn't that just like a man? In fact, that seems to be Marie's point. All that poor princess wants is a little love, but she is completely victimized by the two men in her life who claim to love her, one who wants to possess her forever and the other who is too proud of his masculine strength to use the potion that is right in front of him. She is, in short, a victim of the men who, in a patriarchal society, run her life and make a shambles of it.

"Les deus amanz" is typical of Marie's lais in its concern for the woman's point of view, which receives so little attention elsewhere in the Middle Ages. She never disavows the value of love, but she does question what love means to both the men and women who populate the lais, whether it means the same thing to them or whether there are gender differences in their perceptions. We can see these questions raised in many of the lais. A good example is "Yonec," which begins by describing an older man who has taken a younger wife. Undoubtedly that situation occurred often in the Middle Ages, and there is nothing obviously wrong with an older man taking a young wife, though such marriages are often a source of humor, as in Chaucer's Merchant's Tale, which describes a May–January wedding with sexual and humorous overtones.

There is nothing humorous about the marriage in "Yonec," however. At the very beginning we learn that this old man has married for a specific reason: He is old and has presumably had a good time throughout his life. Now he is ready to have children — heirs — and he marries a beautiful young woman. We must understand that this match is not based on love, for the lady later curses her parents for having married her to the loathsome old man, probably in return for some financial consideration. In short, she has probably been sold to him for breeding purposes, much the way one might sell a cow. Thus, when we are told that he loved her because of her beauty, we are entitled to doubt whether he is using the word "love" in the same way that she would. He loves her as one would love a possession, which is precisely her status, and he shows his love by locking her up in a tower. It would not be going too far to see that tower as a phallic structure representing the patriarchy that keeps her legally and practically imprisoned.

The biggest irony in the story so far, however, is that after seven years of marriage, this couple remains childless. The implication, borne out later in the story, is that the old man has been incapable of impregnating his wife, that he has waited too long and that what he thinks of as love is ultimately a form of sterility. We might laugh at the irony and at the old man's foolishness, but we cannot overlook the lady's misery, locked up as she is in her tower. When she laments that she cannot even attend church, the effect is even more serious, for by keeping her away from church, her husband may be affecting her chance for salvation, a serious matter indeed. And like Chrétien at the beginning of *Yvain*, but perhaps with more justification, she thinks back to a legendary time when noble knights and fine ladies practiced love as it should have been practiced. The old man has transformed her into an object in two ways: She is a breeder, a baby machine, and she is a treasure to be locked up. And we can imagine that her plight in this lai reflects the real plight of real women.

Fortunately for her, if not for those real women, she inhabits a world in which miraculous things can happen. Thus, when she finishes her lament, a hawk flies in through the tower window and becomes a handsome knight who expresses his love for her. Surely Marie is not proposing as a solution for oppressed women that they fall in love with enchanted knights, but she is contrasting the old man's selfish love with the more romantic and generous love of the hawkman. Perhaps, too, she is making the point that such love exists only in fairy tales and that women should not expect such love in the real world.

The lady reacts to the appearance of her hawkman lover in an interesting way. She tells him that she can only love him if he believes in God, so they pretend she is ill and send for a priest, who gives the knight communion. How the priest gives him communion without being aware that he is where he should not be is not explained. Perhaps in a story in which a hawk becomes a knight, such details need no explanation. What is important, however, is that the lady will only indulge in what amounts to an adulterous relationship with someone who believes in God, whose law forbids adultery. Is this lady, like Chrétien's Lancelot, simply a hypocrite, or might there be another explanation for this paradoxical behavior? Marie clearly understood the evils of adultery. In one of the other lais, "Equitan," a king has an affair with his seneschal's wife, and the lai ends with both lovers being scalded to death in a tub of boiling water, a fate that the narrator views with some equanimity. In "Yonec," however, the situation differs. This lady's husband behaves perfectly legally. As a husband, he owns his wife and can do almost anything he wants with her, as befits such a patriarchal society. Marie, in this fairy-tale lai, challenges that patriarchal view. She knows that adultery is forbidden, but she also understands the immorality of the husband's actions. From a patriarchal point of view, the view that makes the laws, his actions are perfectly justified. But from the woman's point of view, being sold into marriage, treated like a breeder, and locked into virtual solitary confinement are actions that are not justified. In fact, in all but the most legalistic terms, they negate the marriage and justify her affair with the hawkman.

The conclusion of this lai bears out this interpretation. The hawkman dies after the husband becomes aware of the affair; but the lady bears the hawkman's child, who many years later slices off the husband's head, thereby avenging the lovers. Nowhere in the lai is either the hawkman or the lady blamed for their adulterous affair. All the blame accrues to the husband, raising the question of whether a woman who is subjected to such a husband can really be considered married. We must recognize that Marie makes a revolutionary point here. According to both secular and religious law, they are obviously married, but Marie questions the validity of laws that have been made by men for the benefit of men. We might think here of the words of Chaucer's Wife of Bath, written two centuries after "Yonec" but equally applicable:

> Who peyntede the leon, tel me who
> By God! if wommen hadde written stories,
> As clerkes han withinne hire oratories
> They wolde han written of men moor wikkednesse
> Than al the mark of Adam may redresse.
>
> (692–96)

The Wife's point is that all of the misogynistic stories about women — and, by extension, the misogynistic laws — have been devised by men. If women had written the stories and the laws, they would be far different, more sympathetic to women and less so to men. To us, this point may seem obvious: Those who have power control the discourses of power. Medieval women (and, as we will see in a later chapter, other minorities) had little power and therefore little opportunity to take part in the discourses of power. The Wife's words and Marie's lai challenge patriarchal power. They may have had little effect on actual social conditions, but the mere fact that they raised the issue is remarkable. It certainly reminds us that people in the Middle Ages were aware of social injustices and did not just accept oppressive conditions as inevitable or as the will of God. "Yonec" may seem like a fairy tale, but like the other lais, it addresses serious issues.

A similar lai is "Guigemar." In this lai, Marie announces her name, states that her stories will be told well, and asserts that they are all true. As we saw in "Yonec," that last assertion may stretch credulity, if we understand her to mean that the events really happened. On the other hand, if we think back to Chrétien's warning at the beginning of *Yvain* that we should hear not only the story but also what lies beneath it, we may be more willing to accept that the stories lack historical veracity but that what they say is true. "Guigemar," like "Yonec," indicts a system that oppressed women, though it does so somewhat less harshly.

"Guigemar" contains a number of elements that we can find in other medieval works, conventional elements that appealed to medieval authors. For instance, Guigemar is taken to and from his lady by a mysterious ship that has no crew but goes where it must under its own direction. Such magical ships appear in a number of Arthurian stories, like *The Quest of the Holy Grail*. Another common motif presents the young man who refuses to have anything to do with love. Troilus in Chaucer's *Troilus and Criseyde* is such a person, and so is Marie's Guigemar. Troilus, sadly, comes to a bad end; Guigemar is more fortunate.

First, however, Guigemar is injured when he shoots a deer and the arrow ricochets. As the animal dies, and in a clear blow at historical veracity, it curses Guigemar, saying that his wound will never heal until he finds a woman who will suffer the greatest pains of love for him, pains that he will feel as well. As if this curse were not bad enough, we learn that Guigemar has been wounded in the "thigh," which, in medieval literature, serves as a euphemism for the genitals. (In *Perceval*, the Fisher King has been wounded in the thigh, which fits in with the wasteland motif— he shares the curse of sterility with the countryside). Guigemar's wound reflects a physical manifestation of the sterility that he has already shown by rejecting love. Happily, he finds the magic ship that will take him immediately to the lady who can effect his cure.

That lady, like the lady of "Yonec," is a prisoner of an old, jealous husband. Her prison, though, is not a tower but a room whose walls are covered with paintings about Venus, the goddess of love. This appearance of Venus—she will appear again in *The Romance of the Rose* and elsewhere—is an example of the mythography, the use of mythological figures to embody Christian beliefs, that we saw in the introductory chapter. Venus is a particularly difficult figure to understand in her medieval guises, largely because love itself is such a difficult and complex subject. As we have seen, the medievals made significant distinctions among the varieties of what we often call love, and Venus was used to embody all of those varieties. Just as we may have trouble knowing what kind of love we see when someone says, "I love you," so we may have similar trouble knowing what kind of love Venus represents when we encounter her, unless an author provides some kind of clue. In *The Romance of the Rose*, Venus, when we first meet her, will be carrying a torch with which she inflames lovers, which gives us a pretty good idea that in that poem she represents something other than pure, spiritual love. So, too, in Chaucer's *Parliament of Fowls*, when we see Venus half-naked in the garden, seductive and sensual, we recognize her as the goddess of fleshly, carnal love; but when Chaucer invokes Venus under one of her other names, Cytherea, even though Cytherea also carries a "fyrbrond," he calls her "thow blysful lady swete" (113) and cites her as the muse of his poem. These two manifestations of Venus show different aspects of her and therefore of love. The problem for human beings is that those manifestations are often ambiguous: We cannot always distinguish as clearly as we should the kind of love we are confronting.

So it is for the lady in "Guigemar." Apparently her controlling husband has deemed these paintings appropriate because they depict Venus in terms of the responsibilities that go along with love. In one painting, Venus casts into the fire one of Ovid's books on love, undoubtedly his *Ars Amatoria, The Art of Love*, a scurrilous treatise on love that was widely read despite being widely condemned in the Middle Ages. The jealous husband wants his wife to have nothing to do with the kind of romantic, sexual love that Ovid described, so Venus tosses it into the fire. But because Venus is such a tricky figure, this image might well lead the viewer in other directions. The mere presence of Venus, of course, is a reminder of her power, and the association of Venus with fire, with the heat of passion, is particularly — well, inflammatory.

The lady, then, finds herself imprisoned, accompanied by her husband's niece as a companion and served by a priest who is a eunuch, which means that he is no priest at all, since a eunuch could not serve as a priest. The constant reminders of Venus that she sees on her wall probably do nothing to reconcile her to her situation, which is as fruitless as that of Guigemar. Naturally, the magic ship brings him to her. She and her companion care for him, washing his wound (!), and soon he and the lady are in love, though they are reluctant to tell each other, so they suffer in silence until the niece brings them together and they discover the mutuality of their feelings. Marie makes it very clear at this point that Guigemar and the lady are not playing games with love, not just flirting and trying to seduce each other but truly falling in love.

Fortune, another of those medieval personifications who appear so often in the literature, constantly changes. In this lai, the major change is the discovery of their love by one of the husband's servants. Guigemar and the lady devise an interesting way of assuring their love for each other before he is forced to flee: She ties a complex knot in the tail of his shirt and says that he may love any woman who can untie the knot without cutting it. And then he winds a belt around her naked loins, making the same condition. (One might think that this belt would interfere with certain natural functions and disrupt the lady's daily life, but then I remind myself that these stories are not meant to be realistic. After all, Guigemar is there because of a talking deer.)

Once Guigemar is safely away and regains his health, numerous women try to undo the knot in his shirt, without success. And finally his lady rebels against her condition, which the husband has made worse, and escapes, taking advantage of the magic ship, which has returned to pick her up and take her to Brittany, where a nobleman befriends her and then, of course, falls in love with her. She naturally remains true to Guigemar and shows the nobleman the belt around her thighs, explaining why it is there. He tries to remove it, without success, and then, incredibly, invites all of his knights to try. This is one of my favorite scenes in Marie's work: The troop of knights clusters around the poor lady, struggling to remove this belt from a very personal part of her body. It must have been quite a sight. (I should, in all fairness, note that the Old French word "flanc" could be translated differently — and less personally — as "hip.")

Eventually Guigemar and the lady are reunited, with the implication that they lived happily ever after. Strangely, Marie never refers again to the lady's marriage or to the husband from whom she has escaped, as if they either no longer exist or are irrelevant. As we saw in the case of "Yonec," in an important sense her husband and her marriage actually are irrelevant, made so by the cruelty and possessiveness of the husband. That magic ship that appears several times contributes to this perception. In *The Quest of the Holy Grail*, the magic ship has clear religious overtones, but that whole romance has such overtones. "Guigemar" is not the same kind of work, but by having the ship take Guigemar to the lady, rescue her from the jealous husband, and bring her to Guigemar, Marie implies that they are fated to be together, that they belong together. Both of them have faced serious trials — his wound, her imprisonment — but love has triumphed.

Indeed, in several of the lais, Marie does show love triumphant, while in others, like "Equitan" and "Bisclavret," she shows the unhappy outcomes of misguided love. In those two lais, two wives commit adultery, but their husbands are not the cruel monsters of "Yonec" and "Guigemar" and provide no justification for the adultery. It is true that the husband in "Bisclavret" is a werewolf, but he is never cruel and his adulterous wife receives universal condemnation for her behavior towards him. In other lais, Marie looks at different aspects of love. "Chaitivel," a lay that has barely any plot at all, illustrates the complexity of Marie's views of love. We have noted earlier that the titles of many medieval works are modern inventions, given to the works by modern editors. While many medieval writers did not necessarily care about titles, Marie did. In lai after lai, she comments on her titles, but the most interesting discussion about titles comes in "Chaitivel."

Marie begins the lai by saying that it has two names. Most people call it "Le Chaitivel," which Glyn Burgess and Keith Busby in their excellent translation render as "The Unhappy One," though the connotation of "Chaitivel" in Old French involves being a captive or a prisoner. But, Marie tells us, other people call this lai "Le quatre deuls," which means "The Four Sorrows." We might be inclined to wonder what difference the title makes, but as we will see, the title focuses on the central question of this lai and of several others.

There was once a lady who, like all the ladies in the lais, was beautiful and well bred, so that every knight fell in love with her. She enjoys the attention and turns none of them away, not because she is a flirt, Marie explains, but because while a man can do what he likes in affairs of the heart, it is dangerous for a woman to refuse a knight's attention lest he decide to seek vengeance for being rejected. Marie's comment may be justified, but its ultimate effect is that the lady has a surplus of boyfriends. Four of them in particular court her, and she is reluctant to discourage any of them. Each of them believes himself to be her sole wooer, and she does lead them on; but at a tournament, three are killed and the fourth is severely wounded in, of all places, the thigh. The devastated lady provides suitable funerals for the deceased and gets the best doctors for the survivor, but clearly his wound has left him impotent. Together they lament, she over the sad deaths of such valiant men and he over the fact that he is the lone survivor and yet his wound allows him to do nothing with his lady but talk to her. She says she will write a lai and call it "The Four Sorrows," while he says that it should be called "The Unhappy One" (or "The Captive"). And that is the whole story.

In terms of action, then, there is very little, but a closer look shows some fascinating aspects of the lai. The whole lai, in fact, is the story of the naming of the lai, thereby making the entire story into a kind of circle. If "Chaitivel" is indeed the lai that the lady wrote about what happened, as it implies, then the lai is about giving the proper name to the lai that the lady wrote about giving the proper name to the lai.... This postmodern game could go on forever. Why would Marie do such a thing? As the lai makes clear, those two titles reflect different perspectives on the action in the lai. From the perspective of the lady, who has lost all four of her lovers, it is "The Four Sorrows"; from the perspective of the knight, who loves her but can no longer act on that love, it is "The Unhappy One." Each of them, the man and the woman, regards the same story from a vastly different perspective. As is so often the case in the *Lais*, those differing perspectives depend to a large extent on gender. As Marie says, this lai is more commonly known as "The Unhappy One," reflecting the dominant male perspective of her story; but we must never forget the equally important and equally valid female perspective that we see in the lai that Marie herself calls "The Four Sorrows."

These Lais of Marie de France are so wonderful that one is tempted to discuss all of them in detail, but only one more will receive that treatment, another lai about adultery but one whose ending strikes modern readers as bewildering, if not bizarre. "Eliduc" is the longest of Marie's lais, and it is another with two names, either "Eliduc" or "Guildelüec and Guilliadun," the first the name of the hero and the second the names of his wife and his mistress (who becomes his second wife). The lai, befitting its length, contains several adventures, but basically Eliduc is a happily married knight who, in exile, falls in love with another woman. When his wife discovers the affair, she gives the couple her blessing and becomes a nun. He establishes an abbey for her and marries his girlfriend. After happy years together, he builds a church, which he and his men enter as clergy, while the second wife enters the abbey with the first, and they all pray for each other.

It would be easy for us simply to laugh at such a story and dismiss it, but from a medieval point of view, Marie's story makes a certain kind of sense. In all of the lais, Marie offers a variety of views on the subject of love, a favorite subject in medieval literature from the twelfth century on. Many of the "loves" she describes are actually perversions of love, and some describe what we might like to call true love. The ladies in "Yonec" and "Guigemar" truly love their knights, who truly love them in return; and particularly in "Guigemar" we have every hope that the lovers live happily ever after. Romances often, though certainly not always, have such endings. We like the sense of wholeness and happiness that such conclusions convey. They make us feel good. But happily-ever-after endings are generally deceptive. However wonderful the happy couple's lives may be for however long they may live, we know that they must die eventually. In our mostly secular contexts, that ending is sad, but we tend to ignore it when we think of the happy "ever after."

Marie offers us a different view. We may condemn Eliduc for taking a girlfriend while he is married or we may excuse him because he is in exile, but his wife, whose behavior we regard as strange, shows what true, unselfish love really means. She cares more for his happiness than for her own possession of him. By not rejecting him and by not demanding that he remain with her, she shows the depth of her love. Her love, in fact, approaches the ideal. Some readers may dismiss such statements as a male fantasy: How happy the man is whose wife allows him to marry his mistress. Marie, however, is serious, as she shows when she has the husband and his second wife enter holy orders as well. They have all turned away from selfish human love and turned instead to the love of God, and in the light of that divine love, they all care about each other and pray for each other. They have found a contentment that will outlast their mortality, so that not only will they live *happily* ever after, but they will also live happily *ever after*.

As with so many of Marie's lais, we might wonder how seriously we are to take this story. She has told us on numerous occasions that the stories she is telling are based on fact when plainly they cannot be. We know there are no magic ships or knots that can only be untied by specific lovers. We can enjoy these stories, but we know that we must look beneath the surface of the literal meaning to hear what Marie is saying. Does she really recommend that wives of adulterous husbands embrace their rivals? Probably not. Does she really say that true love should be completely unselfish and transcend the ordinary concerns of human existence? Probably. Does she believe that everyone, or even most people, could behave in such a way? Undoubtedly not. Her approach may seem silly to us, or it may make us feel uneasy, but ideals frequently make us uneasy, because we recognize our inability to achieve them.

Marie, then, like so many medieval authors, writes about a world of flawed human beings. They know, or should know from their religious background, how they should live; but because they are flawed human beings, they cannot fully do so. Some may attain happiness and love, which often amount to the same thing; but human love, unless it has something of the divine about it, is not enough. Again, this tension between what we know we should do, those ideals that were public knowledge, and what we actually do pervades medieval literature.

Marie, in her brief lais, presents and examines a variety of approaches to love. We, as her audience, have to decide on the nature of those varieties, on their desirability and on their implications for our lives. She knows that people, depending on their gender and a host of other factors, regard love from a multitude of perspectives. But she also knows that there are proper and improper ways to regard it. Her lais challenge us to consider our perspectives and to see whether we accept her ideals and then, if we do, whether we can achieve them. These poems are obviously shorter than Chrétien's romances, but they are, in their own way, as challenging and enjoyable as those longer works; and they allow us to see important aspects of medieval life through the eyes of a perceptive and outspoken woman.

IV. *The Romance of the Rose*

A Medieval "Best-Seller"

In the twenty-first century, we have many ways to determine the popularity of a book. We can check whether it is on best-seller lists, see if it is being made into a movie, or follow its author's progress on a series of television and radio programs. How can we determine the popularity of a medieval work in its time? One way is to see how often other authors borrowed from it. Today we would regard such borrowing as at least verging on plagiarism, but in the Middle Ages literary borrowing was regarded as a kind of flattery or even homage to an important work. We can also try to determine how many manuscripts of the work survive. We know that, however durable medieval manuscripts may be, many have been destroyed[1]; even so, the numbers of manuscripts can be revealing. According to both of these criteria — borrowings and manuscript survival — *The Romance of the Rose* (*Le Roman de la Rose*) was one of the most popular works of the entire Middle Ages, and for very good reasons.

As is so often the case with medieval literature, we have to give special consideration to the authors of this work. *The Romance of the Rose*, which is not a romance in the same sense as Chrétien's poems are romances, has two authors, Guillaume de Lorris and Jean de Meun. Guillaume began the poem in the early part of the thirteenth century and wrote almost 4060 lines. Some forty years later, Jean continued the poem, adding almost 18,000 lines to what Guillaume had written. That Jean's continuation is more than four times as long as the original poem should give us pause, as should Jean's explanation of why he continued the poem. According to Jean, Guillaume died before he could complete the poem, so Jean took the responsibility of doing so himself. Jean's assertion has generally been believed, but we have good reason to question it. We might wonder how, after forty years, Jean knew this information about Guillaume. There could hardly have been records of Guillaume's life and death, and the poem does not show signs of being incomplete, although, as a result of Jean's words, many readers have assumed that it does. It is clear, however, that in his continuation Jean is having a good time, while making serious points, and it would certainly fit in with the rest of his poem if we assumed that he invented Guillaume's death as a justification for having commandeered the poem.

And why should anyone want to commandeer a poem? From the evidence in Jean's continuation, it appears that he disagreed not only with what Guillaume had to say about the central subject, love, but also with how Guillaume presented the subject. His continuation seeks to correct Guillaume's errors. Some scholars have seen in the differences between the two parts a reflection of a change in sensibilities between the earlier and later parts of the thirteenth century, but that kind of global statement may go too far. As we have already seen in the poems of Chrétien and Marie, there were many views of love, some more genuine and others more cynical, even in the twelfth century; that diversity of views would continue into the following centuries. Even in our time, we seem not to have made a great deal of progress in dealing with the complexities of love. In fact, we face many of the same problems as did people in the Middle Ages, which means that we can all profit from reading and understanding the two parts of *The Romance of the Rose.*

FOCUSING ON LOVE

Before we begin, however, we need some context. Love may have been as much a problem for them as for us, but some things have changed. One element that has changed is what has been called courtly love. "Courtly love" is not a term that anyone in the Middle Ages ever used in any language. It was invented in modern times to name a particular approach to love. Modern devotees of courtly love, however, go too far in codifying the conventions of such love, in trying to make it an organized system. We have conventions regarding love and courtship in our time as well, but anyone who has ever read a book or article describing how love and courtship should be approached knows how inaccurate those books can be. Either the conventions that they describe are corny and unrealistic, or they apply to everyone but the reader and the reader's beloved. What we see so often in medieval literature is the confusion caused by love, the paradox that love, which is a good thing, even potentially a divine thing, causes suffering and misery.

And once again, one of the problems for medievals was that they had the model of divine love as an ideal to which they could never measure up. According to the religious thought of the Middle Ages, the highest sexual state was virginity, and the second highest was widowhood, that is, a state of sexual non-involvement after marriage. Married love, which was, of course, blessed by the Church, came third, and there were even people who urged that married couples should abstain from sexual activity. In any case, sexual activity was viewed as legitimate only if it was intended for the engendering of children. The pleasure of sexual activity was viewed as a consequence of the Fall — St. Augustine says in *The City of God* that had Adam and Eve not sinned, conception would have taken place without pleasure and birth would not have involved pain. The Church demanded sexual purity.

But even if we think that such sexual purity is good, we must recognize that it is also very difficult. Many people in our time think that it is unnatural, but in the Middle Ages it was held up as an ideal, once more raising that tension, which we see so often in the period, between the ideals and the failure of ordinary people to live up to those ideals. In dealing with the subject of love, we have to keep that tension in mind. There were, naturally, people at both extremes: Some urged absolute adherence to Church teachings while others, as represented by French fabliaux, were at the other end. The fabliaux are short poems, somewhat like Marie's lais except that they are bawdy, full of explicitly sexual situations and dirty jokes. Body parts, especially sexual parts, are given voices and personalities, and only the imaginations of the authors limited what those parts could do. But most people occupied an area between the Church and the world of the fabliaux; and for them, love and sex were confusing subjects.

A good example of this confusion can be seen in the work of Andreas Capellanus, Andrew the Chaplain, a contemporary of Marie de France and Chrétien de Troyes. At the request of Marie de Champagne (the patron of Chrétien's *Lancelot*), he wrote a handbook of love, *De arte honesti amandi*. Although the title literally means *The Art of Respectable* (or *Proper*) *Love*, it has been translated as *The Art of Courtly Love*. Andreas divides his book into three parts, the first two of which offer all sorts of rules about how love affairs are to be carried out. In these sections, Andreas is like the Emily Post of love, explaining what is and is not done by whom and to whom. Then in the third section, he condemns everything that he has so carefully explained in the first two. The reader is entitled to wonder what is going on, and the answer is that we do not know. Possibly he meant the first two seriously and then, remembering that he was a chaplain, a man of religion, he felt compelled to add the third section. Or perhaps he used the first two sections only to set up the condemnation, which is what he really believed. Or perhaps something else. We simply have no way of knowing how we should read the work, and its ambiguity reflects the ambiguity of so many medieval works about love. People accepted the religious ideal as an ideal, but they also lived their everyday lives without attaining, or even necessarily trying to attain, that ideal. Consequently, they had to regard love with a certain amount of ambiguity. (It should also be noted that Andreas' work does not seem to have been well known in the Middle Ages.)

In Guillaume's portion of *The Romances of the Rose*, the narrator is a young man who loves and courts a young woman, and he does so very delicately. Some scholars have charged that the lover is after nothing but sex, as though there were something unnatural about him, but there is not. We can find an analogy in a fancy dinner party, where each place setting consists of numerous forks and spoons. How many forks do we need in order to eat? Some people might say one, but in the Middle Ages they managed just fine without any. Why, then, do we need three different forks for dinner? The answer is that we do not. We need those forks for something else. Eating, after all, is an animal act, but if we can create table manners and use individual implements for each course, we make it seem less like an animal act. We disguise, even from ourselves, our animal natures. The same is true of courtship. This argument is not meant to disparage notions about romantic love, but the goal of romantic love is another animal need, the need to procreate. We create elaborate rituals for courtship and marriage, but the ultimate goal is to have sexual relations and produce children. This argument may strike some readers as crass, but, as we will see, it summarizes the differences between Guillaume's and Jean's views of the ambiguous subject of love.

GUILLAUME'S DREAM

This brief discussion of love is in no way complete, but it should prepare us for *The Romance of the Rose*. First, though, there is one more factor to consider. *The Romance of the Rose* is the first example we have come across of a very popular medieval literary form, the dream vision.

Inexperienced writers will occasionally create a story without knowing how to end it, so they fall back on, "Then I woke up and realized it was all a dream," a conclusion that sends chills up the spines of writing teachers. But in the Middle Ages, dream visions, more skillfully used, were extremely popular. Naturally the sources for dream visions are both biblical and classical.

In the Bible, there are many famous dreams and dreamers: Joseph, who has dreams that tell the future and who also interprets other people's dreams; Daniel, who describes and interprets a dream; and the prophets, whose visions, according to some commentators, came to them in dreams. These stories all proved that dreams could predict the future. The classical world, however, offered a more detailed description of dreams. The great Roman orator Cicero wrote a long book based on Plato's *Republic*. That book, unfortunately, has disappeared, except for its last chapter, "The Dream of Scipio." Scipio was a Roman general, and Cicero describes a dream he had in which his grandfather, also a Roman general, appears to him and teaches him certain truths about the values of earthly life. The reason that we still have "The Dream of Scipio" is that a fourth-century writer named Macrobius wrote a long commentary on it, thereby preserving the text and at the same time presenting, in his commentary, concepts that would be used throughout the Middle Ages. Among those concepts is Macrobius' classification of dreams.

Many of those medieval works that we call dream visions rely on Macrobius' classifications. In later chapters we will look at such dream visions as *Pearl*, *Piers Plowman*, and some of Chaucer's early works, but there are far more dream visions. One of the most famous, and influential, is *The Romance of the Rose*. Macrobius refers to five categories of dreams, but he adds that any dream may belong to more than one category. We can argue, therefore, that *The Romance of the Rose* belongs to several categories, but the most important for this brief introduction to the poem is the prophetic, called in Latin the *visio*. The section of the poem attributed to Guillaume is primarily prophetic in that it reveals things that were to happen.

The poem actually begins with a discussion of dreams, as the narrator tells us that although many people dismiss dreams, he believes that dreams may come true and that they may reveal truths. He tells us that when he was twenty, he had a dream, all of whose elements have come true in the time since he had it. He will now recount that dream in *The Romance of the Rose*, which will contain the whole art of love. In this introduction to the poem, the Dreamer effectively presents the thesis of his poem: What we are about to read was a dream that came true, and it will teach us about love. Whatever happens in the poem, we must never forget these points. Not only did he dream that it was May, but it was May when he did so; it was spring, the time of rebirth, a common time for dream visions. In his dream he heard birds singing, as he describes in detail; and we cannot forget that bird songs are actually mating calls, just as, we will see, *The Romance of the Rose* is a mating call. He jumps out of bed, gets dressed (including, in medieval style, sewing the sleeves onto his shirt after he has put it on), and heads toward the river, where he looks at the river bed, then follows the river to a garden. Here we may recall the garden that we saw in Chrétien's *Erec and Enide* and its association with the Garden of Eden and with scenes of love in other medieval literature. This garden, too, is enclosed, but at first glance it seems uninviting because the wall is covered with paintings of such disagreeable personifications as Hate, Avarice, Envy, and Old Age. In fact, these personifications are pictured on the outside wall because they represent the qualities that cannot be allowed inside the garden, which is where the Dreamer would like to be, though he has trouble finding the small, hidden entrance. Clearly the garden is somewhat exclusive, but the Dreamer is admitted by a young woman holding a mirror who introduces herself as Idleness and who tells him that he is in the garden of Pleasure.

These early pages of the romance introduce us to some of Guillaume's techniques. The most prominent is his use of personification allegory, that is, characters with names like Old Age, Idleness, and Pleasure, who stand for those qualities. Guillaume uses these allegorical figures very carefully throughout his poem. Later in the poem we will meet many more personifications, including many that represent the internal qualities of the lady loved by the Dreamer—figures such as Fair Welcome, Shame, and others. These figures may at first seem strange to us, but they need not. We speak very easily about such psychological qualities as the id, ego, and superego, but these are not identifiable parts of the brain. No brain surgeon has ever said in the middle of surgery, "Look at the ego on this guy." Id, ego, and superego are, in effect, allegorical figures that suited the time when they were defined, just as Fair Welcome or Shame suited the psychological needs of the Middle Ages. Furthermore, these personifications are not necessarily simple figures. What exactly constitutes Fair Welcome? What does it mean for the Dreamer to be in the Garden of Pleasure and for that garden to recall the Garden of Eden? The answers to these questions are complex. For instance, we know that medieval Christianity expressed deep suspicions about earthly pleasure and that questions about love were regarded with some seriousness, yet the Dreamer says that he wants to find Pleasure and entrance to the garden is provided by Idleness. We could simply conclude that the kind of love presented in the poem is rooted solely in pleasure and requires plenty of free time, but that conclusion would make the poem into a trifle, hardly worthy of consideration. And the Dreamer actually seems to find little pleasure in the Garden of Pleasure. Instead, the love he discovers there causes him great pain. Perhaps Guillaume is acknowledging the fact that the pain of love is paradoxically one of its pleasures. Discerning readers have interpreted the poem in numerous ways, but the point of this discussion is that Guillaume's use of personification allegory is far from simplistic.

As the Dreamer wanders through the garden, Guillaume depicts a whole allegorical world. The Dreamer sees characters like Courtesy and Joy and he describes some of them in detail. Idleness holds a mirror, for instance, an indication of her self-centeredness, Courtesy is most courteous, and Joy makes all who see her happy. And by her side is the god of love, whose robe, made of flowers, shows the plenitude of nature. Like the garments of Philosophy in Boethius or of Nature in Alan of Lille's twelfth-century *Complaint of Nature*, Cupid's robe is highly symbolic, making the point that love is an integral part of nature, that without love, nature would not be so prolific. When the Dreamer says that the god of love looks like an angel from heaven, he is not simply exaggerating. In *The Complaint of Nature*, Alan of Lille had developed the idea that Nature was God's assistant whose responsibility was to keep the natural world operating and that Nature had appointed Venus, mother of the god of love, to oversee procreation. The god of love, then, ideally should be doing divine work, ensuring the continuity of species. That he does not always do so is a perversion, but that perversion does not negate the necessity of his job. Once again, then, we are presented with an ambiguity about love. It can be divine or perverse.

And what does it mean when the Dreamer says that the life he sees in the Garden of Pleasure is eminently desirable, that it would be worth forgoing a greater good to lead such a life, that having a lover puts one in paradise? The Dreamer himself brings in the religious language of angels and paradise, so he himself raises these troublesome questions. By having him do so, Guillaume seems to be making parallels between human and divine love. In describing the garden, the Dreamer has been describing life the way young people have often thought of it. Strict Christian standards would condemn such a life, but, Guillaume says, perhaps there is truly nothing wrong with it. Perhaps it just reflects the way people really are and human love can have something of the divine about it.

As the Dreamer continues to explore the garden, he is trailed by the god of love, with his bow and arrows. Again we see the profusion of nature, this time in the trees, until the Dreamer comes to the spring of Narcissus. This spot is the most important place in the garden, for it is where the Dreamer falls in love, but its allegorical meaning has a tremendous effect on how we are to regard that love. There have been fascinating scholarly debates about the spring and its significance, with scholars interpreting it in various ways. Most interpretations hinge on the mythological story of Narcissus, the beautiful young man who saw his reflection in the spring, fell in love with himself, and pined away until he died of self-love. Obviously the spring of Narcissus is a potentially dangerous place, and the Dreamer pauses to warn young women that they should not be so self-absorbed that they abandon their lovers, as Narcissus abandoned Echo.

It is odd that the Dreamer addresses his warning to women, since Narcissus was a man. We will soon see why he does so. But first, he looks down into the spring, all the way to the bottom, where he sees two crystals in which he sees his own reflection and a reflection of the whole garden, including a rose bush covered with roses. Immediately he is attracted to one of the roses.

This spring inspires those who look into it with love, but the kind of love differs according to the way the lover approaches it. Narcissus looked into the spring in a too limited way: he saw only himself reflected, as one sees oneself reflected on the surface of a body of water. Narcissus' consuming self-love resulted from a shallow look at the spring. The Dreamer's case is different. If we think back to the poem's opening, we remember the river that the Dreamer followed. He mentioned both the flow of the river, its changeable surface, and the rocks at the bottom, which did not change. An observer who only regards the surface will see only the changeable, the transitory; but the observer who looks past the surface sees the permanent and unchanging, as the Dreamer does. At the spring of Narcissus, we are presented with the same phenomenon. Narcissus could see only the surface and he died, both physically and spiritually; but the Dreamer, who has been warned by Narcissus' story and who is able to see below the surface, sees even beyond his own reflection in the crystals. By seeing past the flow of time and past his own self, both of which snares trapped Narcissus, the Dreamer finds his love, who he hopes will be constant.

Unfortunately for him, it appears that she has not been constant, because he notes that the mirror deceived him. This reference to deception also takes us back to the poem's beginning, where Guillaume mentioned that he had two audiences in mind for his poem. One is a general audience, whom he hopes to entertain; the other audience is his beloved, whom everyone should call Rose. He is writing both to and about his lady. He is sending her a poem that describes, in great detail, the background and course of their relationship, how he fell in love with her and what happened afterwards. Clearly he is in some difficulty with her, and he hopes that his poem will find favor with her and bring him back into her good graces. Thus, at the spring, he warns her — she is one of the ladies he addresses — that she should be true to her lover, to him, and that she should once more be as she originally appeared. If she thwarts their love, if she is so interested in herself, so proud, that she allows her lover to die, surely she will be divinely chastised. The Dreamer is telling his lady, his Rose, that their love needs to be unselfish and that if she continues to behave as she has been behaving, she will be punished.

Guillaume's poem, then, is his attempt to win his lady back. How did he lose her? After seeing the reflection of the roses, the Dreamer goes to the actual bushes and finds one bud that stands out. It is difficult to know how to interpret this bud allegorically. Some argue that it is a particular feature of the lady, either physical or spiritual. It might be her essence, that aspect of the lady that makes him fall in love. He is tempted to pluck it (which has sexual overtones), but its thorns keep him away. Then, from under a fig tree, the god of love shoots him with his arrows. Why a fig tree? After Adam and Eve ate the fruit and recognized that they were naked, that is, became sexually aware, they covered themselves with fig leaves. The Dreamer, like them, has just become sexually aware.

Love's arrows enter the Dreamer's eye and go to his heart. This path relies on the medieval conception of the heart as the seat of passion. In effect, the Dreamer sees his lady's Beauty, her Simplicity — those qualities represented by the arrows — and they make him fall in love with her. Immediately he surrenders to the god of love, having put up no struggle at all, and becomes his vassal, his loyal follower, even allowing love to lock up his heart. All of this, of course, is an elaborate way of saying that he has fallen deeply in love with his lady, that he will be true to her and that she rules over him. His loyalty to her is eternal, and he implies that her response should share that quality.

So far the Dreamer has presented his love in terms of medieval power relationships. Now he moves to a more religious analogy, as the god of love offers him a series of commandments. We could interpret these commandments — including avoiding pride, being clean, and not saying bad thing about others — as parodying the Ten Commandments, in which case Guillaume would be making a devastating attack on the culture of love, implying that it uses the trappings of the true religion for base and perverted purposes. Or we could interpret the commandments as Guillaume's attempt to make a serious connection between religious life and ordinary human life, seeing human love, imperfect though it may be, as a reflection of perfect divine love. Or we could recall what the Dreamer told us at the poem's beginning, that he would present in addition to his story a treatise on the art of love, and see the commandments as part of that treatise. These possibilities, and others that have been proposed, are not necessarily mutually exclusive. As is always the case in interpreting a text, a great deal depends on where the interpreter stands in relation to the text. As part of his presentation of the art of love, Guillaume might be doing something similar to what Andreas Capellanus did, presenting the ambiguities of love, for love can be either divine or perverse. If we take the Dreamer's story at all seriously, if we believe that he truly loves his Rose and hopes to persuade her to return that love, we can well believe that he is drawing the parallel between secular and divine love, though we, like he, must always be aware of how easy it is to cross from love as a divine power to love as a mere fleshly pleasure.

When the god of love compares the lover to a prisoner who hopes to be rescued and who gladly suffers his martyrdom, we see again this coincidence of love and religion. Both the lover and the Christian — who in religious writing is often described as a prisoner in this world awaiting release into the next world — are sustained by Hope. Clearly the Dreamer, who tries to win over his Rose, is being sustained by Hope, which prompts him to write the poem we are reading.

After the lengthy lessons of the god of love, which amounts to Guillaume's treatise on love, we return to the action. The Dreamer has fallen in love, and now he begins to take action. When he approaches Rose, she apparently smiles at him, for, in his allegorical way, he says that he is greeted by Fair Welcome. Of course, no one expects a love affair to proceed so smoothly, and the Dreamer acknowledges that despite the greetings of Fair Welcome, he knows that more threatening qualities linger nearby. One of these is Evil Tongue (Malebouche, literally Evil Mouth), who is likely to spread harmful rumors about the prospective lover. Accompanying Evil Tongue are Shame and Fear. A young woman being courted by someone like the Dreamer in the thirteenth century had legitimate causes to be afraid. Her reputation would have been of paramount importance to her, and if that reputation were to be sullied, were she to be too closely linked to her swain, she might well suffer irreversible damage. As the Dreamer tells us in a mini-allegory, Shame is the daughter of Reason, sent to protect Chastity. In plain words, the lady's chastity must be protected not only from actual assault but also from rumor; and the fact that Shame is the offspring of Reason indicates that the lady's concerns are reasonable.

The fourth nearby quality is a character whose French name is Dangiers, which has been translated into English as Danger or Rebuff. Literally it means something like dominance and clearly is the opposite of Fair Welcome. If Fair Welcome welcomes the Dreamer's attentions, Dangiers rebuffs them. Thus, when the Dreamer declares his love and tells her that the god of love has inflicted five wounds upon him (recalling the five wounds that Jesus suffered!), she panics, assuming suddenly that he represents a threat to her chastity. Appropriately for the allegory, Dangiers immediately appears. Because of her concern, Fair Welcome, allegorically her smile, her receptivity, is replaced by Dangiers. She becomes less welcoming and more upset at his forwardness. The Dreamer, quite naturally, becomes very upset at this sudden transformation.

If we step back from the allegory just a bit, we can see a quite ordinary scene that Guillaume has analyzed in great detail through the use of personification allegory. A young man has fallen in love with a young woman. She has initially regarded him favorably, inviting him to take the next step and declare his love, but when he does so — and remember, all he has done is to say he loves her — she becomes alarmed and turns on him. Naturally he begins to wonder about what he is doing, which Guillaume presents in another allegorical conversation, this time between the Dreamer and Reason.

Reason — we might say his rational self — tells him that he is behaving foolishly, that he should forget about love and get on with his life. Of course, because love is irrational, Reason cannot possibly understand it. Guillaume's allegory captures perfectly the steps in this love affair. The rejected young man asks himself whether this love business is worth all his suffering, a very reasonable question, and he decides, quite unreasonably, that it is.

We might want to accuse him of being guided by his hormones rather than by his brain, but we also have to acknowledge that all love is irrational, even the love that God showed by undertaking the Incarnation and offering fallen mankind the means for redemption. This analogy between God's love and the Dreamer's love should not be pushed too hard, but it does indicate that the Dreamer's rejection of Reason is not a case of simple foolishness.

At the urging of a Friend, the Dreamer finally wins over Dangiers. Some time has passed and the Rose is more beautiful and more mature than ever, so much so that he asks for a kiss, which she, under the influence of Chastity, at first refuses. But then Venus, the enemy of Chastity, appears with her flame, igniting the lady's passion and prompting her to grant him the kiss.

Immediately she regrets her action, as we know when Evil Tongue, Jealousy, and Shame appear and decide that in order to protect Chastity, they will have to control Fair Welcome. The poem ends with Fair Welcome imprisoned and the Dreamer in despair, hoping that he has not lost Fair Welcome forever.

In other words — and one point of allegory is that it is told "in other words" — he kissed his lady, who became embarrassed at her indiscretion and has withdrawn from him. He can only hope to win her back, to regain her favor. He has written this poem, incorporating into the dream vision the various stages of their relationship, in the hope that she will be convinced about the sincerity of his love and take him back. Because we do not know how the affair turned out, the poem may seem to be incomplete, but that appearance has been fostered by Jean de Meun's fiction about Guillaume's death. In fact, the poem is complete, since the Dreamer has taken it as far as he can. He can write no more until his Rose responds; and if she responds favorably, if she again presents the aspect of Fair Welcome, he will be busy doing other things than writing a poem.

Guillaume's *Romance of the Rose*, then, is a complete poem, a delicate presentation of some of the conventions that surrounded the issue of love, an astute and detailed analysis of courtship and an examination of the problems raised by love. We can argue that there is an essential purity and even a kind of holiness about the love that he expresses, or we can maintain that the poem is actually a condemnation of love, that the appearance of Venus with her torch undercuts any pretensions to sanctity.

Whichever stance we choose, there is no denying the power and charm of Guillaume's allegory. The Middle Ages may not have been prepared for the probing interiority of a Henry James, but Guillaume, using medieval techniques, does a good job of presenting the Rose's psyche, those internal qualities that make her act in particular ways.

JEAN TAKES OVER

If the poem is complete in itself, we cannot really say that Jean de Meun completed it. More precisely, he took a poem that of necessity had an open ending and hijacked it. Jean's views of the issues raised by Guillaume differ significantly from Guillaume's, and his lengthy continuation of the poem transforms it into *The Romance of the Rose* by Guillaume de Lorris (if such a person ever existed — we have no proof that he did) and Jean de Meun. Guillaume's poem is delicate and subtle, two qualities that Jean seems to have found boring, if not ludicrous. Jean's poem is funny, episodic, violent, and horrifying. Obviously it was intended to take a very different course than Guillaume's work.

Although we have no external evidence that a person named Guillaume de Lorris wrote the *Romance*, we do know about Jean, who was responsible for a number of other works, including a translation of Boethius' *Consolation of Philosophy*. His reputation, however, rests on *The Romance of the Rose*. It is impossible for us to know whether the first part of the poem would have been popular without the second part, but we do know that the two parts together were enormously popular and influential.

Jean's *Romance* is an extended satire, though there is no single target for that satire. Jean lashes out in many directions. One of his major targets, however, seems to be the kind of delicate, refined love that Guillaume depicts in his poem. Guillaume's Dreamer loves and respects his Rose. He also fears her, as he is reduced to despair by her withdrawal of Fair Welcome. From some perspectives, he undoubtedly appears to be an ideal, courteous lover. From Jean's perspective, he seems like a wimp, so Jean changes him. Guillaume's Dreamer relied on Hope, but Jean's Dreamer knows that Hope is insubstantial and untrustworthy. Guillaume's Dreamer rejected Reason; Jean's Dreamer confesses that he knows that Reason is correct, but ultimately he rejects her anyhow, as he becomes increasingly irrational and driven by his animal urges.

The Dreamer's conversation with Reason in Jean's poem is not, however, as straightforward as we might expect. At one point, for example, Reason tries to dissuade him from loving by listing all of love's bad qualities, a list that, in the fashion of satire, goes on and on, piling up indictments. The problem is that this extended passage (*ll.* 4263ff) parodies II Corinthians 13: 4–13, in which St. Paul lists the desirable qualities of *caritas*, unselfish spiritual love. Paul is clearly talking about *caritas*, the specific word he uses, but it is not clear what Reason is talking about until she explains that love is a mental affliction that has nothing to do with procreation but only with sexual pleasure. As we saw, sexual pleasure is a subtext in Guillaume's poem. In Jean's poem, it becomes the focus. Reason condemns the Dreamer for wanting sex, a fleshly, earthly desire that violates the teaching of Boethius (whom Jean had translated).

At this point, Reason's argument is surely reasonable, but the Dreamer responds that what she demands is impossible. Once again we see this theme that runs through so much medieval literature. Reason, citing Boethius and other authorities, is surely correct in what she says. The problem is that what she says goes beyond human capabilities. The Love that St. Paul described is indeed an ideal; but because it is an ideal, human beings cannot attain it. Reason, like all of Jean's characters, is rather long-winded, but almost everything she says reflects idealized thinking about people's place in the world and about how people should interact with the things of this world. Her speech is a storehouse of accepted truths. If the Dreamer were capable of accepting those truths, the poem would end, in terms of the ideal, very happily. When Reason says that she wants to replace the Rose as the object of his love, she is not expressing the kind of jealousy that we usually find in romances. She offers him something quite different from what the Rose has to offer. She offers spiritual love rather than the carnal love that he has been pursuing.

The Dreamer, almost despite himself, rejects that offer, partially because he does indeed want sex and partially because he seems not very bright. At one point, Reason tells the story of the birth of Venus, a story that involves Jupiter's castration of his father Saturn, and in telling the story she uses the word "testicles." Several pages later, after her continued moralizing, the Dreamer's only response to her challenging speech is, "You said a naughty word," a complaint to which he returns over a thousand lines later. Jean here illustrates the usefulness of Reason's reasonable advice: It is hardly useful at all. She preaches the ideal, and she provides philosophical support for that ideal, while all the Dreamer can think about is that she said "testicles." For such a person, and he surely represents a large class of people, the ideal means nothing. Not only does he not understand what Reason says, but he does not care that he does not understand. His mind is elsewhere. We might accuse him of "thinking" with his hormones, but we might also ask ourselves how often we are guided purely by Reason. We may rationalize, as the Dreamer will, but as a species we are not known for being reasonable.

This discussion with Reason characterizes Jean's whole poem. He knows how things are supposed to be, and he knows how they really are;

like any good satirist, he never tires of pointing out the discrepancies. Love should be pure and people should be reasonable. But love is complicated by sex and the need to procreate, and reason goes against our bodily desires, so almost by necessity we end up behaving badly. After the Dreamer again dismisses Reason, he gets a lot of bad advice from his Friend, who advises him to deceive his lady and along the way repeats many of the traditional and stereotypical complaints about women, about how greedy, unfaithful, and oppressive they are. As is so often the case, this advice comes from someone who reveals himself to be greedy, unfaithful, and oppressive, among other things. Once more the Dreamer's failings become obvious, as, having rejected Reason, he pays attention to his Friend.

In addition to the Dreamer's transformation from Guillaume's courteous lover to Jean's impressionable dolt, another change becomes clear as we move along. He is no longer interested in the refined love of Guillaume's poem. Increasingly his focus moves directly to sex. The beloved lady is there to be used, or abused, and all that really matters is his own comfort. Thus, when the god of love reappears, he is transformed into a threatening character who brings his army and helps Guillaume to besiege the lady. This siege imagery alone reveals the difference between Guillaume and Jean. Guillaume's Dreamer tried to win the lady; Jean wants to conquer her. As upset as Guillaume's Dreamer may have been, he never contemplated violence. In Jean's poem, False Seeming, a type of hypocrisy, chokes Evil Tongue and cuts out his tongue, after which love's army kills the drunken soldiers who are supposed to be guarding the Rose. As anyone can see, all the charm of Guillaume's poem has vanished. Jean's poem is brutal. His subject no longer even pretends to be love. Rather, he uses a distasteful assault on the Rose, on the lady, as a pretext for lashing out at the evils he sees predominating in his world.

For example, one of Jean's major targets in his poem is the friars. We need to be clear on the difference between monks and friars.[2] Even in the Middle Ages, monks had had a long history, having existed even before the beginning of Christianity. Monks go "into the wilderness." Sometimes they actually went into wilderness or desert areas in order to withdraw from the everyday world and devote themselves to spiritual matters. Other times they simply joined communities — monasteries — where life was highly regulated with spiritual aims in view. The monastic movement, from the early days of Christianity through the rest of the Middle Ages, went through a series of periods of corruption and reform, and monks were often the target of satire and harsh criticism when they abandoned their ideals and prospered rather than eschewing the things of this world. The friars, or the fraternal movement, began in the early thirteenth century, the century in which *The Romance of the Rose* was written. Begun under the influence of St. Francis and then of St. Dominic, the friars did not join a community. Rather, they vowed to give up the things of this world and to lead individual lives of poverty and begging, trying to serve all who were in need. Like monasticism — like so many human institutions — the fraternal orders very quickly abandoned their stated ideals. There were, of course, many dedicated religious friars, but too often the good they did was overshadowed by the corruption of their fellows. In the General Prologue and elsewhere in *The Canterbury Tales*, Chaucer provides portraits of corrupt monks and friars, but there was a long history of writings attacking such people. Jean attacks them mercilessly, referring to them as wolves who are attempting to take over the entire Church. His criticism of the friars is largely unrelated to his larger story, except that in both cases he focuses our attention on the corruption of an ideal and on the triumph of hypocrisy over truth.

As we continue to read Jean's poem, we can see it become darker and darker. After love's army has broken down the Lady's outer defenses, we meet the Old Woman who guards the Rose herself. This Old Woman, who served as a major model for Chaucer's Wife of Bath, is truly horrifying as she gives a view of the world based entirely on hypocrisy and deceit. For instance, because so many men have betrayed women — she provides examples such as Aeneas, Paris, and Jason — she says that women are foolish if they do not take many lovers. The distance between Guillaume's view of love and Jean's should be clear. Whatever flaws we might find in Guillaume's conception, Jean views love entirely as a matter of power (with the power normally held by the male), cynicism, and ruthlessness. This view of love, combined as it is with so many other targets of satire, provides a fairly dismal picture of the way Jean viewed his society. Jean continues to use Guillaume's personifications, like Fair Welcome and Dangiers, but no longer with the precise allegorical equivalencies that Guillaume had used. In Jean's hands, they become self-serving entities, each out for his or her own benefit. Guillaume's universe, limited in scope though it may be, is shattered by Jean, in whose world love and charity, in the wider medieval sense of the word, play little part.

The last section of Jean's poem becomes increasingly disturbing. Nature first delivers a long confession. One of Jean's major sources for this confession is a work that was mentioned earlier, Alan of Lille's *Complaint of Nature*, a work that was prompted by Alan's concern with homosexuality.

According to Alan, who, in true medieval fashion relies on many other sources, when God created the world, He also created Nature, Natura in Latin, as his lieutenant to oversee the continuing operation of the natural world. Nature in turn created Venus as her lieutenant to oversee the procreative aspect of the natural world; however, Nature complains, Venus has become too involved, and has allowed the world to become too involved, with the pleasurable aspects of the procreative act. Hence the world is full of sexual perversions.

Jean uses this myth to explore further the complexity of love and sex. Jean's Nature, who is quite separate from Reason, urges human beings to procreate, though she does so within acceptable limits. Nature's rambling confession covers a number of popular medieval problems, but it culminates in a bitter tirade against human failings, with an extended list of those failings, a long indictment of human perversity, and the punishments that flow from it. One of those perversities, amazingly enough, is the refusal to procreate, raising once again the problem of the clash between divine ideals and human behavior.

We should not be surprised that so much of Jean's poem shares the theme we have seen in other medieval works, namely our knowledge of what is expected of us and our inability to live up to those expectations. The appearance of this theme is not surprising for two reasons: First, Jean partakes of a common theme, and second, as a satirist, he must contrast what is with what should be. The difference between Jean and satirists from later periods is that Jean does not have to establish the sense of what should be. His whole society, with its foundation in a Christian concept of the world, knew what should be. Jean reminds his readers of those Christian expectations, but he focuses on how far human beings have fallen and he also shows an awareness of an explanation for such behavior in our natural, animal natures.

Jean underlines the complexity of the human situation by having Nature deliver her confession to the figure of Genius. Genius, who also appears in *The Complaint of Nature*, has an ancient history. The word is not related to what we mean when we say someone is a genius. Rather, the word has to do with birth and generation. Nature, though separate from Reason, provides a fairly reasoned argument for the natural urges, especially the urge to procreate, but Jean's Genius, unlike Alan's version of the same figure, is strictly an animal urge, and as such he makes an odd figure as a priest and a confessor. His advice to his followers is "Plow, barons, plow," and he adds "por Dieu," that is, do it "for God"; and he develops the image of sex as a form of plowing in obscene detail. Finally, at the end of his libidinous sermon, which arouses its hearers, Genius and Venus spread a flame that arouses all the ladies.

This extraordinary poem ends with what must be the most explicit allegorical rape scene in the history of literature. Jean not only returns to the imagery of plowing, but he also has the Dreamer refer to his Lady's vagina as a reliquary, a container of relics, holy objects such as the bones of a saint or a piece of the True Cross, that were meant to aid in worship. Guillaume's Dreamer may have gone too far in idolizing his beloved Rose, but Jean's Dreamer goes much further, simultaneously sullying love, sex, and religion. Similarly, the Dreamer describes himself as a pilgrim, someone on his way to a religious shrine, carrying a staff and a scrip, a small sack holding his most important possessions, but clearly the staff and scrip refer to his sexual organs. Ultimately we see that the Rose that he loves has come to represent the Lady's virginity (something that has been hinted at earlier) and finally he plucks it, scattering seed in the vicinity, impregnating his Lady. And with that, he awakens from his dream.

Obviously *The Romance of the Rose* is a long and complicated poem (or pair of poems). The complications arise from a number of factors: the relationship between Guillaume's and Jean's poems, the ambiguity of some of the allegory, the multiple perspectives, and the apparent randomness of Jean's satire. The preceding discussion has tried to provide a sense of those complications, but it has also taken firm positions on a number of points. Readers should be aware, however, that every one of those points has been the subject of extended debates. In fact, the debates began in the Middle Ages. As we have seen, we have very few examples of contemporary critical or popular reaction to medieval literature, but we do have such material about *The Romance of the Rose*. Christine de Pizan, an important author in her own right, raised objections to Jean's depiction of women, and she was answered, in both negative and positive terms, by other writers. Furthermore, Sylvia Huot has examined many of the surviving manuscripts of the *Romance*, looking at the way copyists altered the poem, changing either individual words or longer sections, thereby affecting the poem's meaning. She has also examined the marginal comments that various medieval readers made in the manuscripts. Her research indicates that medieval readers were no closer to having a "key" to the poem than modern readers are. Nevertheless, the fact that the poem has produced so much disagreement, that people care enough about it to engage in critical disputes, indicates its power. The two parts of this poem give us a window into two quite different thirteenth-century minds, two different sensibilities.

V. *The Tale of Genji*

LEAVING EUROPE

One of the wonderful things about studying medieval literature is the breadth of the period, both temporal and spatial. Traditionally, the study of the Middle Ages involves about a thousand years and all of Europe, which was united by the international language of Latin and by at least the pretense if not the actuality of a common religion. For a long time, the study of medieval literature was confined to the works of Christian male authors. Now the works of female writers like Marie de France, Christine de Pizan, and Margery Kempe are regularly included in courses on the Middle Ages; and in the next chapter, we will meet some non–Christian European authors. In this chapter, however, we will be considering a work from Japan that is both interesting and important but that until recently was not thought of in terms of the Middle Ages: *The Tale of Genji* (*Genji Monogatari*), by Lady Murasaki Shikibu. A large variety of medieval lyric poetry from both Japan and China is available in good translations, but there are special reasons for considering *The Tale of Genji*. First, this extremely long work is still thought by many scholars to be the greatest work in Japanese literature, even though it was written in the early eleventh century. It defines Japanese literature in much the same way that Dante's *Divine Comedy* defines Italian literature. And second, it is of interest to see the kind of literature that was being created in another part of the world at about the time we have been studying.

We should begin this discussion by considering two points, one practical and one theoretical. The practical point involves the tale's length. In Edward Seidensticker's readable translation, the tale is almost eleven hundred pages long. Big pages! Many people are not likely to read such a long work. Fortunately, Seidensticker has prepared an abridged version that includes twelve of the tale's fifty-four chapters. Clearly such an abridgement has some drawbacks, but it does allow new readers to get more than just a taste of the work. Perhaps after reading the abridgement, some readers will go on to finish the whole work. The following discussion, however, will focus on the abridged version.

The theoretical point involves the questions of what we mean by "medieval" and whether that term can be applied to the Japan of the year 1000. We in the West think of the Middle Ages as the period between Classical Antiquity and the Renaissance, but since Japan knew neither Classical Antiquity nor the Renaissance, it would seem that applying the term to Japan is little more than cultural imperialism. However, Jin-ichi Konishi, the author of a multi-volume history of Japanese literature, subtitles his second volume "The Early Middle Ages," and he defines the Middle Ages as the "period during which the indigenous Yamato culture was transformed by the infusion of Chinese civilization," a period that he sees beginning in the ninth century (3). Furthermore, Barbara Stevenson and Cynthia Ho, editors of *Crossing the Bridge: Comparative Essays on Medieval European and Heian Japanese Women Writers*, point out that the Heian period, during which Lady Murasaki lived, resembles the European Middle Ages in being based on aristocratic courts and on having a central religion, Buddhism. We may, then, refer to the Japanese Middle Ages if we remember that the term means something very different in Japan from what it means to us.

So if *The Tale of Genji* is a very long work from the Japanese Middle Ages, what kind of work is it? If we think of Western literature that is even very roughly contemporary with *Genji*, we might come up with *Beowulf* or *The Song of Roland*, epic works, or with early examples of romance, predecessors of Chrétien de Troyes, like the *Roman d'Eneas*. *Genji* fits into neither category. If there is a Western genre into which *Genji* fits — and again, discussing *Genji* in Western terms is a kind of cultural imperialism — the closest fit would be the novel. The origin of the novel in the West is sometimes attributed to the ancient Greek romances or to *Don Quixote* or to the eighteenth century, but no one would argue that there are medieval novels. Nevertheless, *Genji*, with its psychological insights, its frequent bouts of verisimilitude, its sense of actual human beings in actual human situations, clearly shows the attributes of the novel. In fact, *Genji* has often been compared to the works of Jane Austen and other well-known novelists. Reading *Genji* is very much like reading Marcel Proust's enormous masterpiece *À la Recherche du temps perdu*.

Lady Murasaki does indeed show an interest in the passage of time, though her interest is quite different from Proust's. The greater similarity, and this is especially the case in the later sections of *Genji*, lies in the characters' introspection, in the analysis of that introspection, and in the attention to the significance of the smallest details. In some spots, the resemblance between *Genji* and Proust's opus is uncanny, though there is one warning that the reader needs to keep in mind: Whereas Proust's work is always concrete, Lady Murasaki's contains built-in ambiguities that even the translator, with good reason, often tries to overcome, though he, too, is not always successful. For example, none of the major characters in *Genji*, including Genji himself, are known by their actual names. Often they are known by words that play significant roles in individual chapters. The best known example is Genji's first wife, Aoi. Aoi is not her name. Rather, it means heartvine, a kind of plant. This plant is mentioned in an exchange of poems in the "Heartvine" chapter. Although Genji's wife has no role in this exchange, heartvine became the name of the chapter; and because Genji's wife dies later in this chapter, the word became associated with her. We never know her given name or the given names of most of the characters.

Some critics argue that *Genji* is a kind of historical novel, based on real personalities who lived in the century before its composition, although this vagueness about the names, along with other details, has made precise identifications impossible. (In fact, even Lady Murasaki's name is not really her name. Murasaki is simply one of the novel's major female characters.) The vagueness, moreover, is echoed elsewhere in the novel. For example, Lady Murasaki frequently constructs long conversations in which it is not at all clear who is speaking. Seidensticker tries to help the reader by clarifying who is saying what, but apparently even Japanese experts are not always able to make definitive judgments.

The effect of these ambiguities is fascinating. In many places, the novel goes into extraordinary detail: specific things and places seem to come alive. At the same time, even the leading characters are allowed to exist with areas of mystery, conveying the sense that no matter how well we know them, there are still aspects of them that we cannot penetrate. To make a facile analogy, they are like some Japanese drawings that suggest rather than delineate their subjects. The characters come to seem more and more like real people, who are always more mysterious and multi-faceted than we can imagine. No matter how much introspection there may be, there is always something we do not know about the characters. If we compare Lady Murasaki's characters with Chrétien's, we can see this point more clearly. In Chrétien, we learn only what we absolutely need to know about the characters, so that they do not entirely seem like characters in any modern sense. Their thought processes, at least as they are represented, are not at all like ours, and the characters, however interesting their actions may be, are as two-dimensional as any medieval illumination. In a sense, they represent ideas more than they do actual people.

Lady Murasaki's characters, on the other hand, do resemble real people, to the extent that characters made entirely out of words can resemble real people. And as is the case with real people, we can never know everything about them. In *Genji*, we cannot even know their names! In fact, Lady Murasaki often makes the point that the characters themselves create barriers between each other. Sometimes they conceal their identities, and frequently they are separated by walls or screens; but many times, as in the case of Genji and Aoi, they create artificial barriers that never allow them to begin the process of knowing each other. This inability to establish full contact becomes one of the novel's major themes.

Lady Murasaki's calculated ambiguity is only one of the reasons that the authors of *The Princeton Companion to Classical Japanese Literature* are quite correct to say that "*Genji Monogatari* is a complexly integral work of a difficulty surpassed only by its greatness" (203). Other areas of difficulty involve the elaborate etiquette of the imperial court, where most of the novel's action takes place, and the equally elaborate protocols that obtain between men and women. In fact, although the action takes place at court, *The Tale of Genji* has little to do with national or international politics and everything to do with personal politics. The book is populated by emperors, retired emperors, princes, princesses, and a variety of government ministers, but, aside from questions of succession, we never hear anything about their official duties. A casual reader might think that these characters have nothing to do but conduct intrigues and seduce each other. Again, however, there is a prosaic explanation for this focus.

The Tale of Genji, we must never forget, was written by a woman. In eleventh-century Japan, not surprisingly, women led constrained lives, perhaps even more constrained than those lived by women in the West. Court women lived separately from men and made few public appearances. Although men and women often speak together in *Genji*, many of their conversations are conducted while the women are seated behind a screen. It is difficult for us to remember this fact as we read *Genji*, but it would have been natural to Lady Murasaki's audience, for whom such indirect communication was normal. We do have to remember, however, that relations between men and women were conducted far differently from what we are accustomed to, though the evidence from *Genji* is that men and women enjoyed trying to catch glimpses of each other.

Thus, although Lady Murasaki was apparently a keen observer, her observations were of necessity confined to the realm of women, which means that she had little or no exposure to national or international politics. She did know, in exquisite detail, the interpersonal politics of the court, which is her focus. Furthermore, the audience for monogatari, the Japanese genre to which *Genji* belongs, consisted of women, and Lady Murasaki obviously catered to that audience, though we have evidence that men read *Genji*, which was the greatest of all such works (*Princeton Companion 206*). In fact, in a later chapter of the novel, the chapter called "Fireflies," Genji himself makes a number of comments about such literature, first dismissing it as a woman's pastime and therefore negligible but then expressing an opinion that begins to describe a theory of literature, finding utility in such stories. Makato Ueda summarizes that theory in an interesting way: "According to Lady Murasaki's view, then, an ideal novelist will do two things: first he will take for his theme the greatest issue of human life and pursue it to the ultimate; and secondly, he will do that in such a way that the feelings of real life will emerge in the process" (35)

We can draw a significant parallel between this comment and Western literature. In fourteenth-century Italy, one of the greatest writers after Dante was Giovanni Boccaccio, who wrote volume upon volume of learned Latin, all of which is known today only to specialists. The book for which he is most famous is *The Decameron*, a collection of a hundred short tales told by a group of young people who were staying in the countryside in an attempt to avoid the plague. In his introduction, Boccaccio dismisses the work as just something intended for women, which is clearly not a flattering thing to say. Boccaccio might have meant this dismissal to have been read ironically, but whether he did or not, the greatest irony is that he is best known for the work that he disparagingly indicates was written only to entertain women, while his "more important" works are barely known at all. Similarly, hardly anyone in the West knows about the accomplishments of the Heian emperors or the men at their courts. What people do know is the work of Murasaki Shikibu, which men in their official capacities might have dismissed as a trifle unworthy of their serious consideration.

Ueda's comment, however, does quite properly describe *The Tale of Genji* as dealing with the greatest issues of human life. No great work, of course, deals only with a single issue, so trying to determining the single issue that Lady Murasaki addresses in the eleven hundred pages of *Genji* is a futile exercise, as evidenced by the variety of opinions over what that issue might be. Donald Keene cites what he refers to as the simplistic Buddhist interpretation: *Genji* is the "story of a man who was punished for his affair with his stepmother when his own wife betrayed him with another man" (489). Reducing the eleven hundred pages of *Genji* to this moral lesson is akin to saying that the lesson of Oedipus is that there are likely to be problems when one kills his father and marries his mother, though that Buddhist interpretation is no more reductive than many Western medieval comments on the lessons to be learned from classical works of literature. Keene cites a better interpretation by the eighteenth-century critic Motoori Norinaga, who described *Genji* as "a work embodying the principle of *mono no aware*, a sensitivity to things … awareness of the sorrow of human existence" (489–90). More recent critics have devised other formulations. Makoto Ueda says that the novel's greatest theme is the "question of Good and Evil" (36), which may certainly be a great theme but is rather too broad to be meaningful.

Other critics rely on the division of *Genji* into three sections, the first dealing with Genji's youth, the second with his maturity, and the third with events after Genji's death (since Genji dies in the forty-first chapter). Ikeda Kikan describes the three sections in terms of "glory and youth, conflict and death, and transcendence of death" (*Princeton Companion* 204), while Jin'ichi Konishi describes them in terms of "reality and clear insight, Karma and predetermined suffering, piety and spiritual blindness" (333), with the last two sections reflecting back on and transforming the themes of the earlier sections.

READING *GENJI*

What should emerge from this discussion is some sense of *Genji's* complexity. *Genji* differs significantly from the monogatari that preceded it, works that were generally designed as pure entertainment, as a means for women, to whom other activities were forbidden, to pass their time. *Genji* would have provided hours (and hours and hours) of entertainment, but it also provided something for the women and men who read or heard it to think about.

We will return to a consideration of the novel's themes, but first, because this work is so unfamiliar to Western readers, we need a brief description of the novel. This will not be a plot summary, which would be inappropriate and which would itself be longer than any of Marie's *lais*. *The Tale of Genji* is, in large part, just that, the tale of Genji, who is the son of the emperor and his consort. Because Genji's mother is of low rank, and because of various court intrigues, Genji is made a commoner rather than a prince. Nevertheless, he remains a star at the court, where he excels in the arts of poetry, dancing, calligraphy — all the things that make life worthwhile. Furthermore, he is irresistible to women, who, unfortunately, often seem to be in no position to resist him even if they want to, which they seldom do. Partially through the emperor's patronage but largely through his own virtues, Genji gathers a large group of admirers as well as a handful of detractors. He runs into particular trouble when the emperor marries a young woman called Fujitsubo because she reminds him of Genji's now deceased mother. Genji himself has an affair with Fujitsubo, resulting in the birth of a son whom the emperor thinks is his own. As if this bit of Oedipal behavior were not enough, Genji also adopts Murasaki, a young girl who resembles Fujitsubo. He raises Murasaki, and later they become lovers. In the meantime, Genji has a succession of lovers, with some of whom he has other children; and, of course, he is married to Aoi, who resents his amorous activities and who dies giving birth to their son. Eventually Genji seems to mature and change his ways, but those changes come later in the novel, long after Seidensticker's abridgement ends, and they are only temporary anyhow. After Genji's death, the story follows other characters, among them a young man who is supposedly his son but who was actually fathered by another man.

This brief description may make the novel sound somewhat absurd, though it is anything but. The novel's slow pace — not as slow as Proust, but still slow — prevents the various amorous alliances from piling up, and the psychological probing and insights make these activities more understandable. The more we get to understand the characters, the more we are willing to accept the things they do as plausible, because we become familiar with the ways in which they think and with the various pressures under which they live.

Furthermore, Lady Murasaki does indeed portray Genji, despite all his many failings, as a remarkable hero, justifiably renowned for his goodness and increasingly aware of the evanescence of the world he inhabits. And, of course, Lady Murasaki writes with particular sympathy about the many ladies who inhabit the novel's pages. Her portraits of such ladies as the Rokujo Lady, the Akashi Lady, the Lady of the Orange Blossoms, Fujitsubo, and Murasaki are beautifully done and make the reader feel that these women have substance and personality.

At the same time, like Marie de France, Murasaki is not shy about revealing the domination of women by men. She is not strident in her analysis, and she never seems to look forward to or to hope for change in gender relationships, probably because such hope would have seemed so far from possible. Nevertheless, she makes clear how disadvantaged women are. For example, Genji has a huge number of lovers, and while he seems incapable of establishing a relationship that is faithful and monogamous, he does treat his past lovers well. He makes sure that they and their offspring are cared for, and he houses many of them in his own residence. (We can see, though, how limited these women's lives are by the fact that they can inhabit the same residence without making extensive contact with each other.) Genji could much more easily have abandoned them, so he should get some credit. Still, everyone acknowledges that Genji has gone too far in his love life.

Even more revealing is his treatment of Murasaki. First, he practically kidnaps her when she is a little girl, largely because she resembles Fujitsubo, who resembles his mother. Then he takes charge of the way she is raised, shaping her in much the same way that one might shape a bonsai. His attempt to make this little girl who reminds him of his mother into the ideal courtesan should disturb us; and of course, thanks to the seclusion in which women normally lived, he is able to keep his experiment with her a secret. When Murasaki grows up and they become lovers, they have no children, perhaps symbolic of the sterility of the relationship, though Genji does prevail upon her to help rear one of his children by another woman.

We can hardly think that Lady Murasaki presents this affair dispassionately. She makes us aware of the unhappiness of Murasaki's life and of Genji's responsibility for that unhappiness. Genji, in this affair as in others, feels his responsibility, but he has no trouble either overcoming, or forgetting about, any regrets he may have. Genji's behavior toward women often goes beyond the generally deplorable behavior of men toward women in the tale. Lady Murasaki does not go out of her way to dwell on this subject, but neither does she shrink from making clear that there are genuine problems in gender relationships.

Another theme that comes through clearly is evanescence, the transitory nature of the world and of human happiness. In one sense, this theme is very much like the *contemptus mundi*, contempt of the world, motif that we find in so much Western medieval writing, from the Church Fathers on; but, of course, it is also quite different. The Christian view, exemplified by St. Augustine, posits a City of God that is opposed to the

City of Man. The Christian's duty is to belong to the former by rejecting the latter. *Genji*, though it relies on Buddhist ideas and though many
of the characters become Buddhist monks or nuns, is not nearly so ide-
ological. Genji seems less like a medieval Westerner and more like a modern one, questioning the values of his acts and the meaning of his life
without worrying about his eternal soul.

Because *The Tale of Genji* covers so many years, we can watch characters grow up, age, and die, and many of them die at a young age, as
was no doubt the case in Lady Murasaki's time. We also get a very strong
sense of the passing of the seasons and of the fading of beauty. These
changes are not necessarily presented with the intention of teaching readers to eschew the things of this world or to prepare for a better world
elsewhere, as they might have been in the West. Rather, they are presented with a sense of sadness and regret, with an acknowledgement that
there is something fundamentally sad about human existence.

Another important aspect of *Genji* involves its poetry. *The Tale of
Genji*, unlike every other work we have considered so far, is written in
prose, but it is full of poetry. It may be difficult for modern Americans
to grasp how central poetry has been in other cultures. In Heian Japan,
poetry, along with other arts, was considered a sign of education, of sensitivity, of the kind of culture that has the ability to raise human beings
to a higher level of existence. The Japanese poetry of Lady Muraski's time
was heavily influenced by Chinese poetry; her characters, men and women
alike, are able to quote extensively from the poetry of both nations. Characters frequently make allusions to poems in their everyday conversation,
and they also address each other with longer quotations. Some of these
longer quotations bear a clear relationship to the subject being discussed,
but often the reader has to struggle to see the connection, which may be
very subtle indeed. Nevertheless, those poetic quotations add immeasur-
ably to the texture of the novel. Readers might be tempted to skip them,
but they should fight that temptation. They should remember that no
medieval literature was meant to be read quickly. It was meant to be read
slowly and out loud. *The Tale of Genji*, especially, will suffer if the reader
tries to get through it too quickly.

While *The Tale of Genji* is obviously unlike anything written in
Europe during the Middle Ages, it still fits well into the study of medieval
literature. One advantage it has is that readers who are new to the Middle Ages already expect medieval works to have a strong sense of "other-
ness," so that the peculiarities and difficulties of this text will not deter
them. Furthermore, the very differences of this work provide valuable

contrasts to the themes of so many medieval European works. Nothing like *Genji* was to be seen in Europe for many centuries.

It is beneficial to read *Genji* in conjunction with the romances of Chrétien de Troyes, particularly *Yvain, Lancelot*, and *Erec and Enide*. All these romances examine facets of love and sexual relationships, just as *Genji* does; and all of them illustrate male power and female subservience. We can make a case that Chrétien is critical of those male and female roles — Enide proves to be quite a heroine, while Lancelot and Yvain are fairly inept in their roles — but in *Genji* the examination of gender roles goes into far more depth. Genji is granted a great deal of latitude in his dealings with women, and he never simply abandons any of the women who have been his lovers. Although his kindnesses do not excuse his philandering, they do put him far ahead of Yvain, Lancelot, and Erec, whose concern for their women extends only as far as their own glory.

It is also worth considering Lady Murasaki and Marie de France as women writing in totally male-dominated societies. We can observe how they both challenge the patriarchy even though such challenges must have seemed hopeless. Both of them, working within their own cultural constraints, see and help others to see the unfairness in gender roles and the lack of a meaningful rationale for those roles. Both express the awareness that those gender roles depend more on getting and preserving power than on any other factor.

Another point of comparison can be found in the psychological portraits that the authors draw. Marie does little psychological probing in her brief *lais*, whereas Chrétien is famed for his internal monologues and the psychological interest that they reveal. Even so, we can hardly deny that many of them, based on a scholastic question-and-answer model, often seem humorous to modern readers, and may have seemed so to medieval readers. Lady Murasaki, on the other hand, is far closer to Henry James. She really gets into her characters' minds and tries to make her readers understand how the characters think, how they perceive their environment, and why they behave as they do. It should hardly surprise us that *Genji* is considered the greatest of the monogatari. It is also one of the great works of world literature.

Although we have only been able to touch on the outstanding qualities of *Genji*, perhaps readers of medieval literature will be encouraged to give this work a try, at least in its abridged form. Reading *Genji*, becoming accustomed to its style and to the conventions it uses, might take some time and patience, but they will be amply rewarded. And perhaps reading *Genji* will prompt readers to explore other non–Western work from the Middle Ages. There are many Japanese and Chinese works to explore, and much great poetry was produced in the Middle East and in Moslem Spain. In a world that professes to value multiculturalism, it is time for such works to become part of mainstream medieval studies.

VI. Jewish Literature

THE JEWS IN CHRISTIAN EUROPE

The Tale of Genji took us outside of the world of Western European Christendom, but even within, that world was not quite so homogeneous as we sometimes imagine. There were, of course, major national and regional distinctions, even though medieval culture was in many ways international. For example, beginning in the twelfth century, the Gothic style of architecture swept across much of Europe, but English Gothic differs from French Gothic which differs from Gothic in other places. At the same time, despite these national differences, Gothic is always recognizable as Gothic.

There was, however, one major minority group in Europe during the Middle Ages whose cultural achievements are often overlooked in studies of medieval literature, the Jews. Today, many people take for granted the value of multiculturalism and diversity. We regard tolerance of differences as a bare minimum for the functioning of society, but we also encourage the understanding and appreciation of cultures and traditions different from our own. Though such views are common in our society, they are certainly not universal. In the Middle Ages, they were nearly non-existent. Whatever virtues existed in the Middle Ages, tolerance was not among them.

We can use Islam as an example. Until the beginning of the Crusades (in the very late eleventh century), most people in Europe knew nothing of Islamic culture, which in many respects was greatly superior to European culture. Nevertheless, Moslems were regarded with some horror and were subject to slaughter by the Crusaders. Even in Dante, Islam is treated as a Christian heresy; well into the Renaissance, literary works are filled with enemy "infidels" and "Saracens." Very few Europeans made any effort to understand or appreciate Islam, even though many European thinkers, like Thomas Aquinas, were influenced by Moslem thought.

The same kind of thinking affected medieval attitudes toward Jews, who, unlike Moslems, actually lived in Europe. Jews believe in the Old Testament but not in the New Testament,[1] which means that they do not believe that Jesus was either the Messiah or the Son of God. For medieval Jews, these beliefs clearly set them apart from the Christian majority, as did their adherence to the biblical dietary laws, the strict observance of Sabbath laws on Saturdays, the celebration of Jewish holidays, and other traditions that Christians regarded as no longer necessary after the Crucifixion. But the most serious liability that afflicted the Jews was the false accusation that they had been responsible for the Crucifixion, that they were "Christ-killers." Modern historians understand that this charge totally lacks foundation, but in the Middle Ages, it was an article of faith. One result was that attacks against the Jews often increased around the time of Easter. And later on that accusation contributed to another, the Blood Libel, which stated that Jews used the blood of Christian children in the production of Passover matzah.

In fact, an overview of Jewish history in medieval Europe looks like an unmitigated series of horrors. At the time of the Black Death, for example, Jews were accused of causing the plague by poisoning the wells. At other times they were deprived of normal rights or subjected to attempts at forced conversion. St. Augustine argued that Jews should be allowed to survive as Jews, but that their lives should be made difficult in order to demonstrate the errors of their ways. In 1215, the Church decided that Jews should be forced to wear clothing that identified them (thus offering a model that the Nazis were to imitate over seven centuries later). At other times they were required to pay special taxes or to go through degrading ceremonies. Probably the lowest point for medieval European Jewry came with the start of the Crusades.

The Crusades have often been portrayed in romantic and idealized terms, but there was little about them that approached the ideal. They were begun not out of religious idealism but as a method of reuniting a Europe that was being split by political and religious quarrels. Many of the Crusaders were younger sons, that is, the offspring of wealthy men who could not inherit the wealth of their fathers, which went to oldest sons. They regarded the Crusades as not so much a religious mission as a chance to pillage and get some wealth for themselves. As they made their way across Europe, they wondered why they were going to attack the Moslems when there was an alien group in their midst, the Jews. In the German Rhineland, in cities like Mainz and Speyer, terrible slaughters of Jews took place, massacres that are recorded in both Jewish and Christian sources.

The Jewish communities were devastated, and word quickly spread about what had happened, leading both to further outrages and to despair among the Jews, a feeling that is reflected in the poetry that was written by European Jews. Often they described themselves in terms of Abraham's offering of Isaac, which, unlike the attacks of the Crusaders, was stopped through divine intervention. David bar Meshullam of Speyer wrote,

> Lambs a year old were sacrificed
> They were sacrificed like the ancient peace offering.
> To their mothers they said, "Don't feel pity
> We have been called from on high to this fiery sacrifice to God."

There are a multitude of poems like this, questioning God for the suffering and yet also affirming faith in God despite the inexplicable tortures the people had gone through. And because these poems are written in Hebrew, they inevitably are full of biblical resonances. The four lines quoted above make extensive references to the sacrificial system described in Leviticus.

A particularly striking poem of this sort is the eighty-line lament "Al'lai li," "Woe is Me," by the twelfth-century Rabbi Menachem ben Ya'akov. We know very little about Rabbi Menachem, but we do know what prompted the poem: the killing of thirteen Jews in Boppard in 1179 as a result of the Blood Libel, and the deaths of several hundred Jews in the northern English city of York in 1190. Jews had lived in England since the late eleventh century, and one of the largest communities was in York, where they lived in relative peace, but in 1189, when the Jewish community of York sent a delegation to Westminster for the coronation of Richard I, they were attacked, against Richard's express commands. Richard tried to punish those who had violated his orders, but his absence from England led to further attacks. In York, a mob attacked the Jews, who were offered protection in the Norman castle. Through a tragic misunderstanding, the sheriff who had offered them protection thought they were trying to take over the castle, and he joined the siege. The Jews, knowing that they were doomed and fearing what would happen when the mob entered the castle, engaged in an act of mass martyrdom, so that when the mob did enter the castle, they found virtually everyone dead.

This incident occurred on the night of Good Friday, the night before the beginning of Passover.

The poem, like many medieval Hebrew poems, uses an acrostic, in this case spelling out "Menachem the son of Ya'akov, be strong; Menahem, be strong in the Torah." The poem is also full of biblical quotations and references that function in complex ways, as the third stanza illustrates:

> How the mighty have fallen and the weapons of war perished,
> My holy ones that are in the land,
> And I am bereaved of children, desolate and horrified.
> Outside shall the sword bereave, and in the chambers, terror.

In this stanza, all four lines are taken from biblical texts. The first, "How the mighty have fallen," is from 2 Samuel 1:27, David's lament over Saul and Jonathan. The second line, "My holy ones that are in the land," is Psalm 16:3; most of the third line, "And I am bereaved of children, desolate and horrified," is from Isaiah 49:22 (with references also to Jeremiah 12:11); and the fourth line, "Outside shall the sword bereave, and in the chambers, horror," is Deuteronomy 32:25. This collection of biblical verses, yoked together as they are, raises the central questions of the poem.

The first line, for example, comes from David's lament. There is something a bit ambiguous about that lament, for we must remember that from practically the first days of his reign, Saul had known, by the word of God conveyed through Samuel, that he had displeased God and that his son would not reign after him. He had spent the last days of his life in semi-madness, trying to reverse God's decree, in part by trying to kill David and remove him as a successor; and yet here is David mourning Saul's death in extravagant and beautiful terms. If Saul has died, did he not deserve to die? Perhaps. But David has not learned, as Dante was to learn many years later, that those who suffer divine punishment deserve their fate and do not deserve our compassion. Thus David can acknowledge Saul's culpability and still mourn his death, just as he mourns the death of his dearest friend Jonathan.

Let us keep this ambiguity in mind while we consider the next line. Rabbi Menachem quotes half of a verse, "My holy ones that are in the land." The other half of the verse, as his audience would have known, is "They are excellent in whom was all my delight." Obviously the lament of the first line applies to the holy ones of the second line, those excellent ones "in whom was all my delight," but while the psalmist meant that the holy ones were in the land, that is, in the country, Rabbi Menachem says that they are in the land, that is, in the earth, buried, and therefore, in the words of Isaiah, "I am bereaved of children, desolate and horrified."

But then, in the fourth line, Rabbi Menachem complicates all that he has said, for the fourth line comes from the end of Deuteronomy 32, where Moses is describing what God will do to a people who "forsook God," who "stirred Him to jealousy with strange gods," who "sacrificed to demons which were no gods." Such people will have evils heaped upon them; they will suffer hunger and heat and pestilence; "outside shall the sword bereave, and in the chambers, terror." Is it possible that the poet is suggesting that the current set of horrors has descended on the people as divine punishment for their sins? Such an explanation, after all, would fit in with a certain kind of religious outlook, an outlook that we know well from other medieval disasters, like the coming of the Black Death. It would explain why such terrible things were happening while leaving intact the belief in divine justice. It would parallel the belief so often expressed in the prophets and in the Talmud that the Temples were destroyed as punishment for the sins of the people. Furthermore, Rabbi Menachem alludes to the same idea in the second stanza, which begins

> The vengeance of the covenant grew on me
> To destroy, to cut off the children from the street

These lines, from Leviticus 26:25 and Jeremiah 9:20, again seem to indicate that divine punishment comes as retribution when the people disregard the covenant. These lines could demonstrate a harsh way of viewing the world, a way that feeds into the Christian notion that the God of the Hebrew Testament is a harsh God, while the God of the Greek Testament is more loving. Even though that notion is quite mistaken, we could imagine Rabbi Menachem contemplating the otherwise inexplicable destruction and murders and coming up with this as a comprehensible, if disturbing, explanation.

But that explanation, as we should know from our own experience with the Holocaust, is too simple; and it was too simple for Rabbi Menachem. To understand what he was trying to do, we must ask who the "I" of the poem is. It cannot be the poet himself, because the adjectives — bereaved, desolate, and horrified — are in the feminine gender. In fact, those words, as they are used in Isaiah and Jeremiah, refer to the land of Israel, to Zion, and we can see them in this poem referring to the people

of Israel in their exile from the land. With this explanation, we can understand the opening lines of the poem:

> Woe is me, for in a moment came widowhood and loss of children
> And I am left empty, in nakedness and want
> The first ripe fig that my soul desires to eat...
> For I am as the last of the summer fruits, and there is no cluster

These lines, taken from Isaiah, Deuteronomy, and especially from the
prophet Micah, paint the despair of Israel, which has been left widowed
and childless. The controlling image of these lines, from Micah 7:1,
describes the prophet as isolated, lamenting his role in the world at a time
when the righteous no longer exist, a time of depravity. So, too, with the
speaker of Rabbi Menachem's poem, Israel, who feels that she inhabits a
world from which righteousness has disappeared, a world in which innocent people can be slaughtered at a whim. Rabbi Menachem goes on to
accuse God in almost blasphemous terms for allowing such atrocities, but
he then allows God a chance at redemption, if only God will destroy the
evildoers.

We do not have to consider all eighty lines of this poem in order to
see how it works. It laments the misfortunes that have befallen the Jews,
it questions how God could have allowed these misfortunes, and it calls
on God to stop the oppression and punish the oppressors, while affirming
the innocence of the victims. In all of these ways, the poem is typical of
the poetry of medieval European Jews, who, unfortunately, had much to
lament. While this poem is touching, others are even more touching,
because they refer to the fates of specific individuals. One such poem,
by the great scholar Eliezer bar Judah of Worms, tells how his wife and
children were killed. Eliezer blames his own sins for the deaths of his loved
ones, apparently because he cannot believe that God could allow such
terrible things to happen without a cause. No one, of course, should criticize what he said in his grief, even after seven centuries, but it is difficult
to understand how saying that his innocent loved ones died for his sins
could have offered consolation.

As this poetry indicates, living conditions for medieval European
Jews were awful. Even when they were not being attacked and killed, there
were oppressive laws and customs to contend with, and life was especially difficult after the Crusades. On the other hand, we also know that
there were times when Jews and Christians seemed to live together in relative peace. In twelfth-century France, scholars at St. Victor, dissatisfied

at having to rely on the Latin translation of the Bible, consulted Jewish scholars in order to learn some Hebrew or at least to learn the literal meanings of biblical passages, a study that had been the focus of Jewish learning at least since the time of the French rabbi Solomon ben Isaac, who is better known as Rashi (1040–1105).

Jewish poets also wrote a large number of religious poems that give voice to their beliefs or that clarify technical points. Many of these poems have been incorporated into religious services. A particularly beautiful example, by an anonymous author, compares human beings to clay, to stone, to an ax, to a helm, to glass, to cloth, and to silver, while God is like the potter, the stonemason, the blacksmith, the sailor, the glass-blower, the draper, and the silversmith who shapes that material any way He wants. This poem, portraying God's complete control over human beings, has become part of the liturgy for Yom Kippur, the Day of Atone-ment, when Jews are particularly aware of their dependence on God.

Despite accomplishments in religious verse and lamentations, how-ever, life for the Jews in Europe was so difficult that their literary activ-ity was minimal. The Jews were expelled from England in 1290, not to be readmitted officially until the seventeenth century, and they were expelled regularly from other countries as well. Under such conditions, literary activity did not flourish.

THE JEWS IN MOSLEM SPAIN

There was, however, an exception. Jewish life in Spain was much different from its counterparts elsewhere in Europe, as were many things about Spain in the Middle Ages. Islam, which first appeared in what we now call Saudi Arabia in the seventh century, quickly spread across North Africa, thanks to the efficiency of the Islamic armies. These warriors crossed the Strait of Gibraltar, conquered Spain, and very nearly made their way further into Europe. They were prevented from doing so by the victory of Charles Martel (Charlemagne's grandfather). But through most of the Middle Ages, Spain was largely under Moslem control. It was finally united under Christian control at the time of Ferdinand and Isabella in the late fifteenth century, at which time they, like so many other Christian rulers before them, expelled the Jews from their coun-try.

But before 1492, under Moslem rule, the Jews had, with some major exceptions, prospered. Medieval Islam was not nearly as hostile to the

Jews as Christianity was. Under Moslem rule, much more than under Christian rule, Jews were able to achieve high political offices and Jewish culture was allowed to flourish. Among the Spanish-Jewish poets whose work has come down to us are Isaac Ibn Khalfun, Samuel Hanagid, Moses Ibn Ezra, Abraham Ibn Ezra, and Todros Abulafia, but for the rest of this chapter we will concentrate on the two greatest Spanish-Jewish poets, Yehuda (or Judah) Halevi and Shlomo (or Solomon) Ibn Gabirol.

There are relatively few characters from Jewish history who could conceivably be described as romantic, but one who could is the eleventh- and twelfth-century physician, philosopher, and poet, Yehuda Halevi. Around the year 1140, Halevi left his family and friends, his prosperous medical practice, and the relative security of Spain to make an arduous and dangerous journey to his ancestral homeland, Israel. According to legend, after a difficult trip, he finally arrived at the gates of Jerusalem, where, as he was kneeling in the dust and reciting his "Ode to Zion," he was killed by an Arab horseman. This legend has a wonderful symmetry and irony, and the only real problem is that it is not true. In fact, the time and place of his death are not known. What we do know is that some time after his fiftieth year, after the death of his wife, he set out on his way to Israel, and that on his way he created a series of poems about the trip. Even before that trip, he had written many poems of all sorts, religious poems, love poems, drinking songs, and a great religious and philosophical work called *The Kuzari*. We will focus on the poems concerning his journey.

Scholars have debated the reasons for Halevi's journey, which apparently puzzled even his friends. Some think he left Spain because he tired of the hostility of the Christians, who were reconquering Spain, and the somewhat less virulent hostility that had grown up among the Moslems. Others think that he went for purely private reasons or because he thought that by going to Israel he could hasten the coming of the Messiah. Because we realize that people seldom do the things they do for single, clearly defined reasons, we might be safe in assuming that all of these figured in Halevi's decision to go. He himself says in one of the poems, "My desire for the living God has urged me to seek the place of my anointed one's throne" (poem 13).[2] Three times a day, when religious Jews pray, they pray for the restoration of Zion and for a Jewish return to their land. Halevi seems to have felt that after his wife's death, with little to keep him in Spain, it was time for him to put his prayers into action.

In another of the poems he says:

My heart is in the east, while I am in the far west.
How can I taste what I eat, and how can it be sweet?
How can I fulfill my vows and my obligations
While Zion is in the cords of Edom and I am in the hands of the Arab?
It seems as easy for me to leave Spain
As the sight of the ruined sanctuary is precious.

(poem 1)

Halevi feels a compulsion to leave Spain and go to Israel, even though the Temple is still in ruins. Will his trip contribute to the restoration of the Temple or to the return of the Jewish people to Israel? He does not know. He only knows that he can no longer function in the alien land of Spain.

Halevi also desires to be in a place where he can more easily and clearly encounter the Divine Presence. We must understand here that Judaism did not share the Augustinian-Christian division between the City of Man and the City of God. Halevi, in line with Jewish thought, regarded the entire universe as a unified whole, all of it capable of holiness. He desires to have the closest possible relationship with God in this world, as we can see in his use of the phrase "the gates of Heaven." In his great Ode to Zion, "Zion ha-lo tishali" ("Zion, will you not ask"), he says to the Holy Land,

There the Presence [of God, in Hebrew "the Shekhinah"]
dwells in you, and
   your Maker
opened your gates to face the gates of Heaven.

(poem 2)

while in another poem he calls Israel

the land that is full of gates
And facing them the gates of Heaven are open

(poem 6)

This image of gates becomes intensely personal elsewhere when he says that he has

Given over my paths to the midst of the sea
So that I might find the footstool of my God

And there pour out my soul and my thoughts,
And I will tread on His holy mountain, and I will match
My gates to the gates of Heaven...

(poem 13)

Yehuda Halevi is not talking here about transcending the world or enter-
ing another world, nor is he describing a passageway through which his
soul can ascend to Heaven. Rather he describes an earthly place, the Temple Mount, where his soul can more easily and clearly encounter the
Divine Presence; he talks about the historic homeland of the Jews and
the dwelling place of God, the site of the ancient Temple, to which he
so often refers.

When Halevi refers to the Temple, we have to remember that he is
speaking of the actual Temple, destroyed by the Romans in the year 70,
only one of whose outer walls was left standing. Thus, in one of his
shorter poems, Halevi describes a kind of dream vision that he had: "My
dream brought me into the sanctuaries of God and I performed His beautiful service" (poem 4). When he awakened from this dream, he "was still
with you, God." If he could achieve this relationship with God in exile,
how much closer could he be in the Holy Land! Yehuda Halevi — the
name means Judah the Levite — must, as a Jew, as one of priestly, Levit-
ical heritage, return to the Temple in order to establish the closest possible earthly relationship with God.

Another motif in the poems, occasioned by the details of his trip,
is the exodus from Egypt. On his journey, Halevi spent time in Egypt,
and he regretted having to leave. Nevertheless, he knows that he must
re-enact the exodus and make the journey from Egypt to the Promised
Land. Like the Temple motif, the exodus is both a symbol and a reality
for Halevi. He is not talking about an allegorical, a tropological, or an
anagogical exodus (the terms in which Christian commentators discussed
the exodus, removing it from its historical context). He is actually making the trip, doing what his biblical ancestors had done so many centuries earlier. He must go, because in Israel, unlike in Spain or Egypt,

there is the Torah, there is the greatness
there is the place of judgment and there is the place of mercy.

(poem 18)

Halevi has a vision of life that we may think of as romantic, a vision that
involves the establishment of a Godly world on earth; and he believes

that Israel is the place where such a kingdom can exist. The Temple was the dwelling place of God's earthly presence, and he must therefore return to the site of the Temple.

To examine in more detail what Halevi's trip meant to him, we can take a closer look at the poem in which he defends himself against someone who disapproved. The poem begins with Halevi admitting that his critic's arguments have a certain appeal. Probably many of Halevi's acquaintances — and he was a well-known person — must have regarded his journey as a sign of madness, and we know from other poems how difficult it was for Halevi to leave the people and places he loved in Spain. Nonetheless, he says, the sweet words of the reproof contain stinging bees. The sweetness is superficial, and beneath the superficiality lies danger.

And what exactly is that danger? It is, from Halevi's point of view, the abandonment of God, which would entail the abandonment of his people and, in a far more profound way than his physical trip from Spain, the real abandonment of his loved ones:

> If the peace of Jerusalem is not to be sought
> While yet with the blind and the halt she is filled,
> For the sake of the House of our God let us seek
> Her peace, or for the sake of friends and of brothers...
>
> (poem 6)

These lines are based on the last verses of Psalm 122, one of the psalms addressed to Jerusalem, in which the psalmist says,

> For my brethren and companions' sakes I will now say
> Peace be within thee.
> Because of the house of the Lord our God I will seek thy good.

In the psalm, traditionally attributed to David, the friends and relatives are mentioned first, then the House of God, while in Halevi the order is reversed. This subtle shift underlines Halevi's outlook. In David's time, the Temple did not yet exist, but the Jewish people inhabited Jerusalem. His prayer, therefore, is for the people who exist there and for the Temple which will exist there. In Halevi's time, the Temple Mount and the Western Wall remained as the holiest places in the holy city of Jerusalem, but the Jewish people were scattered around the world. Consequently, Halevi's prayer, as well as his actions, must be directed first toward the Temple, which functions as a focal point for Jews everywhere. If he accepts the reproof and abandons his journey, he will no longer be acting "for the sake of the House of our God," and in the best interests of himself, his people, and his family.

He goes on to draw the logical result of this position: If the reprover is correct, then the course of the Jews over the past millennium has been sinful, for their prayers and their hopes have been largely directed toward Jerusalem. As he tells the reprover,

> If it be according to your words, see, there is sin
> Upon all those who bend towards her and bow down,
> And sin upon those sires who dwelt in her as strangers,
> And purchased there vaults for their dead.

Of course such a view is untenable, and he goes on to point out that the Jewish people have at least a threefold attachment to the Holy Land: Historically, it is the scene of the great events of their past, as he indicates in his references to Sinai, Carmel, and Bethel, as well as in his use of numerous biblical quotations; politically, it is the only place the Jews can even think of as a homeland—"Have we either in the east or in the west/A place of hope wherein we may trust..."; and finally, as we saw earlier, it is "the land that is full of gates," the land in which humankind can most clearly commune with God. All of these attachments are summed up in the rhetorical question that Halevi poses:

> Have we any heritage save the sanctuaries of God?—
> Then how should we forget His holy Mount?

As a Jew, fully aware of the Jewish historical experience and living in a fundamentally hostile environment, Halevi sees no alternative to his journey. It is the only religiously and intellectually honest course that he can take.

He knows, though, that part of the reprover's problem is what we might today call assimilation. Just as Aristotle's works occasioned hostile reactions in the West, so in Moslem-Jewish Spain they were the cause of bitter disputes. The reprover is evidently a person for whom Greek philosophy has a great attraction, but Halevi rejects pagan philosophy. If he is to be a Jew, to live a Jewish life, he must follow a Jewish path; and that path clearly leads to the Holy Land.

This poem, then, typifies Halevi's Zion poetry in its political and religious nationalism, its dedication to a religious and personal ideal, and its focus on serving God through worldly activity. It is unfortunately impossible to convey in English another element of this and other poems, Halevi's masterful use of the Hebrew language, with its opportunities for intricate word play and biblical references. It is the combination of his words and ideas, as well as the romanticism of the journey itself, that have helped make Halevi such a popular figure over the centuries. Nor can we forget his many other poems, many of them devotional and others expressing ideals of friendship and sensual love:

> Among the trees of Eden you are a flowering myrtle
> And among the stars of heaven you are shining Orion
> God sent you a packet of sweet myrrh
> That He made Himself, not the work of a perfumer.
>
> (poem 34)

Another great poet from Jewish Spain was Solomon Ibn Gabirol. We know that he was born around the year 1022, but strangely enough there is total uncertainty about the year of his death, with some scholars believing that he died before he reached thirty while others think that he lived to about fifty. For a man of fifty, the quality of his writing would be remarkable; for a man of thirty, it seems almost miraculous, though Ibn Gabirol, never one to belittle himself, says in one of his poems, "Behold me in my sixteenth year — yet I have the understanding of an eighty-year old." Ibn Gabirol often seems like a very difficult person, though we know that he suffered from a terrible illness that surely affected his outlook. Furthermore, he really was brilliant. In the nineteenth century, it was discovered that Ibn Gabirol was the author of a work called the *Fons Vitae, The Fountain of Life*, which was translated at some time before 1150 from its original Arabic into Latin. The *Fons Vitae* had some influence on those twelfth-century philosophers who were incorporating Aristotelianism into European thought, and we can only imagine how surprised they might have been to know that they were using the work of a Jewish writer. (To be fair, later philosophers made use of the works of Moses Maimonides, whom they knew to be a Jew.)

Ibn Gabirol wrote poems about friendships and even some poems about wine — a genre that the Hebrew poets adapted from their Arab contemporaries — but his most famous and moving poems are religious in nature. Many of them were written as introductions to already established prayers, while others were later incorporated into the liturgy. One of his most famous short poems reads,

At dawn I seek You, my rock and my salvation
I will set before You my morning and evening prayers
Before Your grandeur I will stand in fear
Because Your eyes will see my deepest thoughts
What can the heart and tongue do
And what power do I have within me
But because man's praise seems good to You
I will praise You as long as there is breath within me.[3]

We can see here his usual deep piety. However highly he may have thought of himself, what we usually find in his religious poetry is a sense of humility and of subservience to God. He recognizes his own insignificance; he knows that God does not need him; but through the prayers he recites and through the poems he writes, he can offer praise to God. Paradoxically, then, his humility is balanced by his obvious pride in his own poetic power.

While many of Ibn Gabirol's poems are small masterpieces, his greatest poem is the *Keter Malchut, The Kingly Crown*, a poem of 640 lines of varying lengths and meters and a highly irregular rhyme scheme. More significant than the stanzaic arrangement, however, is the way in which the poem divides into three major sections. The first section, the first nine stanzas, describes such attributes of God as His oneness, His existence, His greatness, and His wisdom. The description of wisdom in stanza nine, with its discussion of the role of wisdom in creation, leads to the second section, stanzas ten through thirty-two, in which the poet describes the created universe, beginning with the four elements and moving up through the heavenly spheres to the throne of God and to a contemplation of God's indescribable greatness. This contemplation leads to the last section, an extended confession of the poet's sinfulness and unworthiness and a plea for God's merciful judgment on him. This last section comes somewhat unexpectedly and consists of a moving and occasionally terrifying view of the poet's self and of human existence in general.

The poem's last section also illustrates another paradox in Ibn Gabirol's thought, for in the first two sections, God has been presented as infinitely transcendent above and beyond the world. In the third section, however, He is immediately immanent, in an intensely personal way. Ibn Gabirol does not simply contradict himself. Rather, the apparent contradiction in Ibn Gabirol's attitude towards God's relationship with the created world reflects ancient Jewish tradition, in which God is simultaneously absolute Other, transcendent Creator, and an intensely personal deity. Perhaps the best example of this dual attitude toward God can be found in the first two chapters of Genesis. Ibn Gabirol would have viewed these chapters, presenting two apparently opposite views of God, the transcendent in chapter one and the immanent in chapter two, as complementary. In the second section of *Keter Malchut*, Ibn Gabirol describes the created universe more objectively. It is there, created by God, reflecting the glory of God, and operating according to certain eternal laws. But in the third part he deals with God as a personal deity. After describing the sublimity of the created universe, he begins the thirty-third stanza, "O God, I am ashamed and confounded to stand before You." What follows is an extended confession and self-condemnation, a plea for divine aid, and a request for more time to prepare himself for death, to repent.

In the course of the third section, Ibn Gabirol contrasts the transcendent and immanent aspects of God. He says that "Man is born and doesn't know why, rejoices and doesn't know how, lives and doesn't know for how long," an expression of human ignorance in the face of divine knowledge and power; but in the next stanza he says, "If You inquire into my sin, I will flee from You to You, and I will take cover from Your anger in Your shadow." He will take refuge from the stern justice of the transcendent God of creation in the mercy of the personal Deity. Thus his reference to the rebuilt Temple in stanza thirty-nine is a reference to the restoration of Israel from exile, to a time when Israel's suffering will come to an end and the questions about divine justice will be answered.

The poem's last section represents a traditional Jewish view of the immediacy of a personal relationship between God and man. After all of his sophisticated philosophy about the Divine Will in the earlier sections, Ibn Gabirol shows no hesitation in appealing directly to God just as his ancestors did; and as we read *Keter Malchut*, or as we read all of Ibn Gabirol's poetry, we feel that we are in the presence of a deep and very personal piety.

As we study the European Middle Ages, it is important to remember that although the period was dominated by Christianity, it was not exclusively Christian. The Jews of the Middle Ages led an often tormented but vibrant existence. Despite incessant persecution, they survived. They made major contributions to the intellectual life of the Middle Ages by helping to convey the works of Aristotle from Arabic to Latin countries, they helped to focus attention on the literal meaning of the Bible, and they wrote poetry of great power and scope. Unfortunately that poetry can often be difficult to find, especially in readable translations, an indication of how that culture has been neglected in medieval studies; but if we ignore the Jewish culture of the Middle Ages, we ignore an important aspect of the era.

VII. Sagas

ICELAND AND THE SAGAS

Now the scene changes, moves north to Iceland.

At least that is the kind of transition that we often find in the Icelandic sagas, works that add to the variety and wonder of medieval literature. The Icelandic sagas have a great deal in common with other medieval literature, but they also show distinct differences. Most obviously, these sagas are written in prose. In fact, though they contain many poetic passages, they are the first prose works that we have encountered in Europe (aside, of course, from such theological or philosophical works as those by St. Augustine or Boethius). Another, less obvious distinction is that they represent a different kind of society than we have been observing, on at least two levels: that of the nation and that of class.

The works we have examined so far have all come from nations that saw themselves, whether accurately or not, as having long histories. Iceland did not, though again we have to be cautious about the tricks that history plays with our perceptions of time. Iceland began to be settled in the late ninth century and was converted to Christianity in the year 1000, while the greatest of the sagas were written in the thirteenth century. Thus, the sagas tend to focus on events that occurred at least two centuries before their composition. Nonetheless, the sagas have a way of making this history seem very current. Perhaps they do so because while the sagas are set in the past and tell the stories of earlier people, they actually reflect the chaotic situation of thirteenth-century Iceland, a situation that became so unmanageable that Iceland allowed the king of Norway to regain control over the country — an ironic turn of events, since Iceland had first been settled by refugees from Norway who sought to escape from the king of their time. The sagas, taken as a whole, seem to recount most of the early history of Iceland.

That idea of taking the sagas as a whole needs explanation. The sagas are indeed based on the history of Iceland (and Norway, Denmark, England, and other countries as well) in the sense in which history was treated in the Middle Ages. That is, much of it is legendary, not what we would consider history. Nevertheless, in the whole body of sagas, we find that particular characters recur from work to work and maintain consistent characteristics. Egil Skallagrimsson, for example, is the hero of *Egil's Saga*, but he also appears in many other sagas. Undoubtedly the original audiences for the sagas knew these characters — knew who they were, what they were like, who their families and friends were — but for us they can be a bit confusing. Until we get used to who they are, they can seem strange indeed, for a couple of reasons. One reason is that some of them have the same names. In the Penguin edition *The Sagas of the Icelanders*, there are fifteen different characters named Olaf. Not all of these appear in all of the sagas, but sagas do have multiple characters with the same names. In *Njal's Saga*, there are three Hoskulds, three Mords, and three Thorkels. Many of these characters have sobriquets, such as Hoskuld Hvitaness-Priest, and all of the characters have last names; but those last names can also be confusing. According to Icelandic tradition, a man's name consists of his own first name and his father's name, followed by "son" — Hoskuld Njalsson — while a woman's name consists of her first name and her father's name, followed by "dottir" (daughter) — Gudrid Thorsteinsdottir. Thus, in a family of three, mother, father, and child, all three will have different last names. The system takes some getting used to. (Imagine how difficult it would be to use a telephone book.) On the other hand, those last names do gradually help the reader keep the characters straight, and it is always interesting to be reading a saga and to come across a character whom one already knows from another saga. (One finds the same reaction in reading the novels of William Faulkner, in which characters reappear from novel to novel.) The Icelanders considered family relationships to be extremely important, and the pages of the sagas are filled with genealogies and explanations of who married whom and why. We find the same interest in other heroic works, like *The Iliad*, but the sagas take that interest much further, possibly in part due to Iceland's relatively brief history.

That brief history means that even though many of the characters originate in Norway, we can watch Iceland go through the early stages of civilization, much as astronomers can look at distant galaxies and see the early history of the universe. This picture of a developing society, of a nation trying, often unsuccessfully, to become civilized, is unique in the Middle Ages and offers one of the sagas' great distinctions. Even if the sagas are not historically accurate, they provide a picture of how thirteenth-century Icelanders regarded their history.

The second distinctive aspect of these narratives concerns the class to which the characters belong. In the works we have examined so far, the leading characters have all been from the highest classes — Beowulf, King Arthur and his knights, Genji, even the Dreamer from *The Romance of the Rose*. In the sagas we do see kings and queens, but they are neither Icelandic nor the central characters. They are rulers in Norway or England or elsewhere, but there was no king of Iceland. Remarkably, Iceland, early in its history, in 930, developed the Althing, a legislative assembly that met annually to discuss and make laws. (The Althing, incidentally, is the oldest legislative body in the world.) Consequently, while there were legislative leaders and local officials in Iceland, there was no single ruler. Characters frequently travel from Iceland to Norway or to other countries and meet with royalty, but the Icelandic characters, even the greatest heroes of the sagas, are primarily farmers. They will often go on Viking raids, both because they need money and for the sheer adventure, but they usually return to their farms. And some of the biggest quarrels in the sagas — and the sagas are full of quarrels — originate over questions of who owns land or whose cattle graze in a particular spot. Thus, even though we may have reservations about treating the sagas as fully historical works, they probably give us a better idea of how people actually lived than most other medieval works. What we see in the sagas reinforces our suppositions that life in medieval Iceland was quite difficult, that it took not only resourcefulness but also a certain brashness or a supreme self-confidence even to survive. As we read the sagas, it behooves us to keep in mind both the physical and political conditions under which the people lived. The sagas describe the painfully slow process by which they tried to establish order and a rule of law. Given our own often sorry record in this area, we ought to show some understanding of their failings, which, to be fair, they themselves often recognized as failings.

One of the surprising things about the sagas is their tone, which remains dispassionate no matter what is being told. Chrétien's narrator often shows excitement and even comments on the action, but the narrators in the sagas never overtly show excitement or disapproval. They simply tell the story, and the audience must make up its own mind about the content. When Egil cuts off an enemy's head and then gouges out his eye, the narrator recounts the action in the same tone that he uses everywhere else. What happened is what happened. Nor does the narrator probe the characters' inner lives. Chrétien shows us the characters wrestling with themselves. The saga narrators show us the characters wrestling with each other, both physically and verbally. Like many of Chrétien's characters, the Icelanders are trying to understand the difficult world that they inhabit and to decide on the proper course of action, but they reveal their thoughts by talking to each other. They are also quick to take offense, have violent tempers, and have little hesitation about translating their anger into physical action. Often they know that their actions will have serious, perhaps fatal consequences, even for themselves. Nevertheless, that knowledge seldom stops them. They may try to be more careful about what they do, but they do it regardless of the consequences. They seem resigned to a fatalistic view: Whatever happens is what must happen. In this sense, their attitudes mirror the narrators' attitudes. As we will see, this mirroring is not exact, but it does perform an important function in the sagas.

A good example of this attitude in the characters can be found in the *The Saga of the People of Laxardal* (also known as *The Laxdoela Saga*). As part of a chain of vengeance, the time comes for one of the main characters, Bolli, to be killed. When a group of his enemies arrives, everyone knows what is about to happen, and he tells his wife Gudrun to go outside. She does not want to go, but he insists, so she goes out to the nearby stream, knowing that her husband is about to be attacked, and washes some clothes. We then watch a brutal battle scene, all related with narratorial equanimity, in which one character is split in half from his head to his shoulders, another is wounded in the side, and Bolli has to hold a hand over his stomach while he fights to prevent his intestines from spilling out, until he is beheaded. As the killers leave the site of the battle, Gudrun leaves her washing and approaches them; and one of the killers, in a gratuitous insult, wipes his weapon on her shawl, for which one of the other killers reproves him. Gudrun engages them in conversation until they ride off on their horses.

The strangeness of this episode is striking. None of the characters raise their voices or seem surprised at anything that happens. Bolli fights valiantly against his attackers, but everyone knows that even though they take casualties, they will triumph and Bolli will die. No one begs for mercy and Gudrun does not plead for her husband's life, though she really loves him. The tone of this scene is no more agitated than if they were trading horses or negotiating a real estate transaction. Even when one of the killers expresses surprise at Gudrun's calmness and is told that she was just making sure that she knew who the killers were so she could plan her vengeance, the tone retains the same flatness. That tone accomplishes several things: It makes us feel that we are hearing an objective account of events, it makes the narrative sound more historical, and its very strangeness makes us focus our attention on what has taken place, which plays a central role in defining the themes of a number of these sagas. We will approach these themes through a roundabout discussion.

As we have seen, a major focus of the sagas involves the gradual movement toward legal control of social transgression in Iceland, a process that never reaches completion in the sagas. Early Iceland is treated almost like a microcosm, a small world that reflects the nature, history, and concerns of the larger world. Norway was in something of a mess, which led to the settlement of Iceland. The early settlers were not convicts, as the early settlers of Australia were. They were often people who were fed up with conditions in Norway and settled this new land to escape from those conditions. But if they were not convicts, neither were they paragons of virtue. We know from other texts, like *The Anglo-Saxon Chronicle*, how fierce the Norsemen could be as they terrorized the countries of Europe for several centuries. These were not peace-loving, gentle people, and they were no less fierce with each other. Their society, despite the existence of the Althing and of a system of law courts, operated very much on the basis of the *lex talionis*, the law of retribution. These two systems, of course, are incompatible. A legal system cannot work if people constantly take the law into their own hands.

The *lex talionis*, that rule that so often depends on vengeance, contributes to the sense of fatalism that runs through the sagas. If a person is killed, wounded, or even just insulted — no matter whether the offense is intentional or not — that offense sets in motion a predictable chain of events, an escalating series of retaliations on both sides, ending only when one side is either defeated or their strength is depleted. Unless. Unless someone on one of the sides shows the courage and the intelligence to break the chain. Someone has to be willing to forgive the offense — ideally — or even to accept some kind of legal settlement, which might involve financial compensation or condemnation of the opposing side. Those alternatives are always available but seldom used. Or, as in *Njal's Saga*, they are used up to a point, but they prove inadequate. The urge for vengeance, for blood, is generally too strong.

But there is another factor that enters into a number of the sagas. When Iceland was founded, it was a pagan country. Though we see little religious activity in the stories of early Iceland, there are references to pagan customs and we know that the early settlers believed in the Scandinavian gods. But in the year 1000, Iceland, under pressure from the Norwegian king Olaf Tryggvason, adopted Christianity. This conversion is described in detail in two of the sagas that we will be focusing on in this chapter, *The Saga of the People of Laxardal* and *Njal's Saga*. When we talk about such a conversion, it may seem that we are discussing something that happened quickly and completely; but as we know from other examples, national conversions work somewhat differently. When Constantine adopted Christianity as the state religion of Rome in the fourth century, Constantine himself probably understood relatively little about Christianity. He continued to mint coins that depicted pagan deities, and it was not until long after his death that the empire actually became Christian (to the extent that we can say it ever truly did). But in the life of nations, religion plays not only a spiritual but also a political role. Hence we have the simultaneously horrifying and absurd spectacle of people being forcibly and violently converted to Christianity. Such converts are hardly likely to take to heart the teachings of Jesus.

So it was in the conversion of Iceland. In the Laxardal saga, we are told that Olaf Tryggvason has finally reunited Norway and decreed that everyone should become Christian, though many of the people oppose him on this point. Some visiting Icelanders, led by Kjartan, are offered the opportunity to become Christians, and though they refuse at first, Kjartan acknowledges that the king's fair treatment of them has made them view the new faith favorably. This point, of course, is important. King Olaf, by practicing the finer qualities of his faith, sways the pagans, who eventually do become Christians. But then when the Icelanders are ready to return to Iceland, King Olaf instructs Kjartan to convert other Icelanders, even if he has to use force to do so. And when Olaf sends a priest, Thangbrand, to further the conversion, Thangbrand kills some of those who oppose him. The king is infuriated when Thangbrand tells him of his difficulties and he threatens to punish the people of Iceland. Finally, after discussions at the Althing, the entire nation converts, but one wonders how meaningful such a conversion could be. It seems to have little effect on the cycle of violence. Later on, for instance, when Thorsten wants to take vengeance on Halldor, Thorkel says he should not do so at present, but after Lent he can go ahead, and Halldor agrees. We would be justified if we saw in this conversation a misunderstanding of the essence of Christianity, as we would also if we looked askance at violent forced conversions.

Nevertheless, despite these problems, the coming of Christianity to Iceland was important both historically and, for the sagas, thematically.

If Iceland has been operating according to the *lex talionis*, an eye for an eye, the advent of Christianity should teach the people to turn the other cheek, to become less bloodthirsty and more civilized. We might be surprised to find that in a few cases, it actually does have that effect, that at least a few characters, like Njal, forgo bloody vengeance. Of course, even before the conversion, Njal tried to settle feuds peacefully, so the advantages of Christianity are not totally obvious.

Once again, though, we must remember that if these sagas relate legends about the early years of Icelandic society, they were being told and written down at least two centuries later. The year 1000 was an important year in Christian Europe, though scholars are divided over just how important it was. Many of us undoubtedly recall the apocalyptic concerns that some people had when 1999 became 2000. We can only imagine how much stronger such apocalyptic concerns might have been when 999 become 1000. People expected the parousia (the Second Coming of Jesus) or the end of the world. When neither materialized, societies began to reorganize themselves, whether consciously or unconsciously, for the long haul. In the chaos of thirteenth-century Iceland, the authors of the sagas look back to the chaos of the earlier centuries and the conversion of Iceland as though to say that current problems have a solution in the teachings of Christianity, if only people would pay attention to them and take them seriously.

Herein lies another difference between these sagas and works like Chrétien's romances. In those romances, the good guys — Erec or Yvain — always triumph over their enemies, who are invariably clearly evil. They might be giants or dragons or just knights gone wrong, but there is seldom any ambiguity about what their fate should be. Occasionally, as at the beginning of *Erec and Enide*, an evil character will be reformed, but usually they are dispatched with some efficiency. Occasionally two good knights will fight against each other, as Gawain and Yvain do in *Yvain* when they are both disguised; but in such cases, neither is killed. In the sagas, however, while there are characters who are better or worse than others, almost no one is either impeccably good or irredeemably evil, even if they often do things that are evil. In short, they are more like ordinary people caught up in the ambiguities of the world, as we see throughout the sagas.

EGIL AND LAXDOELA

Let us consider, for example, *Egil's Saga*. The saga begins, as so many of the sagas do, by situating us historically. We learn a great deal about

Egil's ancestors, and Egil himself does not enter the narrative for many pages, so that new readers might well begin to wonder why the saga is named after him. When he finally does enter the saga, we watch his development and discover that he is a poet; but if we think of him in any kind of aesthetic sense, we are quite mistaken. Egil is no Oscar Wilde, nor even a Dylan Thomas. He is a warrior and a farmer who happens to be skilled with words. In the last two centuries or so, it has become common for poets (or writers in general) to function as literary heroes. They are often sensitive souls who flout convention and are misunderstood by their contemporaries. In medieval literature, however, we seldom see poets as characters, certainly not as major characters; and when we do see them, they do not resemble our conceptions of what a poet should be. Poets, as we said earlier, were craftsmen. One of the most extensive portraits we have of a medieval poet is Chaucer's frequent depiction of himself as a character, but those self-depictions appear to have little in common with the actual poet named Geoffrey Chaucer.

So Egil is a poet, and *Egil's Saga* is filled with examples of his poetry, which he generally composes in response to a specific action, such as a challenge or a battle. The poems take as their subjects drinking, fighting, and insulting or praising other people. They are not poems that come from Egil's deepest feelings, the "spontaneous overflow of powerful emotion" (as that phrase is generally misunderstood). They are, rather, highly calculated. At one point, when King Eirik is angry at Egil, as he usually is, Egil's life is in jeopardy, and he follows his companion's advice to compose a twenty-stanza poem in praise of the king. With some difficulty he does so, memorizes it, then recites it to the king, whose anger is thereby mollified. The poem is indeed a fine example of the kind of heroic poetry that people enjoyed, but given Egil's true feelings about the king and the danger he faces, we know that he has simply written a suitably heroic poem and applied it to the king. It has nothing to do with his real feelings or his attempt to understand their relationship or any other subject that we might expect from a modern poet.

On the other hand, his poem honoring his friend Arinbjorn shows much more personal feeling. Most touching of all, however, is the poem he writes after the deaths of his sons. Egil mourns their deaths so deeply that first he tries to starve himself to death, until he is tricked into eating by his daughter Thorgerd, who says that she wants him to live long enough to write a poem about her brothers. The long and touching poem with which he fulfills her request actually helps him to recover. In this case, then, we do see a conception of poetry that more nearly coincides with modern ideas.

Still, sensitive poet though he may be, Egil is also a fierce and brutal warrior. Even as a child he exhibits these qualities. After being bested by another boy in a game, Egil splits the victor's head with an axe. We would probably regard such behavior as anti-social, but not the Icelanders. Of course a feud develops and seven men die, but the only overt comment on the affair is that Egil will be a great Viking when he grows up. Still, Egil comes by his temperament honestly. During another game, Egil's father Skallagrim gets so carried away that he kills one of his opponents and nearly kills Egil, killing instead his nurse. Later that day, Egil cold-bloodedly kills one of Skallagrim's favorite warriors, thus evening out the killing of favorites. As a result, Egil and Skallagrim stop talking to each other for a time.

It may seem that we are treating terrible brutality a bit too lightly. In fact the sagas are filled with battles, murders, and general mayhem that is reported in a matter-of-fact tone. On the one hand, as we have said, the authors are reflecting the mayhem of their own time. On the other hand, we can only imagine how tough and even brutal a person had to be to survive in such a society and in such a climate. As *Egil's Saga* illustrates, the people did indeed require taming. Significantly, Egil does not die in an outburst of Viking glory. Instead, he becomes old and decrepit, weak and blind, bossed around even by the cook. Before he dies, he hides a quantity of silver that he had received from the English king before it can become the subject of dispute among his heirs. Interestingly, after his death, his bones are buried in a church, with the implication that Egil displayed Christian virtues. This implication might sound more reasonable if some scholars are correct in assuming that *Egil's Saga* was written by one of Egil's descendants, Snorri Sturluson, the author of *Heimskringla*, the history of medieval Iceland.

Another of the great sagas is *The Saga of the People of Laxardal.* As the title indicates, this saga deals not with one individual hero like Egil but with the events in a whole area in the northwest of Iceland. As we have already mentioned, the conversion of Iceland to Christianity is central to this saga. As usual, the saga contains many scenes of brutality, both before and after the conversion, though the saga implies that after the conversion the people should know better. Some characters do. When the conspirators ask Thorstein to join them in killing Bolli, he refuses and expresses the hope that members of the family will stop killing each other: No one benefits from such a system and everyone suffers. His words seem obvious to us, but if we consider for a moment, we will see that Thorstein's point has still not had an effect on many people.

The Laxdoela saga also illustrates another important aspect of the sagas, the vital role played by women. In Chrétien we encounter many women who are troublemakers, like Guinevere and the maiden who initiates the Joy of the Court. We also find many women who are dependent on men. The women in the sagas are far different. They are, for one thing, not delicate creatures who expect to be waited on, first because they are not members of the aristocracy (which of course did not exist in Iceland as it did in France) but also because Icelandic society was structured differently. France (as Shakespeare reminds us at the beginning of *Henry V*) had the Salic Law, which meant that a woman could never serve as the reigning monarch. In Iceland, by way of contrast, we even find men who take as their second name their mother's name. Thord, for example, is the son of Slum and Ingunn and is known as Thord Ingunnarson. The women also tend to be fairly powerful, especially Unn and Gudrun. Certainly we see powerful women in Chrétien as well, like Laudine, who is a powerful queen, though she clearly requires the aid of a man and therefore marries Yvain in some haste. The women of the sagas seem much more independent. They may require men for deeds that demand physical strength, but they are no gentler than their male counterparts. Thorgerd, who happens to be Egil's daughter, has no hesitation about urging her sons to avenge the death of Kjarstan. Those sons seem willing to try to live in peace, but Thorgerd will not allow them to. In Chrétien, troublesome women seem troublesome, at least in part, just because they are women. The case is different in the sagas. The women behave very much as the men do. We tend to see more of the men, since they do the fighting and the legislating; but the men frequently consult their wives. Surprisingly, perhaps, we see little of the women in regard to the conversion. At the end of the Laxardal saga, Gudrun turns to religion, and eventually becomes a nun, but her case is unusual.

Like the other sagas, the Laxdoela saga also has its share of prophetic dreams and ominous predictions that come true. When a character in a saga predicts that something will happen, the reader knows that it will happen; and when someone interprets a dream, or, as in the Laxdoela saga, a series of dreams, the reader knows that those interpretations are correct. These predictions certainly lessen the suspense of the narrative, but of course suspense is not their point. As is so often the case in works like the sagas, the audience knew the story anyhow. The focus lies on how the story is told. All of those dreams, omens, and predictions add to the sense that there is a fate operating in human affairs and that somehow things work out as they were intended to work out. We can see this sense in the chain of vengeance: If A kills B, then C must kill A and D must kill C, until either the alphabet runs out or someone breaks the chain. The Laxdoela saga, by giving us an overview of a whole district around the time of the conversion, encapsulates many of the themes of the sagas. The greatest of all the sagas, *Njal's Saga*, presents even more of Iceland as its setting, but, like *Egil's Saga*, it also has a narrower focus. *Njal's Saga* is probably the most carefully organized and the most artistically constructed of the sagas, It is indeed a powerful and moving work.

NJAL'S SAGA

What does "artistically constructed" mean? It means that every part of the work helps to elucidate the work's central concerns. In many of the other sagas, we get the feeling that each one is part of a continuum of sagas. *Njal's Saga*, while it mentions characters who appear elsewhere, seems to be a more self-contained whole. A major theme of the saga appears at the very beginning and serves as a focus throughout. The saga begins, as sagas and novels almost have to do, by introducing some main characters. The sagas often accomplish this task by providing genealogies of the main characters. *Njal's Saga* introduces us immediately to Mord Fiddle, but offers no genealogy. Mord Fiddle's reputation rests not on his pedigree but on his skill with the law. After the brief introduction of Mord, however, the saga does something rather strange. Readers of sagas quickly become accustomed to the often rudimentary narrative techniques these works employ. For example, if a character performs a role in a saga and then goes to Norway, the narrator might tell us that that character is now out of the saga. Also, there are few sophisticated transitions between scenes. Scenes tend to be juxtaposed rather than to lead into each other. Thus, Mord is introduced as a fine lawyer, and almost immediately the narrator tells us that the scene is changing to another part of Iceland. We might initially be a bit surprised, because we have not really had a scene so far. Nevertheless, the juxtaposition of these two "scenes" is important, because we are now introduced to two half-brothers, Hrut and Hoskuld. In their case, we do get a full genealogy, going back to Ketil Flat-Nose, whose own family is described at the beginning of *The Saga of the People of Laxardal.* Not only do we get this genealogy, but we learn that Hrut and Hoskuld are great warriors.

At first we might think that the introductions of Mord, Hrut, and

Hoskuld simply allow us to become familiar with the characters, but the abrupt juxtaposition that we have seen signifies more than we realize until we get further into the work. That juxtaposition of introductions calls our attention to the differences between the characters, between the lawyer Mord with his skimpy genealogy and the warriors Hrut and Hoskuld with their more developed genealogy, for much of the saga will focus on those differences: on the need for law and control in the spread of civilization and on the too easy triumph of force, which works against law and contributes to the breakdown of civilization.

Some readers may think that this interpretation of a medieval Scandinavian saga is too modern and too liberal to reflect the thought of the saga's author. In fact, we can trace such thought much further back in history. In Homer's *Iliad*, for instance (which, of course, the saga writer could not have known), the failure of the Greeks and the Trojans to settle their dispute through arbitration or legal means results in calamity for both sides. There is nothing distinctively modern about recognizing that peace is better than war, that wars seldom settle anything, that (as Tolstoy shows us in *War and Peace*) wars seldom proceed according to plan, and that our well-being depends on our ability to settle disputes without recourse to fighting. Nor have we, in the twentieth and twenty-first centuries, been notably better at avoiding wars than were our ancestors in centuries past. Clearly the author of *Njal's Saga* makes these points throughout the saga, starting at the very beginning; and by using so much of Iceland as his setting, he makes clear how widespread the problem is. It affects not only a single family or even a single district but the whole of the country, which, we probably do not need to be reminded, was in a state of chaos at the time the saga was composed. We must not think, however, that the author treats this theme simplistically: War is bad, peace is good. Rather, he explores that theme, he considers complicating factors, and he demonstrates the difficulties that accompany it. But there can be no denying that with all the scenes at the Althing and all the quarrelling and battling, this theme is central to the saga.

Another of the saga's themes also appears at the beginning. Hoskuld has a daughter, Hallgerd, who has beautiful hair. Hrut, her uncle, admires her when she is young, but he comments that she has the eyes of a thief. What such a statement might mean in everyday life is hard to say, but Hrut proves to be prescient, for later on Hallgerd does steal. As a result, her husband Gunnar slaps her. Even later, when Gunnar is under siege, his bowstring snaps and he asks Hallgerd for some locks of hair to be made into a new bowstring. Hallgerd, remembering the slap, refuses him and he dies shortly thereafter. This episode, foreshadowed in the saga's opening, fits into the fate motif that we discussed earlier. Virtually every action and every word has consequences that cannot be foreseen but that are inexorable. One thing leads to another, so that eventually the characters lose control over the actions and things just have to play themselves out, usually tragically. As we continue to read *Njal's Saga*, we may become as prescient as the characters, as we come to recognize the way things work in the world of the saga.

As is the case in the other sagas, *Njal's Saga* contains little in the way of psychological probing. When Hrut returns from a trip to Norway to find that his wife has left him (actually because of sexual difficulties), we learn only that he is surprised. We are not treated to his thoughts, and we are not even allowed to overhear what, if anything, he says to anyone else about his marriage. We do, however, see his actions as he refuses to return his wife's dowry. We can see that Hrut is more hurt than angry and that he seeks not vengeance but the preservation of his self-esteem. We know that Hrut is a kindly character, though he is also a good warrior (because of a scene in which Hoskuld beat a boy who made fun of Hrut, whereas Hrut taught the boy a lesson about kindness). Because of Hrut's character, there is no fighting over the dowry. Gunnar, who manages the affair for the ex-wife, uses legal manipulations at the Althing to force Hrut to repay the dowry, which he does without rancor and without violence. In this important episode, we see how the law can work, if people allow it to, even when a clever lawyer is allowed to play legal tricks.

Gunnar, however, is not himself the clever lawyer. He learns his tricks from Njal, who is one of the cleverest. Njal, as we might expect, is the saga's central character, a relatively gentle man who believes deeply in the rule of law. Njal has one great peculiarity: He cannot grow a beard, a fact to which many of the characters allude, often in a mocking way. Whether such a person as Njal ever really existed and whether, if he did, he was beardless are irrelevant considerations. Characters view his lack of a beard as a sign of effeminacy and therefore of weakness, incorrectly equating the presence of a beard with virility. Nor do Njal's knowledge of and devotion to the law represent weakness; they represent a different, healthier, form of strength. Thus, when Njal's wife and Gunnar's wife begin a quarrel that results in a number of deaths, Njal and Gunnar disapprove and settle the problems caused by each death legally. Naturally, Njal is not naïve. He knows the kind of society in which he lives and has no hesitation about telling Gunnar that if he must fight, he will be safe if he kills no more than one person from the same family. Still, Njal knows that the law must be the foundation of society.

At the same time, the law has its own weaknesses. Njal knows the laws so well that he can manipulate them. As we saw, he did so for Gunnar; but later, when he manipulates the law for the advantage of his own family, his actions lead to difficulties that culminate in his death. It should be stressed that Njal's manipulations are not illegal or even particularly venal, but they do present a challenge to the notion of the rule of law. In this connection we come once again to the introduction of Christianity to Iceland. The new religion, which becomes the national faith, should theoretically bring a lessening of violence, but it does not. Scholars agree that the chapters in *Njal's Saga* on the conversion actually originated in another work, but those chapters are included in *Njal's Saga* for a reason. As in the Laxdoela saga, Thangbrand is described as killing some of his opponents, which is not a promising start. Like the rule of law, Christianity offers an opportunity to end the cycle of violence, but both of these systems, which could work together to bring peace, must be used in the right spirit, which is what the author tries to convey to his thirteenth-century contemporaries.

Njal and his whole family, after a chain of events that follow his manipulation of the law, are killed in a particularly gruesome fashion: Their house is burned down while they are inside it. Even some of the burners have reservations about this action, though they do it anyhow, thereby raising other moral issues; but after the burning, when they go through the ashes, they find that not only have Njal's and his wife's bodies been preserved from the flames, but Njal's in particular seems more radiant than it did in life. At this point, the author has incorporated the kind of element we would find in a saint's life, a popular medieval genre. In these works, righteous people are regularly subjected to horrible physical treatment, which they always manage to transcend, even if they die in the process. The state of Njal's body equates him with such saints. His way of combining reverence for the law and Christianity, even though he may have failings, is thereby shown to be superior to the rule of force.

Significantly, *Njal's Saga* ends on a note of reconciliation. One of the burners, Flosi, even gains the forgiveness of the Pope and is then reconciled with Kari, who has sought vengeance for Njal. The last lines of the saga describe Kari's offspring. The implication perhaps, only hinted at but still there, is that hope remains a possibility, that the values of life rather than those of death might triumph. Many fine characters perish in the course of *Njal's Saga*, and many others suffer because the primitive instinct for vengeance overcomes the civilized use of reason and law. But, the saga says, perhaps people can learn that what is best for the society is also best for them individually. *Njal's Saga* is a brilliant telling of a story that uses all the elements of the Icelandic saga to make a point that remains valid. Like all of the sagas, it presents memorable characters and scenes in ways that make them come alive.

VIII. Dante

Abandon hope, all who enter here.

According to Dante Alighieri, those words are posted over the entrance to Hell. They might also, though in a very different way, apply to anyone who dares try to write about *The Divine Comedy*, which is one of the monumental works of world literature, so monumental that it defies attempts to describe it. One must approach the *Comedy* with a mixture of awe and excitement because of its overwhelming nature. Even its first readers were taken aback: Dante had called his work only *The Comedy*. His fourteenth-century contemporaries called it *Divine*; even today, when students read it, they often find themselves moved, frightened, and resuming, at least temporarily, their church attendance. The *Comedy* is also a work of supreme egotism, of— though Dante would not have known the term —chutzpah. It includes the whole universe, both spatially and temporally, and it makes staggering judgments about people who were Dante's contemporaries. Although the *Comedy* has had tremendous influence on subsequent literature, no other work has been able to approach its grandeur. Whether or not we accept its theology, we must recognize it as one of the wonders of the world.

The Divine Comedy marks simultaneously the culmination and conclusion of the medieval world. That statement may seem strange. How can the *Comedy* mark the conclusion of the Middle Ages if we still have two chapters beyond this one? The answer takes us back to the discussion of boundaries in the introductory chapter. Historical periods do not begin or end on a single day. They are, rather, part of a continuum. Thus we cannot say that the Middle Ages ended and the Renaissance began on a particular day. The Middle Ages shaded into the Renaissance, and that process took place at different speeds in different places. It happened first

126

in Italy, where the successors of Dante, writers like Petrarch and Boccaccio, herald the Renaissance while maintaining medieval characteristics. The process happened later in England, where we generally view the Renaissance as beginning in the very late fifteenth and early sixteenth centuries, after the Wars of the Roses. Chaucer is considered a medieval author; but Chaucer, unlike most medieval people, was well-traveled, having been to France and Italy, where he came in contact with literary works (and often their authors) that reflected the new spirit. Chaucer's works, therefore, are primarily medieval in spirit but show a familiarity with the new movement. Dante's masterpiece, on the other hand, has a strictly medieval orientation.

The *Comedy* is difficult to read for several reasons. Dante was not only a great poet, but he was also a highly political person, who was quite involved in the political struggles of his day. And in his native Florence, politics appears to have been something of an obsession. Florence, in both the Middle Ages and the Renaissance, must have been a remarkable place. It was, in modern terms, fairly small, but it produced an extraordinary number of outstanding writers, philosophers, and artists despite its tumultuous history. Dante himself was on the losing side of a major political clash and found himself exiled from his beloved city. Not only was the *Comedy* written during this exile, but Dante used his poem to comment extensively on Florentine and Italian politics (though we must remember that Italy was not a unified country — it would not achieve that status until the nineteenth century). Dante's multiple references to contemporary events and people require that modern students of the poem read an edition that provides detailed notes. The reader does not have to become intimately familiar with all of those contemporary references, but it is important to gain a general sense of what Dante is talking about. Otherwise the poem begins to seem so far removed from us that it loses its appeal.

Furthermore, Dante, like many other medieval writers, was quite learned. Consequently, the poem is filled with all manner of classical and biblical references. Many of Dante's classical allusions would have been well known to medieval readers, but even they might have been stumped on occasion. Again, an annotated translation is essential.

The best way to read Dante's poem might be to read the summary of each canto, then read quickly through the notes at the end of the canto (regardless of the edition being used), and then finally read the canto. And, as is always the case in reading a new work, the reader should not worry about understanding everything the first time through. No one ever has. In fact, no one has ever understood everything about the poem, which is part of what makes the study of literature so much fun.

Dante, we know, was born in 1265, because he tells us so at the beginning of the *Comedy*, where he says that at the time of the action he was halfway through the journey of his life. Since the poem takes place in 1300 and the accepted biblical standard for a life span was seventy, he must have been thirty-five. We know, too, that he died in 1321. Even knowing those dates means that we know more about Dante than we do about any of the writers we studied earlier; and in fact, we know much more about Dante. In this chapter, however, we will only consider things that Dante himself tells us in his poetry, which appears to be, and has always been accepted as, autobiographical. Dante wrote a number of works in both Italian and Latin, but we will focus only on the *Vita Nuova* (*The New Life*) and the *Comedy*. These works were so important to the history of Italian literature and to Italy as a whole that the dialect in which they were written, Tuscan, went on to become the basis for modern Italian.

The *Vita Nuova* is a short, fascinating work that serves as an introduction to the *Comedy*. In it, Dante describes the beginning of one of the world's great love stories, his love for a young woman named Beatrice. (Authorial intrusion: Both the *Vita Nuova* and the *Comedy* have at their centers Dante's love for Beatrice, but, as we will see, Dante had very little actual contact with Beatrice, who died young. We do know, however, that Dante was married, and I have often wondered what Mrs. Alighieri thought about all this Beatrice-inspired poetry.) As we will see, the *Comedy* makes extensive use of number symbolism, which was part of the medieval view that the whole world had allegorical significances. In fact, the whole of the *Vita Nuova* might be described as Dante's attempt, looking back over his life so far, to discover the significance of things that have happened. The work, like Boethius' *Consolation of Philosophy*, consists of a mixture of prose and verse; in Dante's case, most of the poems appear to have been written earlier and the prose passages added later. Now, with the advantage of hindsight, he has put them together, and he uses the prose passages to explain why the poems were written, how they fit together, and how we ought to read them. Part of that act of reading, of course, involves the use of allegory.

The numbers that figure most prominently in Dante's work are nine and three. He first sees Beatrice when she is at the beginning of her ninth year and he is at the end of his ninth year. Nine years later, at the ninth hour of the day, she greets him, and that night he has a dream that begins nine hours before dawn. So why nine? As he explains later, nine is the Trinity times itself. Given the central role that Catholicism played in everyday life in the Middle Ages, we cannot overestimate the significance of the Trinity, which was one of the great mysteries of Christian life. Nine, as the Trinity times itself, becomes for Dante a number fraught with significance. We might say that it raises the divine to an even higher degree, though saying that makes Dante's allegory seem more mundane than it is. As is so often the case with Dante (or other great poets), we diminish what he says when we try to explain it, however necessary those explanations may be.

That nine that is so often associated with Beatrice, however, should make us aware that she is special. Of course, people always think that there is something special about those they love, and there were certainly many Italian poets, many of them friends of Dante, who wrote reams of poetry about their various beloveds. At first, because Dante did not "read" the allegory that surrounded him, he though that his love for Beatrice, whom he hardly dared to approach, was like the love shared by his poetic friends. His dream reinforces that feeling, for in it he sees a masterful figure carrying a nearly nude Beatrice. The mysterious man holds Dante's heart, then gives it to Beatrice to eat, after which they ascend to heaven. We might well be reminded here of *The Romance of the Rose,* that long dream vision in which the god of love becomes the Dreamer's master; and this impression might be reinforced by a later dream, in which Dante sees a man dressed in white, who tells him, in Latin, "I am like the center of a circle, equidistant from all points on the circumference, but you are not" (17). Again, Dante, when he has this dream, thinks that he is like any normal lover who follows the pattern that had been established for lovers by works like *The Romance of the Rose* and in the works of his friends and mentors. He has come to realize, however, that his love is nothing like those other loves. In the *Vita Nuova*, Beatrice dies, and Dante discovers that there was truly something divine about her, that his love is not a species of carnal love, no matter how refined, but that it is somehow heavenly.

If we take this knowledge back to the beginning of the book, we can see how all of those nines and those dreams, among other elements, indicated the divine nature of Beatrice, if only he — and we, as readers — had been alive to the allegory. Those dreams might recall works like *The Romance of the Rose*, but their resemblances to that poem are superficial. The dreams also recall biblical images, which we probably overlooked because we expected a work about love, specifically about worldly, fleshly

love. The Dante who has experienced this love, who has come to understand that his love, real love, is divine, is ready to begin a *vita nuova*, a
new life.

Strangely enough, then, this short work, which in the hands of Guillaume de Lorris would have seemed terribly tragic, with the death of the
beloved lady, concludes on a most positive note. Dante, the character in
his own poem, promises that he will write something worthy of his divine
Beatrice, a kind of work that has never before been written about a
beloved lady. He also expresses the hope that someday he will again see
Beatrice, which is another way of saying that he hopes he will spend eternity in Heaven, where she dwells now and forever.

But something goes wrong. Despite his knowledge of Beatrice's true
nature, despite his hope to see her in Heaven, Dante goes astray. We cannot be sure until late in the *Comedy* what mistake he made, and even
then certainty cannot be guaranteed; but we do know that he has gone
astray, jeopardizing his soul. *The Divine Comedy* tells the story of how
he is rescued and led back to the proper path. It involves a journey
through Hell, Purgatory, and Heaven, and it reveals the physical and theological structure of the universe. One might almost call it an encyclo-
pedic summary of medieval beliefs in which Dante deals with questions
of theology, physics, philosophy, biology, history, politics, and other fields.

Hell

The poem opens as Dante is lost in the woods on Good Friday, having left the road he should have taken. Since we should now be experts
in recognizing medieval allegory, we know that he means that he has lost
his way in the world, that he has left the path that would lead him to
salvation. As he tries to find his way, he is confronted by a leopard, a lion,
and a wolf. Again, we have a strong feeling that these animals are allegorical and that they represent significant obstacles. Over the centuries, commentators have explained them in a variety of ways that are worth
considering, but none of the explanations has been fully satisfactory.
Whatever they represent, Dante is in trouble, until he is rescued by a man
who identifies himself as Virgil. Dante seems relatively unsurprised, even
though Virgil has been dead for over thirteen hundred years. Instead,
Dante acknowledges his debt to the dead poet, who explains that the Virgin Mary and St. Lucia sent Beatrice to ask him to rescue Dante.

We might wonder from the outset why Beatrice did not come herself and why, of all people, Virgil was chosen. Actually Beatrice will become Dante's guide later on, toward the end of Purgatory and through Paradise, but Virgil's guidance is significant on many levels. Virgil, the Roman poet who lived from 70 to 19 B.C.E., was a key figure in medieval thought. He had written *The Aeneid*, that great epic that the Middle Ages interpreted allegorically as depicting the soul's journey from the City of Man to the City of God. This poem contained not only one of the major love stories of antiquity, the story of Dido and Aeneas in Book IV, but also the famous descent of Aeneas into the Underworld in Book VI, where he sees the punishments of the wicked and the rewards of the righteous. (Such a descent also occurs in *The Odyssey*, but the text of that poem was not available in Dante's time.) Aeneas' descent resonated in the Christian Middle Ages and is even referred to in the "Dies Irae" that forms part of the Requiem Mass, where the biblical David is mentioned along with the Sibyl, who gave Aeneas his directions.

Furthermore, Virgil also wrote a series of eclogues, one of which, the fourth, is a paean to the infant son of one of his contemporaries. To the Christian Middle Ages, that poem sounded like a prediction of the coming of Jesus. Many people in the Middle Ages believed that Virgil had been so wise that he could detect the coming revelation purely through his reason; and though he got some of the details wrong, he had at least an inkling of the Truth. (There was, though, another tradition that Virgil was nothing more than a magician.) Consequently, Virgil is the ideal figure to guide Dante through Hell and Purgatory: He knows the geography, he is wise, and he was a forerunner of Christianity. And finally, Dante truly admired *The Aeneid* and viewed himself as an epic poet in the tradition of Virgil, though his poem is a Christian epic. Thus, Virgil's concern for him, which grows throughout the poem, is the concern of a great poet for one of his disciples. We could say that in thus depicting himself, Dante again lets his ego show. On the other hand, as the poem indicates, Dante was right, so we can hardly fault him.

Because the *Comedy* is long and complex, it will not be possible to give a complete overview of it. Instead we will concentrate on some highlights of the poem and try to indicate their relationship to the whole. But, as is true of all the work we are discussing, nothing can substitute for reading the poem.

As we read the *Comedy*, we must always distinguish between two different Dantes, as Mark Musa frequently reminds us in his excellent translation. There is Dante the Pilgrim, the character we see in the poem. This Dante learns much, largely because he has so much to learn. At the

beginning of his journey, he understands relatively little, while by the end
he is worthy of seeing God. The questions he asks of his guides begin in
naiveté or even ignorance, but by the end his questions demonstrate the
sophistication of his thought. The other Dante is Dante the Poet, the
person who knew before he penned the opening words where the poem
was going.

As Dante and Virgil enter the underworld, they see huge crowds of
souls waiting to enter Hell. Dante is shocked at the number, and so
should we be, for they are all sinners and their number indicates how evil
the world has become. We are also introduced at this point to one of the
principles of Dante's world, that the punishment fits the crime. Here at
the beginning we see a group of souls who are not even allowed to enter
Hell, and we learn that these are the souls of people who refused to take
a stand, to do what was required of them. Their hesitancy to commit
themselves has resulted in the refusal of Divine Justice to commit itself
to them. Everywhere in Dante's world we will find that punishments fit
crimes (and that rewards fit virtues). Another striking example comes in
Canto 20, in which we meet the soothsayers, people who claimed they
could see the future. These souls are punished by being forced to walk
forward while their heads are twisted to face behind. In other words,
these people, who claimed to be able to see the future, cannot even see
where they are walking. As we see these punishments, we must remember that they are eternal. There is no reprieve for the souls in Hell. They
will be there, suffering their punishments forever. The only change they
can expect will be at the time of the Last Judgment (which Dante, like
most people in the Middle Ages, thought was imminent), when the bodies will be restored to the souls and the punishments will therefore become
even more intense.

We might pause briefly to wonder about such suffering in the face
of promises of Divine Love, for such love appears nowhere in Hell, which
is ruled by Divine Justice. Many aspects of Dante's Hell trouble modern
readers, who tend to profess greater levels of mercy; but to Dante's medieval Christian understanding, all of these souls had their chance to do
good or else to repent when they were alive. They have chosen their own
fates, which Divine Justice merely enforces. To our understanding, the
situation is not so clear. For instance, in Canto 4, Dante and Virgil come
to Virgil's dwelling place, the part of Hell that is called Limbo. Limbo
is a dark place — the reader should pay attention to the way Dante uses
light throughout the *Comedy*— but nothing very bad happens there. As
Virgil explains, the souls in Limbo are not there because of their sins.

They are in Limbo because they were never baptized, and they were never baptized because they lived before the Incarnation of Jesus, when baptism was unknown. In short, they are there for reasons absolutely beyond their control, a situation that strikes modern readers as unjust. If a teacher were to refuse to accept a student's paper and then failed the student for not handing in the paper, we would expect a lawsuit to follow, but here we have the same situation and Dante calls it Divine Justice. St. Augustine dealt with a similar problem: Christianity teaches that people must be baptized, but what happens to the soul of a newborn baby who dies before it can be baptized, something that probably occurred often? Augustine wrestles with the question, because he wants those innocent babies to be allowed into Heaven, but he knows that without baptism they are not truly innocent. They are stained with Original Sin, so that they cannot enter Heaven and must go to Limbo.

The punishment in Limbo does not consist of physical torture. It consists of distance from God. God dwells in the furthest reaches of Heaven, and Hell is in the Earth. The further down one goes, the further from God one goes, and since the Earth was thought to be in the center of the universe, the center of the Earth was as far from God as it was possible to go. (Incidentally, they knew the world was round.) The only punishment in Dante's Limbo, then, is that the souls cannot move closer to God. Otherwise Limbo is not so bad, and Dante sees there, along with other people, a group of famous poets, among whom he again numbers himself. He also hears about the Harrowing of Hell, the descent of Jesus after the Crucifixion so that He could take the souls of good biblical figures, like Adam, Noah, and Moses, to their permanent dwelling place in Heaven. We should note that Virgil never refers to Jesus by name. He still cannot understand the fullness of Christian teaching, and the name of Jesus cannot be mentioned in Hell.

Another important episode occurs in Canto 5, when Dante sees his first actual punishment. In the second circle of Hell (which is divided into nine circles), he sees the punishment of the lustful, who are blown through the air in a whirlwind, just as they were controlled in life by their lust. Here and through the rest of the poem, Dante will encounter one or more souls with whom he discusses their punishments (or, later, rewards) and their significance. In Canto 5 he sees many famous lustful souls, like Cleopatra, Helen, and Paris, and he feels pity for them. Then he speaks at length with Francesca da Rimini, who describes herself and her love for her brother-in-law Paolo in the language of love poetry from Dante's time. She makes herself an appealing character, unless we are smart enough to see the lust lurking behind her words. Dante — along with many other readers, including Tchaikovsky, who wrote a tone poem based on this scene — is moved by her words. In fact, Dante faints when she finishes her story.

We might applaud Dante for his sensitivity, but, as he learns, he is quite mistaken. After all, if Francesca is in Hell, she is there because God put her there. To feel pity for her is to question God's judgment. As Dante proceeds through Hell and learns more about Divine Justice, he frequently becomes upset, but less because he feels pity than because he regrets the evil that people have done. He regrets the sin, not the punishment. Thus, in Canto 8 he wishes even greater punishment on a particular sinner, and in Canto 20 Virgil tells him that it is pious to show no pity in hell. Finally, in Canto 32, where the souls are punished by being buried up to their necks in ice, Dante kicks and otherwise abuses one of them. Again, his behavior might seem gratuitously cruel, but we must remember that the soul he kicks is in one of the lowest circles of Hell, indicating the severity of his sin. Nothing that Dante does to him can be too cruel.

There are many memorable scenes in the Inferno. Among the most notable is the forest of suicides in Canto 13. When Dante and Virgil enter the forest, Virgil instructs Dante to break a branch from one tree. As the tree bleeds, it speaks to Dante, explaining that when a person commits suicide, that person's soul avoids the usual judgment process. Instead, it falls directly to the seventh circle, where it quickly grows into a tree on whose branches sit harpies, who munch the leaves. This episode illustrates another of Dante's techniques, his use of classical literature. The talking tree comes from *The Aeneid*, as do the harpies. Dante adapts these classical references to his Christian poem, thereby honoring Virgil and showing the unity of all thought in the service of Christian doctrine. Elsewhere, as in Canto 5, he uses classical figures as examples of sinful behavior; in other places he uses them as infernal parodies of Christian doctrine, as he does in Canto 6, where Cerberus, the three-headed dog, parodies the Trinity.

The whole of the Inferno is morbidly fascinating, as Dante uses his journey through Hell to criticize his Florentine enemies, the abuses of the Church, and other evils. At one point, he foreshadows the descent to Hell of Pope Boniface VIII, who was the pope in 1360. Dante really hated Boniface, both for personal and political reasons, but predicting that the Pope will suffer in Hell is pretty brazen.

The center of Hell, contrary to popular opinion, is not hot but freezing. At the center sits Satan, who has three mouths (another infernal parody of the Trinity) in each of which he chews forever on one of the archtraitors of history: Judas, Brutus, and Cassius. Judas we can easily understand, but Brutus and Cassius, the chief conspirators in the assassination of Julius Caesar, are a little less clear. Judas betrayed Jesus, and he is therefore a model for all those, like Boniface IX, who Dante thinks have betrayed the Church. But Dante also thought that the Church should stay out of political affairs, and he wanted to see a strong secular leader who could unify Italy. Several times in the *Comedy* he refers in allegorical terms to the imminent coming of such a leader. Brutus and Cassius betrayed and killed just such a leader and are therefore in Hell.

The Inferno, thanks to the normal perversity of human taste, has always been the most popular section of the *Comedy*. It tends to be the section of the poem that is most frequently taught and read. It holds all the fascination of a bad accident. Dante's depictions of the punishments for sin (not all of them original with him) offer the excitement of a terrifying roller-coaster ride. The other two sections are less popular. Purgatory describes a place that people have trouble understanding, and Paradise becomes highly abstract and philosophical. Thus, the Inferno seems to be the most interesting section, just as Satan seems to be most interesting character in *Paradise Lost*. Even so, there is much to interest us in Purgatory and Paradise, and we can never forget that Dante's early audiences took not only the poem but also these divisions of the afterlife quite seriously.

PURGATORY

So what is Purgatory? People whose sins fall into certain categories and who died unrepentant go directly to Hell. As we saw, they are plentiful. Souls that are perfect go directly to Heaven, but they are scarce. The rest, those whose sins are not so serious or who have repented, go to Purgatory, where those sins are purged through various punishments and the souls are purified, after which the souls can ascend to Heaven. Dante conceived of Hell as a deep pit divided into nine circles. That pit was created when Satan was thrown out of Heaven and fell to Earth, where the force of his landing created the wedge-shaped pit of Hell. That wedge of earth was pushed out of the other side of the planet, creating the mountain of Purgatory. (Geologists will probably all agree that this account is implausible, but there were no geologists in Dante's time.) The mountain of Purgatory has nine levels, two in Antepurgatory and the other seven corresponding to the seven deadly sins. At the top of the mountain, Dante finds Eden, the Earthly Paradise, and there, finally, he is reunited with Beatrice.

As he did in Hell and as he will do in Heaven, Dante continues to meet individuals he knows, either personally or by reputation, and his conversations with them and with Virgil clarify additional points of doctrine on topics ranging from politics to religion to how babies are conceived. When Dante begins his ascent of Purgatory proper, his forehead is engraved with seven P's, representing the seven sins, *peccata* in Latin. As he passes through each level, a P is erased and Dante is purified. He feels himself becoming lighter as these burdens are lifted from him, and he is finally able to enter Eden and then, in the next section, ascend to Heaven. Nevertheless, he knows that after he dies, he will have to return to Purgatory where he will have to be purged especially of the sin of pride, an acknowledgement that he suffers particularly from that sin (as we may already have guessed).

In Purgatory, as in Hell, the punishment fits the crime. On each level, we, and the souls who are being purged, encounter examples of the sins, again largely from biblical and classical sources, as well as examples of the sins' opposites. Thus, on the level of pride, where the once-proud souls are punished by having to walk bent over while carrying heavy weights on their backs — to atone for their haughtiness in life — they are exposed to negative examples of pride and positive examples of humility. Repeatedly in Purgatory the souls explain to Dante that their stay in this region can be made shorter by the prayers of people who are still alive. We may associate this doctrine with the abuse of indulgences that became one of the causes of the Reformation, but Dante means something much more positive. He does not intend that people should shorten the time in Purgatory of their loved ones by paying large sums to the Church. He means that they should pray, sincerely. Sincere prayer will have an effect not only on the souls of the dead but on the souls of the living. It will, at least in theory, cause them to examine their own lives, to behave better, to reform themselves and the world. It will help both the dead and the living. Consequently, soul after soul asks Dante to report back on their status and seek the prayers of their relatives.

How long does one need to stay in Purgatory? Dante never says, but at one point the mountain trembles and voices are heard praising God, the signs that a soul has been released from Purgatory. (That only one soul achieves this release during Dante's time in Purgatory is a little peculiar, perhaps, but Dante needed only one for his purposes.) When that soul encounters Dante and Virgil in Canto 21, it turns out to be the soul of Statius, who had died some twelve hundred years earlier. That sounds like a long time to stay in Purgatory, but compared to eternity it is really rather brief. And of course, while the souls would like to be released from Purgatory to Heaven, they never complain, for they know that they are fulfilling Divine Justice and that they will eventually be allowed into Heaven.

The appearance of Statius, however, reintroduces another key theme. Statius was a Roman poet, the author of another epic that was popular in the Middle Ages, *The Thebaid*. Statius died about a century after Virgil, but Dante either made up or actually believed that Statius had been a Christian, which would explain his presence in Purgatory. When Statius, this soul on his way to Heaven, learns that he is in Virgil's presence, he kneels at the elder, pagan poet's feet, a reversal of religious but not of poetic roles. In Canto 22, Statius explains that he became a Christian thanks to Virgil's fourth eclogue, so that both his poetry and his salvation were inspired by Virgil. As the two dead poets walk together, speaking of poetry, Dante trails behind them, listening. Just as he associated himself in Limbo with a cluster of famous poets, so he does here, though with more humility.

By introducing Statius at this point, Dante has introduced poetry as a major focus of the poem, which combines with another focus, love. As we recall, love and poetry were important themes in the *Vita Nuova*. Now, in Canto 24, Dante meets an Italian poet, Bonagiunta, who recognizes Dante and even quotes one of his poems from the *Vita Nuova*. Dante acknowledges the compliment and says that his poetry is inspired by love, and Bonagiunta admits that therein lies Dante's superiority. (Remember, Dante will spend time being purged of his pride.) The implication seems to be that Dante, having had the experience he described in the *Vita Nuova*, is inspired by true love, which is spiritual, divine, and unselfish, unlike the other poets, whose love poetry follows well-established rules about worldly love.

In fact, love has been a major theme throughout the *Comedy*. We saw it, of course, perverted in the story of Paolo and Francesca; but Dante's whole journey has resulted from the love of the Virgin Mary, St. Lucia, and Beatrice. The figures in Hell loved selfishly or loved the wrong things, making love into something evil. In Purgatory, the souls, though suffering, acknowledge that their suffering comes from divine love; and in Heaven, everything is suffused with love. Thus Dante brings together poetry and love as intertwined themes. We might want to conclude that this combination of themes helps to explain Dante's need for his journey. Having learned about true love in the *Vita Nuova*, his knowledge should have guided his subsequent activities. Apparently, however, it did not. Instead of focusing on that true love, he must have returned to other kinds of poetic love, which were artificial and often immoral, forgetting Beatrice and all she means.

This interpretation would explain the peculiar nature of their encounter from Canto 30 to the end of Purgatory. Dante is now in the Earthly Paradise, a place that may well remind us of the garden in *The Romance of the Rose*. We would expect Dante and Beatrice to run into each other's arms, to weep with joy, to be ecstatic. We would be wrong.

Beatrice appears after Dante sees an odd allegorical procession that represents the whole of the Bible, from Genesis, with its story of the creation, to Revelation, with its vision of the End. In other words, the procession represents all of earthly history, and near the middle, uniting the Old and New Testaments, is a griffin, half-lion and half-eagle, representing the nature of Jesus. At this point, Virgil vanishes, because human reason unaided by revelation can go no further. Now Dante's guide will be Beatrice, and is she ever angry with him! She acts like a jealous lover, but we can hardly assume that jealousy motivates her. She speaks to Dante as though to a child, rebuking and insulting him. Her anger, however, is righteous. If he has indeed been using his poetic gifts to write ordinary love poetry, with all of its carnal implications, rather than using what he had learned earlier, her anger is justified. Furthermore, her anger results from her true love for him, from her desire to assure that he will spend eternity in Heaven, which, if he continues on his present course, will be impossible. He cannot get there if, to return to the poem's opening lines, he is lost in the woods.

The conclusion of Purgatory, then, always comes as a shock. Our romantic expectations — not just the expectations of our time but the expectations that more than a century of medieval romance had created — prove to be incorrect. Instead of romance, we see rebuke; and Dante does not argue. He knows that Beatrice is right. Not only does his own individual salvation depend on her lessons, but the whole world is also in jeopardy. Canto 32 is one of the most confusing in the whole poem, as it presents a series of tableaux that chronicle the corruption of the Church, which endangers the salvation of everyone. In this light, Dante's personal story takes on a universal significance. As Dante indicates throughout, people are making incorrect choices, and they are influenced in those choices by corrupt leaders. As he explains in Canto 17, our decisions must be based on love in its purest form. As Dante knows, that course sounds easier than it is.

PARADISE

Paradise at first seems like the dullest section of the *Comedy*, for obvious reasons. No one is being tortured or even punished, and virtue is a lot duller than vice. Much of this section consists of doctrinal exposition. The souls do not tell their own stories as the souls in Hell and Purgatory did, first because to do so would be more egocentric than heavenly souls should be and also because those stories could not be as interesting as the earlier accounts of sinful behavior. Instead, they explain things, and their explanations often reveal for us medieval ways of looking at various phenomena. For instance, according to medieval theory, things on earth are transitory and imperfect, whereas from the sphere of the moon out to the Empyrean, where God dwells, things are perfect and not subject to time. According to this theory, then, the moon should be perfectly smooth; but when we look at it with the naked eye, it seems to reflect light unevenly. Dante asks Beatrice about this peculiarity and she provides a detailed explanation that naturally has nothing to do with what we know as the real explanation but that would probably have satisfied a medieval inquiry. (An interesting sidelight to this episode is that in *Paradise Lost*, which was written after Galileo had looked at the moon through his telescope and saw its mountains and valleys, Milton provides a different, equally unscientific explanation.)

In the course of Paradise, we meet numerous well-known characters, including some whom we have encountered in this study, figures like St. Augustine, Boethius, Bernard of Clairvaux, and Hugh of St. Victor. We also see an assortment of biblical characters; and always these souls are engaged in singing praises of God.

There is another difference between Paradise and the other sections that we should consider. In both the Inferno and Purgatory, the souls are assigned to particular places. In Hell, their places are fixed for eternity; a soul in the fourth circle will always be in the fourth circle suffering the appropriate torment. In Purgatory, the souls move from one place to another. A soul that has finished its purgation of pride will move to the level of the next sin that needs purging. In Paradise, Dante meets the souls as he mounts through the spheres toward the Empyrean, so that souls appear to be in a kind of hierarchical order, with the best being closest to God; but then we are informed that this is only an appearance, that Heaven is a place of undifferentiated good. Thus, toward the end of Paradise, Dante sees all of the souls seated together in a rose-like structure. Beatrice shows him how few empty seats there are, implying that not many people will die before the rose is filled, which will mark the end of the world.

In the concluding cantos of Paradise, Beatrice becomes increasingly beautiful, until she leaves him and takes her place in the rose. Dante finally sees the Virgin Mary, the angel Gabriel, and the Trinity, and the poem concludes with his vision of God, who is presented as pure light. It is truly difficult to describe the conclusion of the *Comedy*. As Dante himself says, what he saw cannot be put into words, and the student of his poem must feel the same way. Regardless of the reader's theological beliefs, the conclusion of the *Comedy* is a transcendent piece of writing, something that goes beyond the power of words. The only analogy that comes to mind is the second movement of Beethoven's opus 111 piano sonata, another sublime work that takes us into a realm that few have entered.

If the contents of the *Comedy* are staggering, its structure is equally impressive. The Inferno consists of thirty-four cantos (actually an introductory canto and then thirty-three cantos) while Purgatory and Paradise consist of thirty-three cantos each, for a total of one hundred. Furthermore, we can often find correspondences among similarly numbered cantos (making allowances for that introductory canto). It is an interesting exercise to look at, for example, Canto 26 in the Inferno and Canto 25 in Purgatory and Paradise to see what they have in common. We have also noted a number of nines in the poem (and there are others we have not mentioned, like the nine orders of angels), but the whole poem is built ultimately on the number three. There are, of course, the three sections (or, in Italian, *cantiche*), and the whole poem is written in a form called terza rima, that is, three-line stanzas rhyming aba bcb cdc and so on. Thus, throughout the poem there are constant reminders of the Trinity and of the order of the universe. Scholars often note that the Gothic cathedral is an allegorical representation of the universe. So, too, though in a different medium, is *The Divine Comedy*.

For an earlier view of the *Comedy*, the reader should look at what is often referred to as Dante's Letter to Can Grande della Scala. Can Grande was one of Dante's patrons, a powerful man who helped Dante during his exile from Florence. Scholars are divided over the issue of whether

Dante himself wrote this letter, but regardless of who wrote it, it offers important insights into the poem. For example, it briefly explains the theory of allegory as that theory was applied to biblical texts and then argues that the same theory can be applied to the *Comedy*, which is quite a claim, putting this vernacular poem on the same level as Scripture. Unfortunately — or perhaps fortunately — no one has ever been able to apply that theory to the *Comedy* as thoroughly as the letter implies.

Another important aspect of the letter is its announcement of the poem's subject, which it declares to be literally "the state of souls after death" and allegorically "man according as by his merits or demerits in the exercise of his free will he is deserving of reward or punishment by justice" (*Epistle* 460). Certainly we can see these elements in the poem, but they are just starting points. Aspects of the poem take us from Creation to the Last Judgment (we need only think of that procession that brings Beatrice into the poem at the end of Purgatory) and from the center of the universe, that is, the deepest part of Hell, to its outermost limit, the Empyrean, the dwelling place of God. In effect, the poem contains everything. It is an extraordinary achievement, and the reader becomes Dante's captive from the opening in the dark woods until the final vision of God and the closing reference to the stars. The poem is, in every sense of the term, awesome.

IX. *Pearl* and *Sir Gawain and the Green Knight*

FOURTEENTH-CENTURY ENGLAND

This book will close with two chapters on the fourteenth century in England. The present chapter will focus on *Sir Gawain and the Green Knight* and *Pearl*, and the last chapter will look at Chaucer and some of his contemporaries.

The fourteenth century in England was a particularly interesting time, but to appreciate it, we need to rid ourselves of stereotyped pictures of the period. When we talk about fourteenth-century England, we are not talking about "merrie olde England," a time of dashing knights, damsels waiting to be rescued, and cute little boutiques to visit afterward. Nor are we talking about the England of fantasy novels and role-playing games. As hard as it may be for us to do, we must force ourselves to think about this, or any, historical period as being populated by real human beings who had to face real problems, both the general ones that confront all people and the problems that are specific to each time and place. And the specific problems of fourteenth-century England were formidable.

There were, of course, normal difficulties, like worrying about the food supply every year, and in fact in the early part of the fourteenth century there were a number of years of famine. Famines were disastrous, but they were expected. In the middle of the century, however, a disaster of unprecedented magnitude struck: bubonic plague, the Black Death. Whole towns were destroyed by this quick spreading and quick killing disease, which wiped out a huge percentage of the population of Europe. And because the people had no notion of microbes or of the means by which the disease spread, they often assumed that it was some sort of divine visitation.[1]

Not only did the plague kill large numbers of people, but it also caused profound changes in society. Medieval society was largely agricultural, though as the centuries passed, the cities gained increasing importance. Even so, a very large proportion of the population was engaged in agriculture, working on land that was owned by a relatively small number of nobles. As long as the number of workers was large, the law of supply and demand dictated that they could be paid little and treated badly. But after the devastation of the plague, there were far fewer of them than there had been, and they eventually realized that their services were now at a premium. The upper classes, naturally, opposed the workers' demands for higher wages and better conditions — very little ever really changes — and they depicted those demands as being contrary to divine law, which, from their privileged positions, they interpreted as requiring every person to be content with his or her place. If the nobles were content to bear the burden of being wealthy, why should the workers not be content with their burden of poverty? It is perhaps not surprising that the peasants rejected such reasoning, and in 1381 there was a violent rebellion, the Peasants' Revolt, during which buildings in London were burned down and prominent citizens were killed, while others fled for their lives. Although this episode in itself is fascinating and complex, for our purposes it is enough to note that, because of the plague and its effects, late fourteenth-century English society was in turmoil.

And if the plague had not been enough, there were other sources of dissatisfaction as well. One of them was the kings. The century began with England being ruled by Edward I, who had some positive accomplishments to go along with his failures, but he was followed by his son, Edward II, who was forced to give up the throne and was eventually murdered. He was followed by his son, Edward III, who had been implicated in his father's death. Edward III was quite young when he became king and he ruled England for fifty years. The beginning of his reign was a hopeful time; the vigorous young king offered a welcome relief from the corruption of his predecessors. But as his reign progressed, as England suffered from the plague and from the start of the Hundred Years War that he initiated with France, as his court increasingly became a center of corruption and immorality, Edward became less and less popular as a leader. Edward III's son, another Edward (the family showed little imagination with names), was known as the Black Prince, and because of his early military victories against the French, and despite his later failures, he became a popular figure. But Edward contracted a debilitating disease on one of his military campaigns and died before his father, so that when Edward III finally died at the age of sixty-five as a senile old man, he was succeeded by his twelve-year-old grandson, Richard II.

Once again there was great hope that a young king would restore England's health, and once again that hope was futile. As William Langland wrote in *Piers Plowman*, "Woe to that land whose king is a child." Until Richard gained his majority, the country was ruled by noblemen who devoted their energies not to the good of the country but to the good of themselves. When Richard finally began to rule, although he put down the Peasant's Revolt, he proved incapable of handling the job, and he was deposed by Henry IV in 1399.

With this combination of kings, plagues, wars, famines, and social unrest, fourteenth-century England was not a happy place; but, remarkably, this was a time that saw the creation of a spectacular body of literature. In the fourteenth century, English as a language that most of us would recognize appeared. Among the important writers of the period were Langland, whose *Piers Plowman* provides an extraordinary picture of England's social chaos; Chaucer, who provides a different perspective on life in England, and John Gower, Chaucer's friend who wrote a major poem in each of the three major languages of England: English, French, and Latin. We will get to them in the next chapter; the subject of this chapter is the anonymous poet who wrote *Pearl* and *Sir Gawain and the Green Knight.*

Actually, this anonymous poet wrote four poems, for the unique manuscript that contains *Pearl* and *Sir Gawain* also contains two other poems, *Cleanness* (sometimes called *Purity*) and *Patience*, that are attributed to the same poet. Or perhaps the same poet did not write all four.

If that statement sounds either confusing or confused, it is because the situation is confused. We have a single manuscript that contains these poems (as well as two Latin poems). That manuscript, which is now at the British Library, contains the name of no author for any of the poems, and they might well have been written by four different authors and simply copied together by some scribe in this manuscript. In many ways the poems seem quite different from each other, but there are enough similarities among them that most scholars now think they were composed by a single author, who is usually known as the *Pearl*-poet. Some scholars have attempted to identify the poet, but such identifications are conjectural and too uncertain to be helpful. As is so often the case in studying medieval literature, we must simply acknowledge that we have no idea of the identity of an extraordinary poet. Medieval writers, like medieval artists, did not regard it as their first duty to put their names on their creations. Nor do we know exactly when the poems were written, except that it was in the second half of the fourteenth century.

Another strictly literary problem has to do with the nature of allegory. The people of the Middle Ages may have viewed the world as a snare and a deception, but as we have seen, they also saw it as a vast allegory. Some scholars of the Middle Ages therefore see everything in medieval literature as allegorical, while others are less inclusive. A good example of the problem can be found in Chaucer's *Canterbury Tales*. Chaucer's pilgrims are traveling, as many real pilgrims actually did, from just outside London to the shrine of Thomas Becket at Canterbury. Should we simply regard their journey as the ordinary journey that so many pilgrims made? We could, and in part we should; but we must also realize that many aspects of the journey are unrealistic, in the modern sense of the term. People do not talk or tell stories in rhyming iambic pentameter verses (or even in other verse forms), and a group of almost thirty pilgrims, traveling along narrow paths on horseback, would not have been able to hear each other no matter what they were saying. Should we then regard the journey as allegorical, seeing London as the City of Man and Canterbury as the City of God? We could, and in part we should, though the pilgrims never actually reach Canterbury; and it would be a mistake if we, like the medieval critics of Virgil's *Aeneid*, tried to impose an allegorical reading on every detail of Chaucer's poem. The questions we have been raising are the questions we will have to ask as we look at *Pearl* and *Sir Gawain*, for some readers see every element in these poems (like the pearl itself or the green belt in *Sir Gawain*) as allegorical, while other readers take other approaches. (Incidentally, the titles of these poems are modern inventions. In the manuscript, the poems have no titles.)

Although these poems were written at about the time Chaucer was writing, they are written in the dialect of the North-West Midlands, a dialect that can be very difficult for modern readers. Here, for instance, are lines 121-124 of *Pearl* in both Middle and Modern English:

The dubbement dere of doun and dale3
Of wod & water & wlong playne3
Bylde in me blys, abated my bale3
Fordidden my stresse, dystryed my payne3

The adornment precious of hills and dales,
Of wood and water and splendid plains,
Aroused in me bliss, abolished my woes,
Dispelled my distress, put an end to my pains.[2]

A quick glance at the Middle English will show that each line contains several words that alliterate. In fact, *Pearl* and *Sir Gawain* are among a group of fourteenth-century poems that are often referred to as constituting the Alliterative Revival. Again, because so little is known about these alliterative poets, much of the commentary on them is speculative. We do know that Old English poems like *Beowulf* were alliterative, but we have no clear idea of how that poetic style was preserved from the Norman Conquest in 1066 until alliterative poetry reappeared in the fourteenth century. Undoubtedly it was preserved in oral poetry, but its reappearance in manuscripts remains somewhat mysterious. Chaucer's poetry consists entirely of the kind of rhymed verse to which we are accustomed, and he even finds opportunities to poke fun at alliterative verse. One possibility is that poets like Chaucer, who were associated with the court, where the remnants of Norman-French culture were still important, tended to be more influenced by Continental writers. Chaucer, who clearly knew about alliterative poetry, was far more influenced by writers like Alan of Lille, Machaut, Petrarch, and Dante. Other English writers, separated from the court either by distance or by political beliefs, somehow turned to the more native tradition of alliterative verse. Often these alliterative poems express strong reservations about the course of events in England, and while Chaucer is frequently satiric in a humorous way, the alliterative poets are often satiric in a denunciatory way.

PEARL

Pearl, which is both alliterative and uses a rhyme scheme (a-b-a-b-a-b-a-b-b-c-b-c) is not itself denunciatory, though the other poems in the manuscript tend more in that direction. *Pearl* has a plot, but at first that plot appears so slight that it hardly seems to exist. The speaker of the poem presents himself as a jeweler who bemoans his loss of a precious pearl. Then he falls asleep in the garden where he lost the pearl and has a dream in which the pearl appears to him in the form of a young woman, who stands across from him on the opposite bank of a river. In a scene that recalls Dante's conversations in the Earthly Paradise, they discuss a number of theological questions, he has a vision of the New Jerusalem, and when he tries to cross the river he wakes up, having learned a vital lesson. This literal retelling of the story makes it seem strange indeed. Why is the pearl so precious to him? Why does he fall asleep? Why would he discuss theology with a young woman dressed in pearls? Why does he want to cross the river? What does he learn? These are all questions that we will have to answer.

The easiest question to start with is why he falls asleep, and the quick answer is that almost everyone in fourteenth-century literature falls asleep and has dreams. After works like *The Romance of the Rose,* dream visions became highly conventional, following certain rules and patterns. Of course (as one of my teachers used to say) the greatest authors use the conventions, but they also manipulate them and make them their own. So it is with Chaucer in his dream visions and so it is with the *Pearl-*poet. For instance, following in the tradition of *The Romance of the Rose,* dream visions were often used in poems that dealt with the subject of romantic love, and we can find many poems on the subject, some good and some not so good, that simply rely on the well-established conventions. *Pearl* at first seems to be using these very same conventions. The speaker is alone in a garden where he mourns his loss, for which he blames "luf-daungere" (11), which Sister Mary Vincent Hillman translates as "love-dominion," though in her notes she clarifies the point by saying it refers to "his inordinate love for his earthly treasure" (78). A medieval reader[3] might have thought, "Here we go again," but such a reader would have been in for a surprise. This poem is a dream vision, but its subject, despite the conventional beginning, is not romantic love.

Here we enter once again the world of medieval allegory, for before we can go further, we must understand what the pearl is. It could, of course, be just a pearl, an expensive jewel whose loss a jeweler might well lament; but if this jeweler is so upset over the loss of a pearl, clearly his priorities are misplaced, and we do not need medieval theology to tell us that. Many critics have offered opinions on what the pearl represents, but the simplest explanation seems the best. There are two major clues in the poem that help us to identify the pearl: The jeweler tells us that the pearl maiden "was nearer to me than aunt or niece" (233) and that she lived "not two years in our land" (483). Since the pearl appears to him as a young woman, we are justified in thinking that the pearl is an allegorical representation of a person, a person who was more closely related to him than an aunt or a niece and who died at an age less than two. The possibilities are a sister and a daughter, and commentators have inclined toward the latter. In other words — which is what allegory means — the jeweler is a man who is mourning the death of his infant daughter; and the garden where he falls asleep is not the enclosed garden of so many love visions but is rather the cemetery where she is buried.

Some people believe that in the Middle Ages, because of the high rate of infant mortality, parents did not become too attached to their children. They argue that it was difficult to invest a great deal of emotion in someone who was likely to die young. It is probably impossible for us to know how prevalent such an attitude was, though that attitude still strikes many scholars as counterintuitive. Clearly it was not the attitude of our jeweler, who tells us that he has spent much of his time in this cemetery. In fact, his life has been dominated by his grief, and the "luf-daungere" that he mentions is not the domination of romantic love that we might have expected but is rather the domination of the inordinate grief he feels for his beloved daughter, as he now understands. Looking back, he realizes that he should have taken comfort from his knowledge of Christian teaching; instead, his will, the human faculty that is instrumental in the Christian understanding of human sinfulness, overcame his knowledge of Christian comfort and led him to excessive grief. Here, obviously, is the answer to another of our questions: One of the things he learns is to feel comfort rather than grief over the loss of his daughter. As he says at the end of the poem, after his dream and after having had a chance to reflect on the meaning of that dream, he now understands the Christian teachings about death and he willingly gives up his pearl, his daughter, to God. By giving her up, he becomes reconciled to her death and understands that she is in Heaven so that he may rejoice in her glory.

Whether the poem is autobiographical we have no easy way of knowing. It might be, but it equally might be a complete fiction, invented to teach this and other lessons that the poem incorporates. Ultimately it makes no difference whether the story is true since, for the Christian poet, what the story teaches is true. In this sense the poem is like one of Jesus' parables, a fiction that teaches an allegorical lesson. And here we have at least a partial answer to another of our questions: Why is the young woman dressed in pearls? Why is she called a pearl and why are there so many references to pearls? One answer can be found in the Gospel According to Matthew: "Again, the kingdom of heaven is like unto a merchant man, seeking goodly pearls: Who, when he had found one of great price, went and sold all that he had and bought it" (13:45–46). She is the pearl of great price who helps him to understand and thereby potentially to gain heaven. The jeweler has put too much emphasis on her earthly nature, but his pearl has taught him about her far more important spiritual nature. If he grasps that spiritual nature, then he can be like the merchant in the parable.

Furthermore, the whiteness of a pearl is symbolic of its purity, and its perfect roundness is symbolic of its perfection, qualities that make it ideal for representing both his earthly daughter and her spiritual manifestation in the poem. And finally, there is one more possibility, which is only a possibility. When the jeweler sees the New Jerusalem, he describes the gems from which the city is made, and he says

> & vch ȝate of a margerye,
> A parfyt perle þat neuer fateȝ.

> And each portal of one pearl,
> A perfect pearl which never fades.
>   (1037–38)

The word used for "pearl" in line 1037 is "margerye," a word that he uses elsewhere in the poem, and it is possible that the daughter whose death is mourned in this poem was named Margaret (or something derived from Margaret, like Margery), a name that itself means "pearl."

Of course there is something a little strange about the jeweler being taught the secrets of heaven by his deceased infant daughter, and early in the poem he seems to rebel against this situation. How can she, a mere child, teach him anything? In fact, there is a great deal of tension in the early part of their discussion, largely because of his pride, his unwillingness to recognize her superior knowledge. At one point she comments on his foolishness and accuses him of having made three errors in quick succession. This is a stern rebuke from a two-year-old. Both the jeweler and the reader have to recognize that this two-year-old is speaking from the vantage point of heaven, where she now lives. The situation is similar to Dante's in the *Comedy* (which the poet may have known — we cannot tell for certain): Dante has indicated that the whole of his journey has been prompted by Beatrice's love and concern for him, but when he actually meets her, she seems to treat him with scorn and anger. Both Beatrice and the pearl-maiden are impatient with these men because the men are, at least at first, so obtuse, so convinced that they are more knowledgeable than they actually are and that they are more knowledgeable than their female teachers are. Not only do these men have to learn the heavenly secrets that the women are teaching, but they also have to learn to tame their pride, to be humble, to be true learners. Because Dante's work is so much longer, and because he is allowed in his work to traverse heaven, he has more of a chance to demonstrate the learning process. In *Pearl*, the jeweler and the maiden are separated by the river, which she says he cannot cross. But when he sees the New Jerusalem, when he sees her in the procession of the Virgin with the Lamb, he tries to cross it and the vision disappears. He awakens. Unlike Dante, he cannot enter Heaven while he is alive, and he is punished for his presumption by losing more of the vision. Of course, he would have had to awaken at some time, but much of his learning takes place between the time of the vision and the time when he wrote the poem, an interval during which he could reflect on what his pearl has told him.

Among the points that he must learn on his way to grasping the ultimate truth is that despite his feeling of loss, his pearl is not lost. From his earthly perspective she may seem lost, but that earthly perspective is transient and partial. He must learn not to trust his senses but to trust his faith. He must understand what it means for her to be a queen in Heaven, to be married to the Lamb, and he must understand how it is possible for someone who died so young to occupy such an exalted position. Basically, he must understand the difference between the City of God and the City of Man. As he learns, he is treated to lessons from the Bible, including a long retelling of the Parable of the Vineyard, which helps to justify Divine justice; and finally, perhaps as a kind of incentive, he is granted a vision of the New Jerusalem, though he cannot enter it. Like the author of Revelation, he has the vision, but like all human beings, he must wait for death before he can approach the city. The enthusiasm that prompts him to try to cross the river may indicate his continuing ignorance as well as his tendency to disobey divine orders; by the time of writing, he recognizes his errors and assumes a proper humility. Like each of the poems in the manuscript, this one ends like a prayer, with the words "Amen. Amen." (The other poems end with a single "Amen.")

Altogether *Pearl* is a touching elegy, a lament for his dead daughter, as well as a description of spiritual learning through which the audience can also learn. The poem shows an amazing combination of delicacy and pedagogy, and it also demonstrates the care with which medieval poems could be crafted. As we saw earlier, the poem uses both alliteration and rhyme most skillfully, but its craft goes even further. This poem consists of one hundred and one twelve-line stanzas, for a total of 1212 lines. These numbers are not accidental. Aside from any other symbolism associated with these numbers, the description of the New Jerusalem (like the description in Revelation) is full of twelves: There are twelve bandels, twelve foundations, twelve gems, twelve tiers, twelve gates, and twelve furlongs in each square. There are also 144,000 virgins, with 144 being the square of twelve. The very number of lines, then, makes the poem analogous to the New Jerusalem.

Nor is that the extent of the poet's symbolism. The poem is divided into twenty sections of five stanzas each (except for section fifteen, which has six stanzas). Each of these sections is tied together by a key word that appears in the last line of the first stanza, then in the first and last lines of each remaining stanza in the section, and in the first line of the first stanza in the next section. In short, all the stanzas are linked together, and the poem's very last stanza is linked to the very first stanza, making the whole poem into a perfect circle, like the pearl itself. If the pearl-maiden teaches the jeweler important lessons about death and salvation, then the *Pearl*, which is itself like a pearl, teaches its readers or auditors those very same lessons. The poem becomes the thing it represents.

Pearl may be medieval, but no one who reads it now can think of it as being from a "Dark Age" or from a less sophisticated time than our own. This is an altogether remarkable poem that deserves reading and re-reading, as do the other poems in the manuscript. It deals with a terrible problem, the loss of a child, and examines how such evil can exist, or seem to exist, in the world. Its answers may not satisfy us, but few answers really satisfy us on these points. It is worthwhile for us to watch someone wrestle so touchingly with the question more than six hundred years ago.

Following *Pearl* in the manuscript are *Cleanness* and *Patience*, both of which read much like sermons, the former using numerous biblical examples to illustrate the virtue of purity and the latter retelling the story of Jonah to illustrate the virtue of patience. And then comes *Sir Gawain and the Green Knight*.

SIR GAWAIN AND THE GREEN KNIGHT

Sir Gawain is an Arthurian romance. As we saw when we considered the romances of Chrétien, romances may also contain elements of romantic love, but they do not necessarily have to, and we will have to decide whether such love appears in this poem. But before we can consider this poem at all, we must recall that in many Arthurian works, the Arthurian court is a troubled place, full of rivalries and a variety of unchivalric behaviors. Despite this the Arthurian stories make up an exciting and often moving body of literature in which authors from different times and places have been able to use stock plots and characters in order to convey their own individual visions. There are Arthurian stories from any number of countries in the Middle Ages as well as more modern versions, like Tennyson's Victorian *Idylls of the King*, Marion Zimmer Bradley's *The Mists of Avalon*, which tells the story from a woman's point of view, C.S. Lewis' *That Hideous Strength*, and, surprisingly, Bernard Malamud's *The Natural*, which transforms the Arthurian plot into a baseball story.

One of the interesting facets of so much Arthurian literature is how small the role of Arthur is. In Chrétien, as we saw, Arthur is an odd figure. In *Yvain*, before the main action starts, he toddles off to bed with the queen and falls asleep, and in *Perceval* he is completely helpless when the Red Knight insults both him and the queen. In *Sir Gawain*, too, Arthur plays a relatively small role. Although his court is quite important in the poem, Arthur himself is not prominent. The focus throughout is on Sir Gawain, the knight who was a special favorite of English audiences. But even before we get to Gawain, there is an introductory stanza to the poem that requires some attention. This stanza speaks, oddly, about Troy, about how that city was conquered through treachery, and about how one of the refugees from Troy settled Britain, just as another refugee, Aeneas, founded Rome. Why should a fourteenth-century poem about a legendary British king begin by mentioning the destruction of Troy?

Even though *The Iliad* and *The Odyssey* were not available to medieval European readers, those readers did have other versions of the Troy story, and, like the Arthurian stories, these stories about Troy were great favorites. The most important, of course, was *The Aeneid*, but there were others as well. Since in this stanza our author cites Aeneas as a traitor who was responsible for the fall of Troy, we know that he is using one of those other versions. The question still remains, however: Why start with Troy? There are several possible reasons. First, it had been fashionable since Rome derived its origin from Aeneas for nations to trace their origins back to other Trojan heroes. Such derivations established both their antiquity and their nobility. In this stanza the author cites Trojan forebears for both Tuscany and Lombardy before he mentions Felix Brutus, the alleged Trojan founder of Britain. Furthermore, the references to treachery and the fall of Troy lead us to look for elements of treachery and weakness in Arthur's court. After all, if we are not to notice such things, why would the poet mention them? And finally, this stanza, and especially its last four lines, which describe ongoing unrest in England, tell us that we should not focus only on the legendary Britain of Arthur's time but on the Britain that the poet inhabits as well — which implies, of course, that the poet's Britain was also a place of treachery and weakness. The introductory stanza indicates that we should look for these matters in the poem. Unlike the French Vulgate Cycle of Arthurian stories, there are no hermits here jumping out from behind rocks to explain the poem's significance, so readers must rely on their own judgments to see how these elements operate in the poem.

The poem's second stanza is also introductory, but this time it introduces us to Arthur's court. The speaker seems to say that Arthur was "the most courteous" of the British kings, which might be a high compliment. But the narrator qualifies that praise by saying that Arthur has the reputation of being the most courteous. There is a major difference between saying that he was the most courteous and that he was reputed to be the most courteous. Was he or was he not? Were those reports true or were they not? Our initial view of the court in the third stanza is not promising. The action opens at Christmastide, and Christmas in Arthur's court is surprisingly like Christmas in our time; there is little mention of the religious import of the holiday. Instead, the lords and ladies are gathered together for an extended party, including jousting, dancing, and other activities that have little to do with the birth of the Savior.

The emphasis here on their pleasures is important, and its importance is underlined when the narrator refers to Christ. These men are knights, and they have special responsibilities. There is controversy today over the extent to which chivalry was actually practiced in the Middle Ages, but certainly it existed as an ideal. Chivalry, however, did not merely mean politeness. It meant actively undertaking good deeds, even if they were difficult to perform. In addition, there was a religious dimension to knighthood. When Paul mentions in Ephesians "the whole armor of God ... the breastplate of righteousness ... the shield of faith ... the helmet of salvation, and the sword of the Spirit" (6:13–17), he equates knighthood (or its equivalent in his time) with Christian idealism. These men (and the women, too) should be looking to those ideals at their Christmas celebration, not devoting themselves to such frivolities as the kissing game described in the fourth stanza. If Arthur's court, with its high level of frivolity, is the most admired of all such courts, then the poet is certainly making a pointed criticism of court life.

Lest this judgment seem too harsh, we should look at what happens when the green knight arrives. We can only guess where the poet got the idea of the green knight. He might come from vegetation myths or Celtic legends or somewhere else. Whatever his origin, though, he is an imposing and frightening figure, a giant green knight riding a green horse into Arthur's court, where, without uttering any words of greeting, he challenges any knight in the court to exchange blows with him. He is, of course, imposing to us, but both we and he should expect that the great-est knights from the greatest court in the world might respond to his chal-lenge. The court, however, responds to both his appearance and his challenge with silence. The poet, in his subtle way, hints that at first some of the knights remained silent as they awaited Arthur's response, but when he says that not all of them were silent out of fear, he implies that some, perhaps many, were indeed frightened into silence. The green knight is certainly not impressed with these knights, whom he refers to as "beardless children" (280), just as Beatrice referred ironically to Dante's beard when she addressed him as one would address a child (Canto 31). And when the court becomes even quieter after his challenge, the green knight expresses his incredulity that this gathering of partygoers is the much-praised court of King Arthur. Since our expectations of Arthur's court are as high as his, we, too, might be astonished. Finally, when no one else responds to the challenge, Arthur accepts it, and only then does Gawain claim it.

So far, Arthur's court has been less than impressive, and the situa-tion does not improve. After Gawain cuts off the green knight's head, and before the knight picks it up and rides off, the courtiers kick it around in what appears to be a kind of Arthurian soccer; after he leaves, Arthur and Gawain laugh and smile about the episode, while the whole court returns to its previous gaiety. They express no opinions about this star-tling episode or about what it might mean. It is simply another excuse for laughter in what surely appears to be a shallow and unchivalric court.

Sir Gawain and the Green Knight is divided into four sections or "fitts." In the first fitt, no one makes a good impression. In the second, however, when Gawain prepares to set out to find the green knight, he gains in stature. The passing of a year is described in both natural terms and in terms of the Christian holidays that pass, and after Gawain is armed, he goes to mass. Furthermore, Gawain's shield is described at great length, in accordance with the tradition of knightly descriptions that the designs on armor are described in detail. The design on Gawain's shield is simple but full of allegorical significance: It is a star with five points in which all the lines are connected, a pentagram. As the narrator tells us, each point represents aspects of knighthood: the knight's five senses, his five fingers, the five wounds of Christ, the five joys of Mary, and five knightly qualities. Here we have what we looked for in vain in the first fitt, that combination of chivalric and religious features that should char-acterize the true knight. Gawain's adventure is no longer a game, and the other knights, certain that Gawain will be killed on his adventure, bewail his having agreed to the challenge, though what his other options may have been, especially in the face of their reluctance to accept the challenge, they do not say. Gawain, however, is solemn, not because he is afraid but because he is beginning to recognize the seriousness of his enterprise.

The description of Gawain's journey into the north is justly famous. The landscape becomes more desolate, he fights monsters, and the weather gets colder, which must have made wearing a suit of armor terribly uncomfortable. The poet is also playing with the idea that the devil lives in the north, though Gawain is guided by Mary. And when Gawain prays to Mary that he might have a place to hear mass on Christmas, suddenly he sees a castle.

Clearly this journey is more than a simple trip to the north. As the weather and the landscape become increasingly bleak, Gawain's journey takes on more threatening overtones, and we can hardly wait for his encounter with the green knight. Meanwhile, Gawain is welcomed into the castle, where he finds none of the frivolity that we saw at Arthur's court. Instead, the people visit the chapel and sing Christmas hymns, and it is in the chapel that Gawain sees the two ladies of the castle, one young and beautiful and the other much older and far less attractive. We are still in suspense over Gawain's fate, but for the present he is comfortable, and he is even willing in this section's concluding stanza to agree that while his host goes out hunting on the next day, Gawain will stay at the castle. At the end of the day, they will exchange whatever they have won, though it is not clear what Gawain might win in the castle.

We find out what he can win in the third fitt, the longest and most problematical in the poem. It describes three hunts (for deer, boar, and fox) on three successive days, along with more detailed descriptions of how dead animals were prepared for human use than many readers need, though modern hunters often comment on the accuracy of the descriptions. It also describes what happens to Gawain in the castle on those three days. Some critics have tried to find thematic significance in the allegorical meanings of the animals that are hunted and what happens to Gawain on each of the days, but those arguments seldom convince. We might want to be critical of Gawain for sleeping in on those days, but after all, he has had a difficult journey and he has not been invited to hunt. And he is understandably nervous about meeting the green knight. We would be better advised to smile at his discomfiture when his sleep is disturbed on each of these days by the beautiful lady of the castle, who is clearly trying to seduce him. Gawain, in almost every version of the Arthurian stories, is known as a great lover, and, in accordance with medieval custom, he is unlikely to be wearing pajamas — or anything else — under the blankets, so his temptations must be pretty strong. Perhaps he is more worried than we think about his approaching challenge, but he does manage to resist the lady's temptations even though she arrives each day in a more revealing outfit. And every kiss that he gets from the lady, he delivers to the lord of the castle at the end of the day.

Gawain appears, then, to be doing pretty well in meeting his challenges. Not only does he resist the lady's advances, but he also refuses to accept her offers of a ring and a green belt (sometimes referred to as a girdle) — until she tells him that the belt is magical and will protect the life of anyone who wears it. Since Gawain has been so nervous about his meeting with the green knight, he accepts the belt and promises not to tell anyone he has it. At this point, the story seems to be following the "rules" of courtly romance, since lovers, especially illicit lovers, frequently exchange tokens in such stories; but the author of this poem uses that convention in an unusual way. Gawain clearly feels relieved and goes to confession, after which he spends the rest of the day dancing. When his host returns, Gawain gives him the three kisses he had received that day from the lady, but he makes no mention of the belt, just as a lover would not mention the token he had received from his beloved.

This part of the story raises a number of problems. When Gawain finally reaches the Green Chapel, having resisted the temptation to run away, he fortunately does not have his head cut off, but he is punished, however slightly, for his transgressions. The green knight, who, it turns out, was his host at the castle, explains that everything that has happened since Gawain's arrival at the castle has been a test for Gawain, a test that he has passed, though not with straight A's. What exactly was his transgression? On the most basic level, he was guilty of having taken the belt without then giving it to his host. He has broken his pledge; in Gawain's knightly society, a knight was expected to keep his word. But Gawain's failing goes even deeper than that. He broke his word for a particular reason: He was afraid that without the belt he would lose his life. He was also, therefore, guilty of two further sins, a lack of faith in God's ability to protect him (or in God's desire to protect him) and an excessive love of his earthly life. What is remarkable, though, is the host's understanding attitude toward these sins. He points out what Gawain has done wrong, but he also understands that Gawain, as a human being, has his share of human frailty. Gawain is not condemned for his failings so much as he is instructed about them. Once again we see a medieval work about the ideals and our human inability to live up to those ideals.

Gawain, of course, is not immediately grateful for having been put through this ordeal, and he quite irrationally launches into a speech in which he blames women for the bad things that happen to men. Clearly he is looking for someone else to blame, however illogical his blame might be. But then he gets control of himself and accepts the belt as a gift, saying that he will wear it as a reminder of his failures and of the pride that led to those failures.

Suddenly the belt has taken on a new significance. It may not have had the magical powers that the lady described, but it now has the power to help Gawain in his quest for salvation. It may not save his physical being, but it can save his spiritual being. Through his ordeal Gawain has received an education. He has learned about himself and about his place in the world, and when he returns to Arthur's court, he tries to convey to the king and his peers some sense of what he has learned. At this point, Gawain is no longer simply a great warrior. Now he is truly a great knight, someone who combines chivalric and religious ideals. Unfortunately, Gawain is the only character in the poem who grows, for when he finishes telling his story, the king and the rest of the court laugh, and then all agree that they will all wear such a token, though they do so for the wrong reason.

If we remember what Arthur's court was like at the poem's beginning, we should not be surprised that they trivialize Gawain's story. They respond to his seriousness with laughter and decide that they will all wear green belts, not as reminders of pride and human failure but only for Gawain's sake. In a sense, the belt becomes for them not a religious image but a fashion statement. Arthur's court is as frivolous at the end as it was when the green knight's head was used as a soccer ball; the poem's concluding references to Troy and to Jesus remind us of both the internal weaknesses that lead to the collapse of kingdoms and the religious ideals that should preserve but that will also outlast kingdoms.

The conclusion of the poem, however, poses a number of complications that scholars love to discuss. For example, the green knight tells Gawain that the whole scheme was devised by the old woman that Gawain had seen in the chapel, who is actually Morgan le Fay, Arthur's half-sister. In some versions of the Arthurian stories, Morgan is on Arthur's side, but in others she is his enemy. In all of them, though, she has magical powers, which help to explain the green knight's changes of complexion. But the green knight says that Morgan devised the scheme in order to frighten Guinevere. Guinevere may have been as frightened as anyone else when the green knight first appeared, but her fright plays no other part in the story. Instead, the scheme turns out to be a test for Gawain that he passes with difficulty, and a test for Arthur's entire court, which does not pass. Arthur's court is like Troy, internally weak and ready to fall, despite the new awareness that Gawain has brought back from his adventure.

The problems become even more complicated when we consider what might be the very last line of the poem. In the manuscript, after the poem's concluding "Amen," there is a line in French: "Hony soyt qui mal pence," "Shame be to him who thinks evil of it." Since we do not know if the manuscript was written by the poet or by a scribe, we cannot tell who added this line, but it is interesting that the line is the motto of the Order of the Garter, an order of knights that was founded by Edward III. Members of that order were entitled to wear a blue garter, not a green belt, but the presence of this motto, along with the references to Troy's destruction, to treason, and the frivolity of Arthur's court, seems to add to the impression that this poem, in addition to demonstrating Gawain's education, is offering criticism of Edward's court, which pretends to a chivalric ideal that it does not truly uphold.

In *Pearl*, the jeweler thinks that his love for the pearl is a kind of ideal, and he has to learn, through his dream vision, what really constitutes the ideal: faith in God and in divine justice. In *Sir Gawain*, Gawain is regarded as an ideal, and he, too, has to learn that his behavior is not what it should be. But in *Pearl*, the jeweler is alone, whereas in *Sir Gawain* we see the hero operating in a social milieu which is also found wanting and which bears a resemblance to the actual court of the actual king of England. It is difficult, therefore, not to see *Sir Gawain and the Green Knight* as a work of social and political criticism. It builds in a number of ways on the other poems in the manuscript and has a great deal of contemporary significance.

In this connection, it is worth noting that *Sir Gawain* is written in a complex verse form. Each stanza consists of a section of alliterative verses whose number varies from stanza to stanza. These verses are followed by something called a "bob and wheel," a very short line and then four lines of three beats each, rhyming a-b-a-b. This verse form is very flexible and the poet uses it masterfully, but what is really interesting is that there are, altogether, one hundred such stanzas, just as there are in *Pearl*. The careful construction of this poem and of *Pearl* indicates that these poems were intended to complement each other; and like so many of the poems in the alliterative revival, they offer a very critical perspective on fourteenth-century life.

Chaucer, too, as we will see in the next chapter, is critical of the life around him, but his criticism is generally delivered with a smile. There are few smiles in alliterative poetry, and most of the ones that are there are bitter. What is most fascinating about these poems, however, is how distant and different those people were from the way we are. And how similar they are to us.

X. Chaucer

We have no way of knowing why particular ages give rise to multiple literary giants while other ages seem bereft of such figures. The late sixteenth century in England, for example, produced Shakespeare, Spenser, Sidney, and Donne, among others, while the writers of the fifteenth century are, aside from Malory, known only to specialists. The late fourteenth century also produced a series of giants, including the *Pearl*-poet, William Langland, John Gower, and Geoffrey Chaucer. The ostensible subject of this chapter is Chaucer, but first we will give brief consideration to Langland and Gower.

In many college English departments, it has long been traditional to require that English majors take a course in Chaucer, Shakespeare, or Milton. It is, of course, valuable for students to study a single author's works in depth, and the focus on these three authors acknowledges the magnificence and importance of their works. At the same time, it is important to understand these writers, and all other writers, in their own contexts. All three of these geniuses were aware of the literature that preceded them and of the history that surrounded them. Chaucer, who was employed by the king, had a personal involvement in the events of his time, and his extensive use of other authors' works provides evidence of this literary knowledge. He mentions John Gower, whom he clearly knew personally, in his poetry; and he could hardly not have known William Langland's masterpiece, the work we call *Piers Plowman*.

Actually we do not know if such a person as William Langland ever really existed. The speaker in the poem calls himself Will, but in a poem that operates on so many allegorical levels, "Will" might simply be another allegory. "Langland" derives from a line in the poem, but again, it might well not refer to the author's name. Whoever wrote the poem, we can refer to him as Langland; and we can agree that he made things difficult for general readers but exciting for literary scholars. Not only is the poem complex, but it exists in three (some would say four) distinct versions, which are cleverly known as the A-, B-, and C-Texts. All attempts to date these texts and to explain why three versions exist are conjectural, but clearly Langland, for a variety of reasons, became dissatisfied with the texts he had written and spent his life rewriting them. If we consider how difficult and expensive that rewriting must have been — having to copy the text by hand — we can get some idea of how important Langland must have thought his poem was. The A-Text is relatively brief, and we can safely assume that when Langland discovered that he had more to say, he expanded it into the much longer B-Text. We can tell that the B-Text was well known because at the time of the Peasants' Revolt in 1381, the rebels referred to Piers Plowman as though he were a real person. After the revolt, Langland produced the C-Text, which is somewhat shorter than the B-Text. Some scholars think that the C-Text is also less inflammatory than its predecessor, a conclusion with which other scholars disagree. Despite the differences between them, the B- and C-Texts still have much in common.

Piers Plowman, or *The Vision of Will Concerning Piers the Plowman*, consists of a series of dream visions. Will, the narrator, falls asleep so often — along the road, in church — that we might consider him narcoleptic. He even has dreams within dreams. We may recall that dream visions were often associated with stories of love, but such is not the case here. Will's dreams are more like prophetic visions, not visions that tell the future but dreams that reveal the realities of the present and warn the audience about its own sinfulness and about the suffering that will result from that sinfulness. Langland is keenly aware of the demands of Christianity and of the failure of his society not only to meet those demands but even to acknowledge the rightness of those demands. Constantly in all three texts, Langland points to the ideals, whether by quoting Scripture or by presenting them in his allegory, and constantly he illustrates his society's deficiencies in meeting those ideals.

One of the most fascinating aspects of *Piers Plowman* involves the relationship between the individual and society. Langland does a phenomenal job of picturing his society, especially in the opening vision where he describes the "fair field full of folk," a cross section of the society. Everyone is gathered together in the field, which is bordered on one side by a high tower and on the other by a deep pit, allegorical representations of Heaven and Hell. In the tower dwells Truth, and Will has an extended conversation with Truth's representative, Holy Church, of whom he asks the poem's key question, "How may I save my soul?" At first glance, this question appears selfish. But as the poem progresses, we begin to understand that individual salvation is virtually inseparable from the salvation of the whole community, so that Will's question actually means, "How can we save our souls? How can we, as a community, create conditions that will allow us to achieve salvation?" Langland pays close attention not only to what is good for the individual but also to the common good, and he is outraged both morally and religiously (though he would have considered those to be the same). He sees a kingdom that has gone through the recurrences of the plague, through the resultant social turmoil, and through the disorder at the end of Edward III's reign and the beginning of Richard II's rule. Everyone looks out for his or her own good, not for the common good, with the result that everyone's individual good suffers. The upper classes, including the royalty, care only for themselves; the clergy are corrupt; and the lower classes, lacking both political and religious leadership, are adrift and in danger. Not only do they suffer privation in this world, but their reactions to that privation endanger the possibility of their salvation in the next world.

Langland repeatedly makes these points in the course of his long, angry poem, but perhaps nowhere as well as in the episode of the plowing of the half-acre. In Passus 5 of the B-Text (8 in the C-Text; Langland breaks his text up into chapters called passus), the people resolve to go on a pilgrimage to Truth, on the surface an admirable decision, though there is one significant catch: No one knows the way. Clearly Langland is condemning a society in which no one knows how to get to Truth, to God. Suddenly Piers the Plowman makes his first appearance in the poem and provides the directions, which are a summary of the Ten Commandments and other biblical teachings. In Passus 6 (9 in the C-Text), he volunteers to lead the way if the crowd will first help him sow his half-acre. He divides them up, giving each group a job appropriate for its rank and abilities. The knights, for instance, are there to protect the workers, not to enrich themselves. At first this idealistic division of labor seems to work, but it very quickly breaks down as various groups begin to look out for themselves rather than for the common good and then become subject to Hunger, that is, to a communal punishment.

Most of the rest of the poem, from Passus 8 (11 in C) to the end, consists of Will's search for Dowel, Dobet, and Dobest (Do-Well, Do-Better, and Do-Best). In a series of allegorical encounters with various clergymen and with figures such as Conscience and Study, Langland presents an exploration of some of the most serious issues of his time, all focusing ultimately on that original question, how a society can function for the common good so that the individuals in the society can achieve salvation. Unhappily, the answer seems both clear and unattainable: People have to live in accordance with the ideals set out in the Bible, but people are either unable or unwilling to sacrifice their own selfish, earthly desires for the common good and for the achievement of salvation.

Piers Plowman, then, is an angry poem that points out in denunciatory terms the evils of Langland's society. We can justifiably call it a satire, if we think of satire in its most bitter manifestations. The poem is also quite difficult for modern readers (as it undoubtedly was for four-teenth-century readers). The allegory is often obscure, scenes change with little or no warning, and the overall effect is often surrealistic. Nonetheless, *Piers Plowman* is a powerful poem that can continue to affect us. It was very popular in its time and down to the sixteenth century, and it continues to maintain its status as a major medieval work.

Somewhat less popular today, judging by the number of critical studies it engenders, is the work of John Gower. Gower wrote three major works in three different languages, as we mentioned earlier. Like Langland, he reacted overtly to the challenges of his time, though his reactions differed from Langland's. Langland showed outrage both at the disorder of his society and at the conditions that produced that disorder. Gower also recognized the corruption of his society, but he reacted quite strongly to the Peasants' Revolt. He had no trouble discussing the corruption, but he was horrified at the people's violent reaction, as we see in his Latin work, the *Vox Clamantis*.

Gower's most important English work, the *Confessio Amantis*, is less overtly political, though it does include a lengthy prologue that focuses on political and religious corruption. This very long dream vision takes its central image from *The Complaint of Nature* and *The Romance of the Rose*, in both of which Genius serves as a confessor. Here he serves as confessor to the lover. In Jean de Meun's *Romance of the Rose*, we saw Genius as a figure with an overwhelming interest in reproduction. Gower's Genius is much more like a real priest and certainly displays a higher sense of morality than Jean's Genius did. As Genius and the lover go through the Seven Deadly Sins in order to examine the lover's behavior, Genius tells a series of stories taken from the Bible, from mythology, and from other sources to illustrate those sins.

The individual stories that Genius tells can be quite interesting, and many of them recur elsewhere in medieval literature (including in the poetry of Chaucer), but the overall effect of Gower's poetry can be weary-ing for modern readers. First, Gower tends to belabor his points. We can make the same accusation against Langland, but Langland's issue, the cor-ruption of society, remains current, while Gower's discussion of love seems, perhaps unfairly, rather dated. Furthermore, Langland used allit-erative verse, which works for his themes and which becomes appealing once one becomes accustomed to it. Gower wrote in octosyllabic rhyming couplets. This was the verse form of Chrétien, Marie, Guillaume de Lor-ris, Jean de Meun, and other French poets; it works much better in French than in English, for which iambic pentameter is more suitable. Conse-quently, Gower's poem quickly begins to sound monotonous.

Still, we cannot deny the importance of Gower as a poet who illumi-nates significant aspects of the late fourteenth century. Comparing his work to the power of *Piers Plowman* or to the complexity of Chaucer's poems puts it at a disadvantage; but if we can consider it on its own terms, we can enjoy it and learn from it.

EARLY CHAUCER

And then there is Chaucer. There is a common perception of Chau-cer as a comic, that is, a humorous poet. While Chaucer's poetry does indeed contain funny passages and episodes, we would be safer in think-ing of his work as comic in the way that Dante's masterpiece is comic. Chaucer's poetry, particularly *The Canterbury Tales*, is all inclusive, offers a broad view of the human situation, and at least seems to transcend the limits of the everyday world. At the same time, Chaucer deals directly with the important issues of his time. He addresses many of the same issues that Langland addressed, but whereas Langland addressed them with anger and overt condemnations, Chaucer tends to show a greater understanding of human frailty. Langland held up the ideal and demanded that people try to attain it. Chaucer knew the ideal, but he also knew and accepted the fact that ideals are meant to be unattainable, that the best we can do, unless we are saints, is to fail nobly.

There are, however, several reasons that Chaucer is considered a funny poet. One is the Miller's Tale, which, as we will see, is both humor-ous in itself and as part of the larger context of the *Tales*. Probably because of its memorable conclusion, it tends to be the tale that students retain after they have forgotten the others. Another reason for Chaucer's repu-tation is his willingness to insert humor into his poetry, as when, in *The*

Parliament of Fowls, he quotes the goose, the cuckoo, and the duck: "Kek kek! Kokkow! quek quek!" (499). But the greatest influence on his reputation has probably been the portrait of himself that he paints in his poetry. Not only does he tell us that he is short and stout, a stature that is stereotypically associated with jollity, but he also describes himself as inept and more than a little obtuse. This self-description, of course, is quite misleading. No one thinks that Dante was nearly as naïve or as uncomprehending as he pictures himself in the *Comedy*. We accept that self-description as part of the poem because we, as his readers, have to go through the same learning experience that he went through on his journey. But we always know that the real Dante was the genius behind the poem. In Chaucer's case, however, the self-description is so appealing, so amusing, so like us that we are willing to accept it as accurate. Thus, in *The Canterbury Tales*, the character Chaucer tells one of the worst of the tales. So bad is it that the Host interrupts him with the words, "'Namoore of this, for Goddes dignitee'" (VII.919). Geoffrey Chaucer, the greatest poet of his age, pictures himself as a poetic incompetent. If we find this kind of play amusing, it must have seemed even funnier to his original audience, people who actually knew him and to whom he may even have read the poem. Nevertheless, we must always keep in mind the distinction between Chaucer the poet and Chaucer the character in the poems. They are very different people, so much so that in discussing them we will distinguish between them by calling the poet Chaucer and the character Geoffrey. Geoffrey is an often humorous character in the poetry of Chaucer.

One more point before we actually get to Chaucer's poetry: his language. At the end of the fourteenth century, there were several major dialects of English. These dialects differed from each other in matters like vocabulary and pronunciation. Because spelling had not yet been standardized, people spelled largely according to the way words sounded. Many of these dialects, like the North-West Midlands dialect of *Sir Gawain and the Green Knight*, are difficult for modern readers, but because Chaucer's dialect developed into Modern English, Chaucer's language is not all that difficult. Many editions of Chaucer's works include a pronunciation guide as well as notes and a glossary. Anyone who really wants to read Chaucer should study the pronunciation guide, listen to a recording (or an online clip) of someone reading the Middle English, and plunge right in. The pronunciation and some of the vocabulary and syntax will take getting used to, but they are truly not difficult. There are translations of Chaucer's poetry into modern English, but part of the fun of reading Chaucer lies in reading him in the Middle English (if possible by candlelight, with straw on the floor and a recording of fourteenth-century music playing in the background).

Chaucer, as we mentioned earlier, had traveled on the Continent and knew the works of contemporary European writers. In some cases he even knew the writers themselves. Furthermore, Chaucer lived at court, where Continental values were still considered superior to native English values. Chaucer's work, then, reflects the court's values. Except in very rare instances, he avoids any hint of the native alliterative poetry, and his sources are almost always Continental. (People know that Shakespeare did not invent his own plots. Instead, he borrowed plots from others and developed them in new ways. The same is true for much of Chaucer. Such borrowing was not considered plagiarism. Rather, it was a kind of flattery, an acknowledgement of an earlier authority, and an avoidance of originality, which, no matter how much it was practiced, had to be denied.) Chaucer translated two works that influenced him greatly — Boethius' *Consolation of Philosophy* and large sections of *The Romance of the Rose* — and he used works by Alan of Lille, Petrarch, and Boccaccio, among many others. In all of Chaucer's works, however, we can detect the Chaucerian touch. He is one of the most humane of all poets, a quality that has contributed to his continuing popularity.

Although we will focus our attention on *The Canterbury Tales*, we will begin by looking at Chaucer's earlier works. Three of his earliest works, *The Book of the Duchess*, *The House of Fame*, and *The Parliament of Fowls*, are dream visions; the first two are written in octosyllabic rhyming couplets. *The Book of the Duchess* deals with a theme that would figure prominently in most of Chaucer's work, love, but in a very special way. Having had trouble falling asleep, Geoffrey reads the story of Ceyx and Alcyone in Ovid's *Metamorphoses*, a story about true love between a husband and wife. He then falls asleep and has a dream that is clearly inspired by his reading. In his dream, he meets a man in black, who laments over his lost love. Thus far, the poem seems like a minor variation on any number of dream visions in which the poet laments over his unrequited love, and Geoffrey keeps asking the man in black why he is so sad. We might expect that the answer will also involve unrequited love, but though the man in black hints several times at the real answer, Geoffrey persists in asking until the man blurts out that his beloved has died. After Geoffrey offers his condolences, he awakens.

This brief summary (which omits a great deal) illustrates the seeming simplicity of the poem, but the poem is more complex than it seems.

First, the poem has an interesting tripartite structure: Geoffrey's reading, the early part of his dream, and his lengthy conversation with the man in black. These three sections are closely related, but Chaucer forces the reader to make the connections among them, just as a medieval viewer would have to make the connections among the sections of a triptych, a painting with three distinct sections. And Geoffrey's continual questioning of the man is problematic. Is Geoffrey simply so obtuse that he does not sense the man's grief? That explanation is possible, but we can also surmise that Geoffrey is behaving like a good therapist, forcing the man to confront the grief that overwhelms him, to acknowledge publicly the death of his lady. The situation becomes even more complex when we understand that the man in black represents Chaucer's patron, the king's uncle, John of Gaunt, Duke of Lancaster, whose wife Blanche (which means "white") had recently died. Perhaps, the poem itself is meant to fill for John of Gaunt the role that Geoffrey fills for the man in black, acknowledging Blanche's death and her husband's grief. Then the story of Ceyx and Alcyone, which tells of a wife's grief for her dead husband and their eventual reunion, becomes relevant as a foreshadowing of the reunion of John and Blanche, in Christian terms, in Heaven. In Ovid, Ceyx and Alcyone are transformed into birds, a part of the story that Chaucer omits, but he could safely assume that his audience knew that part of the story and would see in it an element of consolation.

The House of Fame is a much longer poem, but it is highly problematic because it ends in the middle of a line. Without having the conclusion, we can only guess where Chaucer would have taken the poem. What we have of the poem is fascinating; but given our limited space, it may be wisest to pass on to *The Parliament of Fowls*, which is one of the most nearly perfect poems of the Middle Ages. Once again it is bedtime and Chaucer is reading, this time "The Dream of Scipio," which we discussed in relation to *The Romance of the Rose*. Naturally Geoffrey's dream will be related to this work. Like the dream in *The Book of the Duchess*, this one is divided into parts, again creating a tripartite structure, a triptych. In the opening section, Geoffrey describes "The Dream of Scipio," with its emphasis on the smallness of the world and therefore of worldly gain, and its praise of working for the "commune profit" (1. 47), which may remind us of *Piers Plowman*. Then in the first part of the dream, Geoffrey finds himself in a walled garden, guided by Scipio's grandfather Africanus. Here Geoffrey encounters examples of good love — which is generous and directed to the other — and evil love — which is selfish and carnal. Much of the imagery in this section derives from *The Romance of the Rose* and from Dante's *Comedy*, reminding us that those works may not be as disparate as they seem. The third section of the poem, the second half of the dream, is the actual parliament of the fowls. On St. Valentine's Day, the birds, under the auspices of Nature (another vestige of *The Romance of the Rose* and Alan of Lille), are gathered to choose their mates, which, this being the Middle Ages, they must do in the order of their ranks. But there is a problem: The royal birds, the eagles, instead of obeying the natural instinct to mate, become involved in courtship problems, thereby preventing everyone else from mating.

In this scene, Chaucer combines two of his favorite topics, love and common profit. Because the eagles' love is directed not toward the necessity of procreation but toward the pleasures of courtship and posturing, they simultaneously make a mockery of love and interfere with the common profit. Nature finally devises a solution — the eagles will postpone their decision for a year, while everyone else will go ahead and mate — but that solution is clearly unsatisfactory and even unnatural. The upper classes, by their unnatural behavior, have abrogated their responsibilities and have put their role as leaders in question. After all, if their approach to something as basic as love and marriage is so distorted, how much faith can anyone have in their ability to lead in other areas — a question that might well have been directed to members of the court. This poem, which has so much to say about love, has an even stronger focus on the question of common profit, of the necessity for every part of the society to work together for the common good. As we saw in *Piers Plowman*, this theme, which remains relevant now, had a special meaning in the chaos of the fourteenth century.

An interesting aspect of Chaucer's approach, however, can be seen in the stanza in which he repeats Africanus' assertion that good souls find eternal bliss but that sinful souls are whisked about in pain for many years before they are allowed to gain that bliss. Of course, Cicero, who wrote "The Dream of Scipio," was a pagan, but those two fates sound very much like the Christian concepts of Heaven and Purgatory. There is no Hell in this scheme, though Dante used the concept of souls being whisked around in his Hell. Chaucer makes no such adaptation. As a medieval Christian, Chaucer surely believed in the punishments of Hell, but he makes no mention of them here. His interest focuses on the vagaries of human behavior, and while he always makes us aware of the morality (or lack of morality) in human behavior, he never overtly condemns anyone, as Dante and even Langland did. Langland rails at human failures, and from his more biblical perspective, he is quite correct. Chaucer also recognizes those failures. He neither denies nor minimizes them, but he does, often, smile indulgently at them. What else, he seems to ask, can we expect from fallen human beings?

We can regard these three early dream visions as introductions to Chaucer's two major works, *Troilus and Criseyde* and *The Canterbury Tales*, works that are quite distinct even though many of their concerns are similar. *Troilus and Criseyde* is a single very long poem that tells a unified story about a young Trojan warrior, Troilus, who loves Criseyde, a Trojan woman whose father has defected to the Greeks. Troilus is a terribly inept lover, so he turns for help to Criseyde's uncle Pandarus, who is worse than inept, so much worse that his name became the source of the English word "pander." Pandarus engineers opportunities for Troilus and Criseyde to be together, sometimes in compromising circumstances, and eventually Criseyde begins to return Troilus' love, though the reader might wonder why such a sophisticated and intelligent lady would love such a naïve and whining man. Soon, however, her father, who knows that Troy will be destroyed, demands that she be returned to him. She and Troilus promise to remain true to each other, but once she is in the Greek camp, she becomes involved with Diomedes. When Troilus learns of this, he reenters the battle, fights fiercely, and is killed.

Chaucer drew on many sources for this poem, though the source he cites throughout the poem, Lollius, never actually existed. His main source was a poem by Boccaccio, but Chaucer, in his manipulation of the story, creates a much more complex work, as we can see if we simply try to judge the characters. Criseyde, for instance, seems like a villainess in this poem, as she abandons the gentle man who truly loves her for an opportunistic ruffian. At the poem's end, the narrator even apologizes for presenting such a deceitful woman. But is Criseyde really to blame? Troilus is, in technical terms, a wimp; and his reliance on Pandarus, his acquiescence in Pandarus' schemes, reflects a startling lack of judgment. Furthermore, Criseyde occupies a ticklish position: As a widow, she is a solitary woman, a difficult status in the Middle Ages. She is also the daughter of someone whom the Trojans regard as a traitor. Consequently, we can hardly blame her for taking advantage of Troilus' infatuation. As a man and as the king's son, he seems to offer her protection. Still, she has not sought him. Rather, she has been manipulated into loving him; and even, he cannot prevent her from being sent to her father in the Greek camp, where once again she must protect herself.

The point of this discussion is to indicate how complex Chaucer makes the whole situation. The reader has difficulty making judgments about the characters' behavior because there are so many aspects of that behavior to consider. Langland can make stricter judgments because he operates according to a clear moral code, a code to which Chaucer probably also subscribed, though he saw more clearly that the behavior of ordinary mortals could not satisfy that order, that in everyday life things are not so clear-cut. Thus *Troilus and Criseyde*, with its typically complex Chaucerian narrator, is full of speculation over the role of Fortune and free will in human life, although the discussions do nothing to clear away the confusion of the topic. Ultimately, we cannot understand the workings of the world we inhabit. We can only do our best, which is never good enough.

Thus, at the poem's end, Troilus' soul rises toward heaven, and as Troilus sees the world become smaller and smaller, he realizes the triviality of everything that he recently considered so important and he laughs. That laughter reflects Chaucer's attachment to the thought of Boethius, whose ideas figure so prominently in all of Chaucer's poetry; but again, Chaucer does not make things easy for us. The conclusion of *Troilus and Criseyde* confuses us because it consists of several possible conclusions (like the movie *Clue*). Each of those conclusions reflects a legitimate interpretation of the poem, but none of the interpretations can be definitive. Had Dante considered the story, he would have to have made a judgment about where in the afterlife the characters belonged, based on what he considered immutable principles. Langland, too, to the extent that he would have given any consideration to such an obvious fiction, would certainly have been judgmental. But not Chaucer.

THE CANTERBURY TALES

And that point brings us to *The Canterbury Tales*, a work that presents us with many problems and perspectives. One problem, however, is absolutely basic to any study of the *Tales*: Chaucer died while writing the work, which means that despite its length, what we have is a fragment, or, more precisely, a series of fragments. We do not know and we cannot know where Chaucer was going with the work, how many more tales he intended to write, or how those tales could have contributed to the overall effect of the work. In addition, we do not have Chaucer's autograph manuscript. Instead, we have fifteenth century manuscripts (Chaucer having died in 1400), and those manuscripts differ, as medieval manuscripts are wont to do, both in what they include and in the order in which they include it. Great scholars have attempted to determine what Chaucer intended, and their work deserves careful consideration, but it is always conjectural.

A further complication is that we do seem to have part of Chaucer's plan, for in the General Prologue, the Host proposes that each of the pilgrims should tell two stories on the way to Canterbury and two on the way home. The pilgrim whose story is voted the best will be treated to a meal at the Tabard. Obviously the Host is no fool, for if that scheme is carried out, he stands to make a fair profit. The problem, however, is that the Host is a fictional character. His plan may not have been the same as Chaucer's. His plan would require well over a hundred stories, surpassing Boccaccio's *Decameron*, and would consequently have made the *Tales* incredibly long.[1] Even when poets speak in their own voices about their plans for their poems (as Spenser does in his Letter to Ralegh about *The Faerie Queene*), they tend toward inaccuracy. We must be even more careful, then, about confusing the Host's proposal with Chaucer's own plans. In the fragments that we do have, all of the stories are told on the way to Canterbury, none on the way back. In fact, if we think of the pilgrimage allegorically, moving from the City of Man to the City of God, it is inconceivable that there would have been a journey back. The last tale that we have, that of the Parson, is told with the towers of Canterbury in sight and the tale itself, a lengthy sermon on the seven deadly sins, seems like an appropriate conclusion for such an allegorical journey. Of course, it may only seem appropriate because it is all we have and we have become accustomed to thinking of it as the conclusion to the *Tales*. Chaucer just keeps us guessing.

We have referred several times to the *Tales* as a series of fragments. This statement means only that certain tales are properly grouped together. For example, at the end of the General Prologue, the Knight is chosen to tell the first tale, so we know that the Knight's Tale will follow. When he finishes, the Miller insists that he go next, so his tale follows; and when he finishes, the Reeve insists on taking a turn, so his tale follows. After the Reeve's nasty story, the Cook offers to tell another nasty story, but after about sixty lines, his tale stops in the middle. Perhaps Chaucer put it aside, planning to come back to it, and died before he could. Perhaps Chaucer was dissatisfied with what he had written. Perhaps Chaucer finished the tale, but the concluding pages were lost before our fifteenth-century manuscripts were created. We cannot know. All we know is that in the two best manuscripts that we have, the Man of Law's material comes next. But after that fragment, the two best manuscripts diverge, presenting the rest of the fragments in somewhat different orders. Again, we cannot know for sure which, if either, of these orders reflects Chaucer's plan. But if we think, as we must, that the structure of a work is related to its overall import, we must also recognize that in dealing with *The Canterbury Tales*, there are many elements of uncertainty that affect our approach to the work.

In one sense, of course, all of this uncertainty is a drawback. We wish that Chaucer had written more and that we could know where he wanted each part to go. On the other hand, the uncertainty has allowed readers over the centuries to exercise their ingenuity in trying to understand what Chaucer was doing and has prompted numerous interesting and exciting readings. And if we think back to the conclusion of *Troilus and Criseyde*, we realize that Chaucer himself would probably have enjoyed the ambiguities that he created. Certainly the text of *The Canterbury Tales* contains a plenitude of built-in ambiguities.

The Canterbury Tales opens with the General Prologue, which provides the setting for what will follow. The season is spring, when people can begin getting around again. Our narrator, Geoffrey, reports that he was at a tavern just outside of London, where he met a group of people who, like him, were preparing to go on a pilgrimage to the shrine of St. Thomas Becket at Canterbury. Pilgrimage, of course, was a religious act, at least in theory, but as *Piers Plowman* illustrated, it was subject to abuse. Many people certainly went on pilgrimages out of religious convictions, but for others, like some of the Canterbury pilgrims, it was a chance to travel, to have a good time, and to take a vacation from everyday duties. In England, Canterbury was a great pilgrimage center. It was not terribly far from London, the journey there was not overly difficult, and Thomas was a popular saint.

Geoffrey begins his record of the pilgrimage by telling us about each of the pilgrims, and here we encounter yet another problem. We can almost imagine Geoffrey making his way around the tavern, talking to each pilgrim and gathering significant information about them, but we must wonder about how seriously we should take each of these pilgrims as fictional characters. As Jill Mann has demonstrated, the pilgrims are based largely on traditional descriptions of people in the various professions that they represent. Nevertheless, Chaucer depicts them so freshly that they do strike us as characters rather than as types. This question will become more important as the poem continues, for many of these characters will tell tales. Many critics see a relationship between the tales and the tellers as they are described in the General Prologue. Other critics contend that such a view is too modern, that Chaucer utilized types and would not have been able to conceive of the kind of character consistency that such a dramatic presentation requires. The view of this chapter is that the tellers are indeed reflected in their tales and that the dramatic principle functions admirably in the *Tales*. We cannot make pronouncements about what medieval people were capable of and then use those pronouncements to deny what Chaucer actually did. As we read the *Tales*, we must pay close attention to what Geoffrey says about the pilgrims in the General Prologue and then relate those depictions, making allowances for Geoffrey's own peculiarities, as we read the tales. We must also pay close attention to the occasional byplay among the pilgrims that occurs between tales or that even appears as an interruption within a tale.

Naturally, Chaucer did not make our job easy. His love of ambiguity appears first in the way he uses Geoffrey. Many of the descriptions that Geoffrey provides are quite critical of the pilgrims, fitting in with those stereotypical traditional portraits that were their sources. (We do the same thing now when we tell jokes about lawyers or computer geeks.) Geoffrey, however, seems oblivious to the criticisms that his descriptions imply. According to him, virtually every pilgrim is the best at whatever he or she does, though we cannot tell whether Geoffrey is being serious or ironic when he says so. Chaucer's genius allows him to present these pilgrims as both ideal paradigms and targets of satire, and as we continue through the *Tales* we must ask ourselves which of these alternatives we should choose — or whether we need to choose between them at all. Perhaps Chaucer is presenting a cross section of society, and the people he describes share the flaws and lack of self-awareness that still form part of the human situation. Perhaps Chaucer did not feel the need to make the kinds of judgments that were so basic to Dante and Langland. Chaucer the medieval man, the public servant, the witness to the events of 1381, could hardly have overlooked the ills that afflicted his society; but he could have taken a less doctrinaire attitude toward them than did other fourteenth-century poets.

Some concrete examples will illustrate this point. Among the pilgrims are a number of clergy: several nuns, a priest, a monk, a friar, and a parson. There are also two pilgrims who are loosely associated with religious matters, a summoner and a pardoner. Almost without exception, these characters show deep flaws. The Prioress, for instance, occupies a position of some authority. She should be in charge of a group of nuns, but she exhibits behavior that casts doubt on her suitability for a such a job. Her name is Madame Eglentyne, an odd name for a nun. It might seem unfair to say that the name is more appropriate for a romance heroine except that she behaves like a romance heroine. Geoffrey tells us that she speaks French, the language of romance; but Geoffrey apparently knows French well enough to recognize that Madame Eglentyne learned her French in England and has never been in France. If she speaks French to him, then, she does so as an affectation. She wears, of course, a nun's habit, but a very stylish habit. The wimple, the headpiece, is pleated, and she wears it in such a way as to set off her high forehead, which was considered a sign of beauty. Geoffrey also describes her cute little nose, her eyes, and her small, soft, red mouth, elements that we might expect in the description of a romance heroine but not in a nun. We might wonder whether Geoffrey is taken in by her affectations, whether he is falling for this nun, or whether he is only conveying to us her sense of herself. In either case, we can see in her a woman who has gone into the wrong line of work, a woman whose worldly affectations make us wonder about a church that would have her as a prioress. She wears a brooch that carries the motto *amor vincit omnia*, love conquers all. Theoretically the brooch refers to divine love, but this lady seems less concerned with divine love than with its more secular alternatives.

The Prioress also tries to demonstrate ladylike manners. She eats daintily and makes a show of her table manners (at a time when good manners included important points like not blowing one's nose into one's hand during a meal). But for all her daintiness, Geoffrey tells us in a wonderful understatement, "she was not undergrowe" (156). Furthermore, though she cannot stand to see the suffering of even a trapped mouse, she keeps, in violation of nunly rules, a group of dogs to whom she feeds meat, milk, and the finest bread, foods that could more properly be given to the poor.

In the forty-four lines that Geoffrey devotes to describing the Prioress, he never says an overtly critical word about her, but we leave this description with many doubts. She does not seem to be an evil person, someone who sets out to do harm, but she certainly seems out of place as a nun. She does not steal or kill or commit adultery, but she certainly does not meet her responsibilities as a prioress. Although she makes a mockery of the Church's ideals and thereby potentially does harm, neither Chaucer nor Geoffrey openly condemns her. In effect, she condemns herself, but we get the feeling from her portrait that she is a real woman, a woman who probably entered the Church without a true vocation and whose humanity has consequently been sublimated — but not too successfully.

Later on, when the Prioress tells her tale, it turns out to be a horrifying story of anti-Semitic brutality. Of course, that view of the tale expresses twenty-first-century sensibilities; Chaucer's audience might have regarded it differently. At the same time, her tale reflects the pretense of great feeling and underlying cruelty that we saw in her reaction to trapped mice and luxuriously fed pets. Thus the Prioress, despite the traditional stereotypical literary qualities that she reflects, also reflects the qualities of a real person. When we read Langland, we seldom feel that we are in the presence of people. When we read Chaucer, we usually do, which perhaps explains why readers have related more to Chaucer's poetry than to Langland's over the centuries.

We can see the same effects in the description of the Monk. He is not, as we might say, a bad guy, but he is a terrible monk. Monks were supposed to be chaste, dedicated to poverty, to renunciation of the world, and to life in the monastery. This monk has a stable of horses with fine riding equipment, he loves to go hunting, he hates to be in the monastery, and there are several hints in his description that he enjoys sexual activity. He is also fat from eating fine foods. Like the Prioress, though perhaps more consciously, he undercuts his religious vows with potentially deleterious effects on society. The Friar is even worse, and by the time we get to the Summoner and the Pardoner we find that we are dealing with scoundrels and criminals, though even they have some sympathetic aspects.

Many critics contend that among the pilgrims, three present actual ideals: the Knight, the Clerk, and the Parson. We might be correct to say that these characters are less flawed than the others. The Parson, for example, does indeed live up to religious ideals. He lives in poverty and truly cares for his parishioners, among whom he lives rather than running off to London, where he could earn more money. He is what a priest should be. We might wonder, however, how Geoffrey knows so much about him, and the only answer is that the Parson has told him. This answer, of course, assumes a higher degree of verisimilitude than many critics would allow Chaucer. It assumes, too, that the Parson is quite proud of himself. On the one hand, the Parson should be proud, because he does well. On the other hand, pride is sinful, so that if he shows pride in his adherence to the religious ideal, he thereby diminishes that adherence.

Actually Chaucer is having some sly fun with the Parson. There can be no doubt that the Parson is a good character, a religious figure who takes his religious responsibilities quite seriously. At the same time, as his occasional interactions with other pilgrims illustrate, he is a most unpleasant person, a prig who likes to show off his righteousness. Most of us would undoubtedly prefer to travel with the Monk rather than with the Parson, not because we are so sinful (though we may be) but because the Monk would be better company. And it is no coincidence that the Parson travels with his brother the Plowman, whose brief description indicates that he is also a paragon of sorts. But even in an age when people's body odors must have been astounding, the Plowman's close association with dung, the first item mentioned in his description, would have made him more than noticeable. This association of the Parson and the Plowman, the one's self-righteousness and the other's aroma, probably refers to *Piers Plowman*, with its central figure of a plowman, its satire of the clergy, its long sections of preaching, and its overtly judgmental stance. While Langland's poem strikes us (or many of us) as a powerful masterpiece, Chaucer seems to have had reservations about it.

Geoffrey's descriptions of the non-ecclesiastical characters are equally revealing. It should come as no surprise that the Merchant is slightly crooked, though he is "a worthy man with alle" (283). Many of the characters, in fact, are like the Cook. He is an outstanding cook, naturally, but he has one troubling feature: an open sore, which even in the days before antisepsis must have struck people as less than appetizing. Still, he made a fine white sauce. Yum. As we read these descriptions in the General Prologue, we should use an edition that has good notes, because Chaucer embeds a great deal of meaning in even the slightest details. These introductions to the pilgrims, like Langland's fair field full of folk, give us a picture of the society, though Chaucer, through Geoffrey, indicates both the virtues and vices of the characters. We should also notice that Chaucer has not given us a picture of his whole society. Rather, he depicts a rudimentary middle class. No members of the royalty and no members of the lowest classes number among the pilgrims. The Knight, the highest ranking secular figure, has nothing to do with the upper classes; and even the Plowman owns some property. But this middle class has its own divisions, as we see clearly in the tales themselves.

At the end of the General Prologue, the pilgrims draw straws to determine who will tell the first tale. The Knight wins, though Geoffrey hints that the contest might have been fixed by the Host, allowing the highest-ranked pilgrim to begin. The Knight's Tale is a long romance, based again on a work by Boccaccio. It is a great story, but it is also quite formal and the Knight is a bit self-conscious about telling it. The story involves a number of elements that we have seen in so much medieval literature: love, the transitoriness of human happiness and existence, the importance of a Boethian outlook. It is a fine performance that all the pilgrims, and particularly those of higher rank, enjoy. The Host then turns to the Monk for a tale. Having curried favor with the Knight, he now wants to hear from the most prominent of the religious figures, but he is interrupted by the Miller, who insists that he be allowed to tell a story that will match the Knight's Tale. When the Host agrees to this demand, the Miller excuses himself for being drunk and says that he will tell "a legende and a lyf," terms associated with religious stories, about a carpenter and his wife. At this point, the Reeve, who also happens to be a carpenter, tries to stop him, apparently afraid that a story making fun of a carpenter will make fun of him. The Miller tries to calm him down and then tells his tale, but not before Geoffrey tells his readers that he feels compelled to include the Miller's Tale even though it is offensive. He does tell squeamish readers that they should feel free to skip the tale, which is as clear an indication as he could devise that they should pay it close attention.

The Miller's Tale is indeed a masterpiece. On one level, it makes clear fun of the Knight's Tale, translating the kind of refined love that concerns the Knight's upper-class characters to a group of lower-class, often rascally characters, thereby mocking notions of refined love. On another level, however, the Miller engages in a good deal of social criticism of his own, so much so that we may begin to doubt his claim to drunkenness. More likely, he only claims to be drunk so that the targets of his criticism may overlook what he says. And one of his targets is specifically not the Reeve, who reacted so strongly to the Miller's introduction. The carpenter in the story is foolish, but unlike every other character, he is also honest and generous.

The characters in the Knight's Tale are pretty standard: Theseus is the great leader, Emelye is the beautiful maiden, and Palamon and Arcite are the valiant lovers. The sources of the Miller's characters are the pilgrims themselves. He looks around, sees who his companions are, and includes them in his tale. His heroine, Alisoun, shares her name with Alison, the Wife of Bath, an older woman who, as the prologue to her tale will show, is preoccupied with sexual matters. The Miller's Alisoun is very sensual herself, as the imagery from the Song of Songs that is used to describe her indicates. But the Miller's Alisoun also wears a prominent brooch, as though the Miller, looking at his fellow travelers, noticed the Prioress' brooch and included her in his description. By combining the Wife of Bath and the Prioress in his character, the Miller points out similarities between those ladies that are hidden by their superficial differences. The clerk in the story is based on the Clerk pilgrim. The Clerk is described as a model student, interested only in learning. "Oh, no," implies the Miller. The Clerk is a student; students are devious, and they like women. The clerk in his story thus reveals aspects of the Clerk that the Clerk likes to hide, though those aspects become obvious when the Clerk tells his own tale. The parish clerk of the story, Absolon, is based on the Squire, who is the Knight's fancy-dressing son. The Miller's physical description of Absolon is very like Geoffrey's description of the Squire. Finally, the Miller even includes himself in the story. The carpenter's servant is Robyn. He is strong, "a strong carl for the nones" (3469) and he can knock a door off its hinges with his head. In the General Prologue, Geoffrey describes the Miller, whose name is also Robyn, as "A stout carl for the nones" (545) and says he is so strong that he can knock a door off its hinges with his head.

The Miller's Tale, then, not only comments on the Knight's Tale, but it also comments on the other pilgrims, and it reveals a good deal of class consciousness. However, none of the Miller's targets recognize themselves. Only the Reeve reacts, quite mistakenly. Instead of allying himself with the Miller, as he should, he tells a tale that makes scandalous fun of millers. Thus, not only is there conflict among the various levels of the middle class, but even those characters who should be natural allies cannot get along. Chaucer depicts the clashes in his society, similar to those that persist even into our time, clashes that undermine the welfare of communities.

Other tales, particularly the wonderful Nun's Priest's Tale, use the same technique as the Miller's Tale. Others comment in different ways. Many of the tales discuss specific issues involving love, marriage, and gender relationships, and all of these tales comment implicitly, and often explicitly, on each other. The reader of *The Canterbury Tales* must always be alert on several levels. The reader has to pay attention to the individual tales, to the relationship between the tale and the teller, and to the relationships among the tales. *The Canterbury Tales* is an incredibly complex work in which virtually every part is related somehow to every other part, and there is always something new to be discovered. Would that Chaucer had been able to finish it.

If the *Tales* are inherently complex, Chaucer (or someone) added a final complexity by tacking on to the very end of what we have a small retraction in which Chaucer allegedly repents for all of his secular works and prays that he be forgiven for them on the basis of his more spiritual works. No one knows exactly now to regard this retraction. One approach is to assume that Chaucer did not write it, which would render it almost, though not completely, negligible. Another possibility is that Chaucer, living his last days among the monks of Westminster, was overcome by religious sentiment, or became worried about his salvation. And yet another possibility is that the retraction operates ironically: By denigrating his own works, which, at the time the retraction was written could not actually have been retracted at all, he can present those works and simultaneously deny (or seem to deny) their value. Whatever the explanation is — and we will never know what happened — the retraction adds yet another ambiguity to Chaucer's marvelously concrete and yet infinitely slippery poetry.

Epilogue (But Not Retraction): From the Author to the Reader

Many works of medieval literature involve journeys: Beowulf travels to Denmark, Dante and Virgil travel through the afterlife, and Chaucer's pilgrims travel to Canterbury. We, too, have taken a journey, from *Beowulf* to Chaucer by way of France, Iceland, Japan, and Italy. I hope that in the course of this journey I have been able to impart some of the excitement and enjoyment that I derive from reading this literature and that I have been able to infect the reader with a desire to read these and other works from the Middle Ages. As I said at the beginning, literature requires that we learn and that we enjoy. Medieval literature can seem particularly forbidding, but it is not. Rather it gives us a way of communicating with some great minds from the past, of learning their views on problems that still concern us, and of testing their solutions against our own. It offers us not an escape to a fairy-tale land of dragons and damsels-in-distress but a confrontation with real people and with ourselves. And, as I have tried so hard to impart, it is fun.

It may not seem necessary to do so, but I want to add that every assertion and every interpretation in the previous pages is open to challenge. That, too, is part of the excitement of studying literature. The important thing, however, is to begin by reading the literature. Let me close, then, by quoting the words that St. Augustine reports having heard in Book 8 of *The Confessions:* Tolle, lege. Pick it up; read it.

Notes

Introduction

1. One of the best descriptions of life at this time can be found in the first section of a science fiction novel, Walter M. Miller, Jr.'s *A Canticle for Leibowitz.*

2. It is amusing to realize that the term "Gothic," which we apply to such magnificent cathedrals as those at Salisbury, Canterbury, and Notre Dame, was originally a term of disparagement. Early critics of the Gothic style thought that it looked barbaric, like something the uncivilized Goths might have built. There is a lesson here about the prophetic abilities of critics.

3. All bibilical quotations are taken from the Douay-Rheims Version of the Bible.

Chapter IV

1. The manuscripts that have survived, however, can be read without much difficulty. Someone recently pointed out to me that with proper paleographic training, a person can read those medieval manuscripts, but many books that were printed in the nineteenth century are falling apart. And someone who tries to "read" a computer disk on which some important work had been saved in the 1980's would be pretty much out of luck.

2. We need to delineate these differences despite my experience at a church carnival when I went to the Fish and Chip Booth and asked the proprietor if he was the fish fryer. "No," he replied. "I'm the chip monk."

Chapter VI

1. Consequently, Jews do not ordinarily use the terms "Old Testament" and "New Testament." For Jews, the "Old Testament" *is* the Bible. Modern critics often use the terms "Hebrew Testament" and "Greek Testament."

2. Poems are cited from *Selected Poems of Jehudah Halevi.* Ed. Heinrich

Brody. Philadelphia: Jewish Publication Society, 1924. The translations are my own, though I consulted those of Israel Zangwill in this volume.

3. Poems are cited from *Selected Religious Poems of Solomon Ibn Gabirol*. Ed. Israel Davidson. Philadelphia: Jewish Publication Society, 1923. The translations are my own, though I consulted those of Nina Brody in this volume.

CHAPTER IX

1. One of the best descriptions of the plague and its effects can be found in Connie Willis' novel *Doomsday Book*. This science fiction novel may not be scholarly, but it captures the horror of the plague.

2. For *Pearl* I am using the translation of Sara de Ford and others. Although there are excellent translations that are more "poetic," this one is very literal.

3. Given the unique manuscript of these poems and the lack of any reference to them anywhere else in medieval literature, we might well wonder if these poems had any readers in the Middle Ages.

CHAPTER X

1. *The Canterbury Tales* covers three hundred pages in *The Riverside Chaucer*. The Host's scheme would take it well past twelve hundred pages.

Bibliography

This bibliography is not intended to be inclusive. It contains only works that are mentioned the text and editions or translations of the works that are discussed.

Alan of Lille. *The Plaint of Nature*. Trans. James J. Sheridan. Toronto: Pontifical Institute of Mediaeval Studies, 1980.

Andreas Capellanus. *The Art of Courtly Love*. Trans. John Jay Parry. New York: Columbia University Press, 1990.

Beowulf. Trans. E. Talbot Donaldson. 2nd ed. New York: Norton, 2001. Other translations that might be considered are by Frederick Rebsamen (New York: HarperCollins, 1991), R.M. Liuzza (Peterborough, Ont.: Broadview Press, 2000), and Seamus Heaney (New York: Norton, 2002).

Berchorius, Peter. *The Ovid Moralizatus of Petrus Berchorius: An Introduction and Translation*. William Reynolds. University Microfilms, 1971.

Bloomfield, Morton. *Piers Plowman as a Fourteenth-Century Apocalypse*. New Brunswick: Rutgers University Press, 1962.

Chaucer, Geoffrey. *The Riverside Chaucer*. Ed. Larry D. Benson. 3rd ed. New York: Houghton Mifflin, 1987.

Chrétien de Troyes. *The Complete Romances of Chrétien de Troyes*. Trans. David Staines. Bloomington: Indiana University Press, 1990. Also useful is *Arthurian Romances*. Trans. Wm. W. Kibler and Carleton W. Carroll. New York: Penguin, 1991.

Dante Alighieri. *Dante's Vita Nuova*. Trans. Mark Musa. New ed. Bloomington: Indiana University Press, 1973.

_____. *The Divine Comedy: Volume I: Inferno*; *Volume II: Purgatorio*; *Volume III: Paradiso*. Trans. Mark Musa. New York: Penguin, 1984–86.

De Lorris, Guillaume, and Jean de Meun. *The Romance of the Rose*. Trans. Frances Horgan. Oxford: Oxford University Press, 1994.

Epistle to Can Grande della Scala: Extract. *Medieval Literary Theory and Criticism, c. 1100–c. 1375*. Ed. A.J. Minnis and A.B. Scott. Oxford: Clarendon Press, 1988. 458–469.

Gower, John. *The English Works of John Gower*. Ed. G.C. Macaulay. London: Oxford University Press, 1900 (reprinted 1957).

Halevi, Yehuda. *Selected Poems of Jehudah Halevi.* Ed. Heinrich Brody. Philadelphia: Jewish Publication Society, 1924.

Hawkins, Peter S., and Rachel Jacoff, eds. *The Poets' Dante.* New York: Farrar, Straus & Giroux, 2001.

Huot, Sylvia. *The Romance of the Rose and Its Medieval Readers.* Cambridge: Cambridge University Press, 1993.

Ibn Gabirol, Solomon. *Selected Poems of Solomon Ibn Gabirol.* Trans. Peter Cole. Princeton: Princeton University Press, 2001.

_____. *Selected Religious Poems of Solomon Ibn Gabirol.* Ed. Israel Davidson. Philadelphia: Jewish Publication Society, 1923.

Keene, Donald. *Seeds in the Heart: Japanese Literature from Earliest Times to the Late Sixteenth Century.* New York: Henry Holt, 1993.

Konishi, Jin'ichi. *A History of Japanese Literature. Volume II: The Early Middle Ages.* Trans. Aileen Gatten. Ed. Earl Miner. Princeton: Princeton University Press, 1986.

Langland, William. *Will's Vision of Piers Plowman.* Trans. E. Talbot Donaldson. Ed. Elizabeth D. Kirk and Judith Anderson. New York: Norton, 1990.

Mann, Jill. *Chaucer and Medieval Estates Satire.* Cambridge University Press, 1973.

Marie de France. *Les Lais de Marie de France.* Ed. Jeanne Lods. Paris: Librairie Honoré Champion, 1959.

_____. *The Lais of Marie de France.* Trans. Glyn S. Burgess and Keith Busby. New York: Penguin, 1986.

Miller, Walter M., Jr. *A Canticle for Leibowitz.* Boston: Gregg Press, 1975.

Njal's Saga. Trans. Magnus Magnusson and Hermann Pálsson. New York: Penguin, 1960.

Pearl. Trans. Sara de Ford et al. New York: Appleton-Century Crofts, 1967.

The Princeton Companion to Classical Japanese Literature. Eds. Earl Miner et al. Princeton: Princeton University Press, 1985.

The Sagas of the Icelanders: A Selection. New York: Penguin, 2001.

Shikibu, Murasaki. *The Tale of Genji.* Trans. Edward Seidensticker. New York: Vintage, 1990.

Sir Gawain and the Green Knight, Patience, and Pearl. Trans. Marie Boroff. New York: Norton, 2000.

Stevenson, Barbara, and Cynthia Ho. *Crossing the Bridge: Comparative Essays on Medieval European and Heian Japanese Women Writers.* New York: Palgrave, 2000.

Ueda, Makoto. *Literary and Art Theories in Japan.* Cleveland: Press of Case Western Reserve University, 1967.

Willis, Connie. *Doomsday Book.* New York: Bantam, 1992.

Index